Victorian Travelers

and the Opening of China, 1842–1907

Victorian Travelers and the

Ohio University Press   Athens

Susan Schoenbauer Thurin

Opening of China, 1842–1907

Ohio University Press, Athens, Ohio 45701
© 1999 by Susan Schoenbauer Thurin
Printed in the United States of America
All rights reserved. Published 1999

Ohio University Press books are printed on acid-free paper ⊗ ™

05 04 03 02 01 00 99   5 4 3 2 1

Page xvii: Map of China by Tim Knaak
Book design by Chiquita Babb

Library of Congress Cataloging-in-Publication Data
Thurin, Susan Schoenbauer.
    Victorian travelers and the opening of China, 1842–1907 / Susan
Schoenbauer Thurin.
        p.   cm.
    Includes bibliographical references and index.
    ISBN 0-8214-1268-x (alk. paper)
    1. China—Description and travel. 2. China—History—19th
century. 3. China—Relations—Great Britain. 4. Great Britain—
Relations—China. I. Title.
DS 709.T49 1999
915.104'35—dc21   98-43661
                                                        CIP

For Erik

Contents

Illustrations

Preface

The Moon Festival in China, which occurs at the time of the full moon closest to the autumnal equinox, is a special time for cheerful gatherings of families and friends. Those separated by distance are symbolically united by strolling outdoors under the autumn moon and eating a filled pastry called a moon cake. In September 1987, I was surprised by the arrival of scores of jovial letters from my Beijing students of the previous year telling me they would remember me during the Moon Festival. It is the sort of gesture that thrills a traveler and teacher. I can only add that my colleagues and students in China have my deepest gratitude for their many kindnesses and genial acceptance of the foreigner in their midst, and for teaching me so much about their country—both its modern face and its ancient roots.

Beyond the experience of China itself, this book is indebted to the support of many individuals and institutions. Foremost is the University of Wisconsin–Stout for affording me the opportunity to be an exchange professor with the Beijing Institute of Light Industry, and later for a sabbatical that gave me time to complete a manuscript of this book. The Stout Foundation granted me a Dahlgren professorship that gave me funds to complete my research.

I am grateful also to Perry Curtis and the late Roger Henkle at Brown University for their NEH seminar that enabled me to begin researching Victorian travel writing about China, and my English Department colleagues who listened patiently to my thoughts on China and travel writing during "Books and Coffee." Jeffrey Dippmann read my manuscript with a sharp eye and provided me with valuable comments on Chinese history.

My research has been assisted by Michael Bott, keeper of archives and manuscripts at the University of Reading, who found and kindly transcribed some of Cumming's letters to her publisher for me. The British Library, the Royal Geographic Society, the Royal Horticultural Society, the Royal Botanic Gardens at Kew, and the U.S. National Archives gave me reading privileges, and their librarians lent me expert help. Virginia Murray at John Murray publishers allowed me to review the papers of Isabella Bird, dug out old ledgers on the sales of Robert Fortune's books, set me up in a fine old library, and treated me like an honored guest. Faye Neuenfeldt and others at interlibrary loan at The University of Wisconsin–Stout have been unfailingly helpful. Tim Knaak prepared the map of China. Marty Springer provided technical assistance with illustrations. The picture of Canton was supplied by the Peabody Essex Museum, Salem, Massachusetts.

Finally, my biggest debt of gratitude is to my husband and colleague Erik, whose constant encouragement and advice have made completion of this book possible.

Abbreviations

Primary sources are cited parenthetically in the text with use of the following abbreviations:

Isabella Bird (Mrs. Bishop)

GC	*The Golden Chersonese*
YVB	*The Yangtze Valley and Beyond*

Constance Gordon Cumming

WiC	*Wanderings in China*

Robert Fortune

JTC	*Journey to the Tea Countries*
RaC	*A Residence among the Chinese*
TYW	*Three Years' Wanderings*
YP	*Yedo and Peking*

Major Henry Knollys

ELC	*English Life in China*

Alicia (Mrs. Archibald) Little

DCF	*My Diary in a Chinese Farm*
IC	*Intimate China*
LBG	*The Land of the Blue Gown*
MiC	*A Marriage in China*

Archibald Little

GFY	*Gleanings from Fifty Years in China*
MOB	*Mt. Omi and Beyond*
TYG	*Through the Yang-Tse Gorges*

A Note on Chinese Names

In order to respect the integrity of the authors' texts, I use their spelling of place-names. On the whole, their romanization of Chinese conforms with the Wade-Giles system, but there are inconsistencies. I offer a selected list of spellings in the Victorian texts, some of them with variants, and their pinyin equivalents and places renamed after the 1949 revolution.

Victorian Names	*Pinyin Equivalent/Current Name*
Amoy	Xiamen
Canton	Guangzhou
Cheefoo, Chifu, Yantai	Qifu
Che-kiang	Zhejiang
Chengtu	Chengdu
Chungking	Chongqing
Ching, Ch'ing dynasty	Qing dynasty
Chusan, Choushan	Zhoushan
Foochow, Fuchou	Fuzhou
Foh-kien, Fokien	Fujian
Formosa	Taiwan
Hang-choo-foo, Hangchow	Hangzhou
Hankow	Hankou
Hung-siu Chuen, Hung Hsui-chüan	Hong Xiuquan
Hwuy-chow, Hwie-chow, Hui-chou	Huizhou
Ichang	Yichang
Jehol	Chengde
Kiang-nan, Kiangsu	Jiangsu

Kiang-see, Kiangsi	Jiangxi
Kiukiang	Jiujiang
Kuan Hsien	Guan Xian
Manchuria	Divided into the provinces of Heilongjiang, Jilin, and Liaoning
Matang	Batang
Mukden	Shenyang
Namoa	Nanoa
Nanking, Nganking	Nanjing
Nganhui	Anhui
Ningpo	Ningbo
Pei-ho	Bei He
Peking, Pekin	Beijing
Shanghae	Shanghai
Sifu, Suifu	Shuifu
Soochow	Suzhou
Sung dynasty	Song dynasty
Swatow	Shantou
Szechuan, Szechuen, Szechwan	Sichuan
Taku Forts	Dagu Forts
Tientsin	Tianjin
Tze Hsi, Tz'u-hsi	Cixi
Wan-Hsien	Wanxian
Whangpoo River	Huangpu
Woo-e-shan	Wuyi Shan
Woosung	Wusong
Yang-tse, Yang-tsze, Yangtse Kiang, Yangtze River	Chang Jiang, Yangzi River
Yüan Ming Yüan	Yuanmingyuan

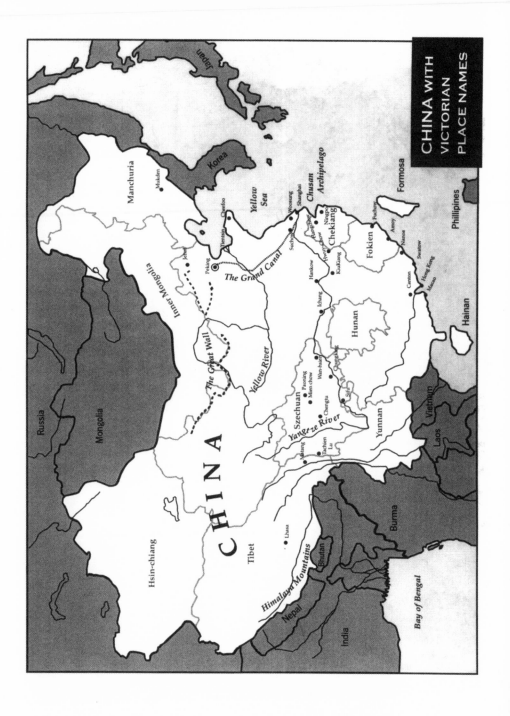

CHINA WITH VICTORIAN PLACE NAMES

"Factories" in Canton in 1841. Courtesy, Peabody Essex Museum, Salem, Massachusetts.

Introduction

Opening China

AT THE END OF the Opium War in 1842, the *Illustrated London News* exulted over the expanse of territory "opened to the speculation of our merchants."[1] The article ended by proclaiming the opening of China as good not only for Britain's commercial interests but also for the Chinese:

> A large family of the human race, which for centuries has been isolated
> from the rest, is now about to enter with them into mutual intercourse.
> Vast hordes of populations, breaking through the ignorance and superstition which has for ages enveloped them, will now come out into the open
> day, and enjoy the freedom of a more expanded civilization, and enter
> upon prospects immeasurably grander. The mighty extension, also, on the

other hand, of the political and commercial influence of England is almost as enormous as the most ample imagination could desire. The expectations of a nation have rarely been opened to more magnificent and glorious views.

The ambiguity in the last sentence as to which nation is being opened to greater expectations cloaks Britain's triumph in magnanimity. The main metaphor also grants China some saving of face: it is not seized, captured, or formally colonized, but "opened." Still, to the victor belong the spoils: The threshold breached, the foreigner demands the run of the house. For China, where hospitality to the guest is an art form, being forced into the position of an unwilling host symbolizes its intense humiliation for its defeat in the Opium War.

The practical result of that humiliation meant that "opening China" was not so easily accomplished for the British as defeating it in war. Its durable society became the object of a seemingly endless quest to explain, explore, convert, tour, trade with, and Westernize it. Throughout the nineteenth century, Britain and other Western nations battled, made treaties with, and forced concessions from it. They built factories, churches, homes, and hotels on its soil. They said that China would catapult to a position of power in the world if only it would open up to Western progress. One hundred and thirty years after the Opium War, with great fanfare and a certain panache, President Nixon "opened" China in 1972. Chairman Mao and the American president toasting one another at a banquet in the Great Hall of the People signaled a momentous change in the relation between China and the United States, yet the understanding with the People's Republic may also be seen as merely the most recent opening of the ever-mysterious "Middle Kingdom."

This book is about six Victorians who, in their individual ways, took advantage of Britain's original opening of China and, elbow in the door, describe what they see inside. They personalize the diplomatic opening by describing their own experiences and the character and customs of the Chinese. Whether their knowledge of Chinese culture and language remains superficial or they become fluent sinologues, they are alike in being convinced they can offer a unique interpretation of the "mysterious continent," as Isabella Bird terms it in *The Golden Chersonese*, describing her 1878 arrival there. Their travel books reveal authors characteristic of their era—mainly adventurous individualists who with a utilitarian purposefulness use their work for research and their leisure for writing. True to the spirit of the time, they link the beginning of modern tourism with the age of imperialism, combining pleasure travel with scientific investigation, business, international politics, and humanitarianism.

The Western View of China

The image of China in the West since the Middle Ages has been based in part on a recognition of China's ancient engineering feats, technology, and cultural achievements.[2] In the third century B.C., the Qin, or Ch'in (from which comes the name China) emperors built the Great Wall and carried out the hydraulic project that turned the Chengtu plain into a fertile field intersected by dikes, sluices, and irrigation ditches. The standardization of a method of writing during the same period and the establishment of a highly centralized government during the Han dynasty (202 B.C.–220 A.D.) contributed to the development of a uniform and cohesive society. In the Middle Ages, China's technology was unparalleled in Europe. Between 605 and 610, the Chinese built a canal system, using locks, that joined several rivers to form the Grand Canal, 2,500 kilometers in length; the British, by way of contrast, did not begin to build their canal system linking industrial centers until the 1770s.

Many of China's practical and cultural productions were adopted by the West. China's silk was long prized in the West; its papermaking and porcelain technology reached Europe in the sixteenth century; and China's meritocracy system, the selection of civil and military officials by means of competitive examination that was established during the Sung dynasty (960–1279), inspired France during the Enlightenment and Britain in the Victorian era. The Jesuits imitated China's examination system in their colleges, establishing the process culminating in the prestigious Cours Général.[3] In England, the Crimean War marked the end of the purchase system for military rank and the initiation of a merit system for selection

3

of officers, and the British civil service examination system was established in 1870.[4] The mythic image of "fair Cathay" in Europe was founded on observation of solid achievements by the Chinese.

The Western image of China was also a product of nearly opposite patterns of contacts between China and the West. Although there was some Chinese exploration of central and western Asia during the Han dynasty, and of Africa during the Middle Ages, far more Westerners found their way to China than did Chinese to the West. Merchants from the Roman Empire traded in South China. The Nestorian Christians arrived in the seventh century, Moslems and Arab traders in the tenth century, and Venetians (including Marco Polo) in the thirteenth century. Discovery of ancient Chinese coins in Viking-era settlements in Ireland speaks to possible trade between northern Europeans and the Chinese.[5] The Portuguese colonized Macao in the early sixteenth century, and the Jesuits gained entry in 1583, maintaining a strong presence for nearly three centuries. Finally, British and European traders began to establish permanent "factories," warehouses, artisan shops, and residences near Canton at the end of the seventeenth century, and the Western mythicizing of China as a land of luxury and exquisite cultural productions reached its zenith.

The Jesuits, led by the brilliant Matteo Ricci (1552–1610) may be said to have first opened China when they arrived at the imperial court with Western learning, technology, and religion. They introduced clocks and modern geography, although the Chinese were always purported to resist the latter.[6] The Jesuits reformed the Chinese calendar, cast modern European astronomical instruments, and designed the Western-style mansions built in Yüan Ming Yüan, the Summer Palace destined to be destroyed by the French and English in 1860.

While Europeans made modest progress in changing China, China made great progress in seducing its foreign guests. Father Ricci had hoped to convert the emperor and thereby all of China, following the model of Constantine and the Romans. Instead, as privileged servants of the emperor and scientists to the court, the Jesuits fell under the spell of the public order and prosperity of China. They forwarded the West's image of China as Cathay, the land of tea, silk, picturesque gardens, and the attractive humanism of Confucius and Mencius. Their tolerance for Chinese rituals only confirmed the emperor's sense that the barbarians had come to pay him tribute, though they did develop a sizable Roman Catholic constituency in Peking and Nanking. The Jesuits' enthusiasm for China was checked in 1742 when the pope ruled against their assertion of the spirituality of ancestor worship, thus solidifying similar rulings in 1715 and 1722. The Chinese emperor was insulted by this chastisement of his Jesuit courtiers, and their long period of influence at the court ended.

The impact on China of these Western contacts before the nineteenth century is a matter of debate, for although the Chinese adopted some Western technology and learning, they remained unmoved by, and perhaps unaware of, the political, economic, and social changes emerging from the age of exploration in Europe.[7] Modern historians believe that China's interest in the West ground to a halt at the end of the Ming dynasty (1368–1643). The Ch'ing dynasty closed in on itself, becoming complacent and resistant to change, and by 1775 began a decline that left it vulnerable to both internal rebellion and external invasion. The White Lotus Rebellion (1796–1804) and the Taiping Rebellion (1850–1864) represent a populist response to serious governmental and social problems. Moreover, the policy of the Ch'ing emperors to control and contain foreign presence in the eighteenth and early nineteenth centuries was a failing that ultimately contributed to its war with England and Western imperialist intrusions after 1842. Administrative inefficiency, widespread corruption among officials, failed leadership of scholars, debasement of the military, a strained treasury, and an inability to meet the pressures of a sharply rising population increasingly plagued the dynasty until its collapse in 1910/1911.[8]

A deterioration of the image of China in the West developed simultaneously with signs of decline in the Ch'ing dynasty.[9] By the middle of the eighteenth century, the tone of allusions to China in British literature began to change, such as in Jonathan Swift's wry comment on the Western appetite for Chinese exports when he satirizes a type of English woman for whom the globe must be "circled three times" so that she can "get her breakfast, or a cup to put it in."[10] In the early nineteenth century, Charles Lamb's description of the design on a china teacup in his essay "Old China" hints at the dismantlement of the mythic image of China by projecting it as delicate but preposterous.[11] As the Opium War ended in 1842, Tennyson contrasted

China and the dynamic British Empire in his often quoted lines in "Lock-seley Hall": "Thro' the shadow of the globe we sweep into the younger day:/ Better fifty years of Europe than a Cycle of Cathay." By 1848, a visit to the *Keying,* a Chinese junk docked for exhibition in the Thames, prompted Dickens to ridicule China as devoid of value.[12] John Stuart Mill, writing *On Liberty* during the Second Opium War, capitalized on the image of China as stagnant, cautioning that the Chinese are "a warning example," a people that demonstrated enormous talent and progressiveness and that then, he says hyperbolically, became "stationary—have remained so for thousands of years."[13] The image of China reached its nadir in fiction such as Shiel's *The Yellow Danger,* published during the Boxer Rebellion, which depicts China as decadent and dangerous.[14]

With the enshrinement of progress in Victorian industry and cultural life, Victorians increasingly viewed China as a static society. They tended to see civil strife in China as an internal problem not particularly important unless it threatened their own security and their own political and economic interests. At the same time, many Victorians had the sense that the various Western encroachments on Chinese sovereignty in the nineteenth century contributed to its problems.

The China Trade and the Opium War

Swift's mordant allusion to tea and porcelain economically brings up England's China problem at the end of the eighteenth century: trade. The trade problem began with tea. Tea became available on the London market in 1657, and the East India Company quickly turned the beverage into a national necessity. However, the European appetite for China's tea, porcelain, and silk was unequaled by Chinese interest in Western goods, and this resulted in a mounting trade imbalance. Between 1781 and 1793, Chinese imports of English woolens, Indian spices, and other trade items amounted to only one-sixth of the Chinese export of tea to England.[15] In lieu of items for exchange, China required payment for its goods in silver. The silver— the cargo of British ships often consisted almost entirely of silver bullion— exchanged hands at Canton. The flow of silver into China as payment for these goods had economic effects in all parts of the world.[16] Although the

British dominated the China trade (tea, silk, and porcelain, as well as goods produced especially for the foreign market, including furniture, wallpaper, and decorative items), other nations, too—the United States, Holland, Sweden, and others—established trading companies in Canton.

In 1759, as a result of internal considerations, the Chinese emperor established Canton as the only port open to foreign trade.[17] The ensuing Canton System of Trade had several elements that set China and the West on a collision course. The Chinese bureaucracy regarded foreign trade as a privilege bestowed on others by the emperor. Numerous regulations controlled both the foreigners themselves and their trade with China. Access to the mainland by foreigners was severely limited. Their "factories"—Western-style offices, warehouses, and residences—were confined to a strip of land on the Pearl River outside the city walls of Canton. In an effort to avert a repetition of the Portuguese colonization of Macao, foreign women were strictly prohibited (and as a result Macao had a large contingent of foreign women). At Macao, foreign ships had to secure a local pilot and gain permission to continue to Whampoa, an island sixteen miles from Canton, where Chinese "compradores" arranged such matters as the transfer of goods to native boats.

The main feature of foreign trade in China was its monopolistic structure. The Cohong, or "hong merchants," were authorized as sole agents to oversee and control all aspects of this trade. The best of them acquired enormous wealth, but they also were exploited by Chinese officialdom and held responsible for any problems arising from the foreign trade. The exaction of various fees, custom duties, and minor extortions were often a source of contention between the Chinese and foreigners. The Chinese system for settling disputes about business practice was cumbersome and exasperated Western traders, though it served Chinese interests in maintaining control over the foreigners. Foreign traders were required to communicate their complaints to the hong merchants, who forwarded them to the "hoppo"—court-appointed officials—who might pass the complaints on to the provincial governor or the court in Peking or do nothing at all. It is not hard to imagine the vexation the Chinese regulations caused the traders, nor the anxiety the drain of resources caused the British government.

China's self-sufficiency, its ancient tribute system, corruption, and the

7

vested interests of the hong merchants collaborated to maintain traditional methods. While the emperor clung to a narrow, highly structured, and authoritarian worldview, the West was pursuing new ideas and new technologies that valued change. Democracy, individualism, and free trade inspired fierce competition among the Europeans and Americans desiring to trade with China. Britain wanted to use modern diplomacy to address its grievances, and toward that purpose sent Lord Macartney to China in the years 1792 to 1794 to arrange a trade agreement and exchange of ambassadors. The story of the Macartney mission has the elements of a Hollywood epic: tremendous spectacle, a clash between two lofty national images, disputes over form, and costly misjudgment. Macartney's entourage included more than eighty officials, artisans, musicians, and others. They took with them a huge and valuable assortment of presents representing the best of Britain's technology and art. Macartney was first housed in the Summer Palace, then escorted with much fanfare to the Emperor Ch'ien-lung at his retreat in Jehol, where a fabulous banquet and exchange of gifts took place in a magnificent tent. A protracted negotiation had been carried out about the kowtow, or the form of Macartney's obeisance to the emperor (refusing to prostrate himself nine times, as required by Chinese protocol, Macartney agreed to genuflect on one knee), but the substance of his mission was assiduously dodged. The emperor remained unfailingly polite and patronizing while agreeing to nothing. Afterwards, Macartney was taken by boat along the Grand Canal to rejoin his ship in the south of China. Until the end he bore hope that his mission would be accomplished. For his part, Emperor Ch'ien-lung, hopelessly mired in a xenophobic, backward-looking state, never had any intention of establishing diplomatic relations with Britain.[18] A successive mission by Lord Amherst in 1816 ended in disaster due to Chinese confusion about the purpose of the mission, and Lord Amherst never even met the emperor. Lord Napier's unfortunate illness and death ended a further effort to establish trade relations in 1839. China had not caught up with the idea of modern diplomacy or treaties with foreign powers.

These matters of business, diplomacy, and cultural difference caused enormous friction in the relationship between Britain and China. The friction might have been eased but for one added antagonism: opium. Opium was the immediate if not the sole cause of the Opium War of 1839–1842; without it, it is safe to say, there would not have been a war. The East India Company had established a monopoly on the opium trade in 1773 by forcing Indian farmers to grow opium for sale in China, controlling the trade from seedling to sale. As Greenberg points out, "opium was no hole-in-the-corner petty smuggling trade, but *probably the largest commerce of the time in any single commodity.*"[19] The size of the trade may be judged by the amount of opium imported from India annually: one thousand chests (a chest equals one hundred thirty-three pounds) in the late eighteenth century and eight-seven thousand chests in 1879.[20] The East India Company's lucrative operation enticed other traders to emulate it. Soon the Jardine & Matheson Company, the American Russell & Company, and several others challenged the monopoly established by the East India Company.

The pawn to these powerful economic forces was the growing number of Chinese addicted to the drug. Although the opium poppy had long been known in China as a medicinal plant, opium smoking began only in the eighteenth century as an indirect result of the introduction of tobacco smoking in the seventeenth century. The addictiveness of opium led to a vicious cycle: increased demand; an increased number of suppliers, both domestic and imported; and further addiction. The causes of opium addiction in China have been attributed to a confluence of social, economic, and political factors that included population pressures, a decrease in living standards, and an increase in government corruption.[21]

Both the British and the Chinese were well aware of the consequences of addiction long before the Opium War. C. Toogood Downing, an Irish physician who served in Canton in the 1830s, noted, "That some of the Chinese entertain very correct notions of the evils of this habit, there is abundant evidence."[22] The evidence he cites are paintings by Sunqua, the "Chinese Hogarth," illustrating the progress of addiction, that were described in the *Chinese Repository* in 1837.[23] For their part, the Chinese emperors had been concerned about the effect of opium among the leisured class and they issued various edicts forbidding opium use, sales, and smuggling in 1729, 1796, 1800, and 1813; however, the opium trade was so profitable and the market so available that neither the foreigners nor Chinese involved in the trade were much troubled by these edicts.

From Britain's point of view, opium was crucial to its commercial expansion. China, on the other hand, saw not only the demoralizing effect of increased addiction but also that opium was cutting into its immense silver reserves built up by the tea trade. In 1839, the exasperated emperor appointed Lin Tse-hsü (Zexu), a strong anti-opium advocate, to be imperial commissioner charged with suppressing the opium traffic. Commissioner Lin, as history knows him, invoked a number of measures to accomplish his goal, including confining three hundred and fifty foreigners to their compounds for six weeks. His most radical measure was the destruction of more than twenty-one thousand chests, about three million pounds of raw opium. The opium was mixed with salt and lime and flushed into a creek that carried the mess to the ocean. It was a dramatic but shortlived victory, for the Chinese were ill-prepared to meet the response to this attack on commerce.

The British launched an enormous military campaign to avenge the insult, lost property, and years of frustrated trade efforts. The military action roused popular support, as indicated by Thomas Carlyle, who writes in *Past and Present* that China itself is to blame for its intransigence in refusing to make trade agreements.[24] Forty-eight ships, including warships, armed steamers, transport, and troop ships, and thousands of troops set upon a technologically inferior and poorly trained Chinese military force. Because the outcome of the Opium War of 1839 to 1842 was never in doubt, Britain's use of excessive force aimed mainly to punish and humiliate China for its uncooperativeness. The English press reports on the progress of the war contrast Britain's modern military might and China's medieval machinery. Illustrations show a strong departure from the serene images and robust figures of the Chinese in the paintings of William Alexander, the official artist who accompanied Macartney in the 1790s.[25] Nearly fifty years later, the *Illustrated London News* used drawings of sampans at rest in a placid bay to depict China's military unpreparedness. As the war drew to a close in 1842, the illustrations were more mocking, such as one entitled "Chinese Artillerymen" that showed soldiers, dressed in the costume of door gods in Buddhist temples, contemplating a giant matchlock—its bamboo sight tied on with a string—mounted on a tree stump.[26] Battle summaries stress superiority in Britain's fifteen-thousand-man fighting force

Nemesis Destroying War Junks. Drawing from *Illus. London News,* 12 Nov. 1842: 420.

that inflicted heavy losses on the Chinese: "We have already slain nearly 8000 Chinamen."[27] Pride in British military power is also apparent in illustrations of its sleek battleship *Nemesis* destroying war junks.[28] Articles in the London *Times* are less sensational, though "Hong Kong Ceded Forever" may be said to overstate the case.[29] Such bravado covers a sense of guilt felt for trouncing an ill-matched opponent. After the Opium War, British involvement with China combines arrogance and shame, and a rank odor wafts over the recurring parliamentary debates on the opium trade.

The Nanking Treaty ending the war forced China into concessions that gave Britain the economic opportunities she wanted.[30] China was forced to open five ports (Canton, Amoy, Foochow, Ningpo, and Shanghai) to British trade, cede Hong Kong, and pay twenty-one million dollars in silver for the lost opium and other damages to British property. Opium was not mentioned in the treaty, thus tacitly allowing the trade. Additionally, a limit was placed on taxation of imported goods, thus curtailing China's ability to profit from free trade. Foreign traders and missionaries who came to exploit the newly opened treaty ports were protected by being exempt from punishment by Chinese law.[31] Similar treaties were soon made with other European nations and the United States, and China became a semicolonial nation for the remainder of the century.[32]

"Chinese Artillery." Drawing from *Illus. London News,* 9 July 1842: 131.

The Lorcha *Arrow* incident in 1856 precipitated the so-called Second Opium War (1856–1860). Events surrounding the Chinese seizing of the *Arrow,* a ship owned by a Chinese resident of Hong Kong but registered with British authorities there, echoed those that ignited the war in 1839. Riots in Canton, attacks on missionaries, and the murder of Augustus Margary, a British official scouting a trade route to Burma, were among causes for further military and diplomatic actions against China and for more treaties and concessions extracted from it after 1842. The Treaty of Tientsin in 1858 was most far-reaching: it legalized opium importation and protected Christian missionaries, set tariffs, opened new treaty ports from Manchuria to Hankow on the Yangtze, and established an ambassador in Peking.[33] The Convention of Peking in 1860 added further clauses, including a large indemnity and ceding the Kowloon peninsula to Britain. The whole of China was now formally open to traders, travelers, and missionaries.

Opium and Missionaries

Britain's success in opening China had its price in that the treaties created a strange link between opium and missionaries. Perhaps nowhere else in the East did imperialism and humanitarian impulses clash so strongly: Britain exploited the opium trade on one hand while justifying it as a means of introducing the gospel on the other. This linkage between the opium trade and Christian proselytizing was recognized early by the Chinese and acknowledged by the British after the Opium Wars. In the 1830s, Downing writes that the Chinese equate opium and missionaries as evils to be eradicated: "At present, they seem determined to exclude equally, and with the same animosity, the introduction of opium, and of novel religious opinions."[34] As the Opium War was drawing to a close, a British war report coupled the opium trade and missionaries as harbingers of change: "Out of evil sometimes cometh good, and the opium trade, which is little understood in this country, may have been the means intended by Providence for introducing the Gospel and altering the condition of that benighted country, for that such an event is sooner or later to take place, no Christian can doubt."[35] It is rare to find such a conscious connection made between evil and its counteracting force, both introduced by the same party. It is a connection that would haunt both missionaries and merchants throughout the nineteenth century, as the treaties made with China deliberately established a role for missionaries seemingly to offset the opium trade.

Before the Opium War, the linkage between missionaries and the opium trade could be attributed to private initiative rather than government policy. The first Protestant missionary in Canton (1809), Robert Morrison, labored twenty years before making a convert, but he put his Chinese to use by writing a dictionary and acting as an interpreter for the East India Company. Morrison was followed by the colorful Prussian Karl Gutzlaff, a brilliant linguist who handed out religious tracts with one hand and abetted opium smugglers with the other, and later became a British consul in Canton. In a quirk of fate, Gutzlaff's translation of the Bible is the one relied on by the man who started the Taiping Rebellion.[36]

In the aftermath of the Opium War, various missionary societies began the process of westernizing China by establishing schools, orphanages, and

hospitals.[37] The China Inland Mission, founded by Hudson Taylor, popularized missionary work and caused a rapid increase in the numbers of missionaries after 1864. Missionaries also became explicators of life in China
and wrote a number of influential books, including those of the Frenchman
Abbé Huc, whose *Travels in Tartary* (1844) and *The Chinese Empire* (1854)
are often cited by Victorians for their unpretentious informativeness. Other
influential books by missionaries include the encyclopedic *The Middle
Kingdom* by the American S. Wells Williams and Arthur H. Smith's controversial *Chinese Characteristics,* which presumes to describe Chineseness.
Some missionaries, such as Annie Taylor, who got almost to Lhasa before
any other Westerner had come near those elevated precincts, added exploration to their religious work, while the Pruens, who went to Yunnan to
convert the Miao, got an anthropological scoop in witnessing the rituals of
an aboriginal tribe, some of whose descendants have recently emigrated to
the United States as the Hmong.[38]

Besides being important contributors to Western knowledge of China,
though, missionaries were objects of touristic interest because of the controversy surrounding them at home and their often hostile treatment by
the Chinese. Every traveler discusses the role of missionaries in China. As
their numbers increased and Chinese attacks against them became more
frequent, "the missionary question" became a matter of public debate in
England. Parliament took up the issue in 1871 after the murder of several
missionaries in the so-called Tientsin Massacre. Travelers visited missionaries partly out of kindness and partly to gather evidence to contribute to
the debate. For these reasons, I have chosen to treat missionaries as a subject rather than as authors.

Victorian Travelers in China

As the Opium War ended, with Hong Kong established as a colony and the
five treaty ports opened to foreign residence and trade, "opening China"
became a quest for thousands of Victorians. Some of these adventurous
souls went out to China in the service of their country, religion, or business;
some went in answer to a more personal call for exploration and travel.
Many submitted to the urge to write about their experience. My search has

yielded about a hundred British travel-and-description books about China between the first Opium War and Britain's agreement to end its opium trade in 1906–1907. In addition to these numerous accounts are a staggering number of American, French, German, Italian, and other travel books on China during this period. The volume of writing about China in the nineteenth century may be indexed by the size of the foreign population there—nearly 8,700 Britons and 4,000 Americans by 1912.[39]

The six travelers who form the basis for this study—three women and three men—represent two streams of travel writers: long-term foreign residents and "globetrotters," the Victorian term for adventure-travelers before the age of mass tourism. The sojourns of these travelers in China span the period of greatest British influence there, from 1843 to 1907. In addition to these broad selection criteria are the purpose, scope, and range of individual travel in China. The contemporary reputation of the travelers, their association with one another, and the significance of their travel accounts are also relevant factors in featuring the six as representative of Victorian interpreters of China and the British presence there.

The timing and itinerary of these travelers offer comprehensiveness to their picture of China. Robert Fortune, horticulturist and collector, spent nearly fifteen years in China, between 1842 and 1861. He saw China from Hong Kong to Shanghai, ventured deep into Chekiang Province, and visited Formosa. Constance Gordon Cumming spent six months in 1878/1879 traveling from Hong Kong to Peking; and Major Henry Knollys spent three months in 1884 touring China from Hong Kong to Hankow. Both Cumming and Knollys kept close to European and American settlements. Isabella Bird (Mrs. Bishop) first visited China briefly in 1878 and then spent fifteen months there in 1895/1896, covering eight thousand miles.[40] Archibald Little, a merchant who spent almost fifty years in China, from 1859 to 1907, and his novelist wife Alicia, who spent twenty years there, from 1887 to 1907, lived in Shanghai, Hankow, Chungking, and Peking, and traveled up the Yangtze River and into the interior of Szechuan, as did Bird. The focus on Hong Kong and the center of China along the Yangtze River from Shanghai to western Szechuan adds unity to these travelers' image of China.

Other criteria for selecting the six travelers include their contemporary reputation and diversity of role or perspective on China. Robert Fortune developed a considerable contemporary reputation and for a brief time in the 1840s held the fate of China's tea trade in his hand. His first two books also captured enough interest to find re-release in a double volume. Quite different from the horticulturist Fortune, Major Knollys, a biographer and military historian, adds a military man's perspective on China. The interest in Cumming's and Bird's views on China derives from their being two of the most celebrated women travelers of their time; and the reputation of the Littles rests on their contribution to China. Archibald Little was a merchant who pioneered steamboats on the upper Yangtze; his wife Alicia crusaded to free China's women from the custom of footbinding. These writers are significant as artifacts of empire in themselves. The three who lived in China for extended periods had a direct interest in the development of Britain's relation with the country; the three "globetrotters" satisfy more personal goals in touring China. As a group, the books of the six illuminate a subtly changing view of China and Britain's role there. They reached a wide audience and thus contributed to the popular image of China.

The six travelers are also linked either by friendship or literary acquaintance, which lends cohesiveness to their commentary on China. They mention one another in their books, but more importantly they use their own accounts to corroborate, take issue with, or add to those who precede them in print. Fortune's books are referred to by Archibald Little and Cumming; Knollys met Archibald Little in Hankow and the men allude to one another in their books; and Cumming and Bird were personal friends whose paths crossed both in China and elsewhere around the globe. Bird stayed with the Littles in Chungking. Cumming alludes to Bird's book, Alicia Little mentions Cumming's book, and Bird refers to Archibald Little's book. Bird and Alicia Little exchanged information and photographs to include in their books. These six travelers form a little community that heightens their credibility as interpreters of China and the British presence there.

Reading China

For Britain, "opening China" included a mix of exploitative goals and generous-minded Western improvements. To individual travelers, opening China meant laying clear its national character, its idiosyncrasies, cultural attributes, attitudes, manners, and customs. Victorian travelers were influenced by the historical events and political climate of their era in addition to their professional interests, gender, and cultural biases. These subjects provide the framework for the chapters that follow.

Victorians were well aware of China's ancient civilization. They were also generally persuaded of the rightness of imperialism, yet they often reflect ambivalence toward and uneasiness about Britain's China policy. As a result, their discourse accommodates the goals both of economic expansionism and humanitarian enterprise and of ideology and morality. Travelers' attention to these concerns results in one of the remarkable features of Victorian accounts of China: a high level of polemics; hence, every book contains, in addition to descriptions of manners and customs, an argument for or against the opium trade and support of or attack on missionary activity. Many books devote entire chapters to each of these subjects. The depiction of China is similarly ideological, but inconsistently so. Most travelers find much to praise as well as fault, at times paradoxically, for example, calling China both backward and the most well-educated society on earth. The travel writers' discourse accommodates a broad spectrum of views both on China and the British presence there.

To analyze the response to China reflected in the books of Victorian travelers, I appeal to an eclectic array of popular and scholarly resources, including contemporary journalism and fiction and current literary theory, history, biography, and ethnography.[41] Since my primary interest is literary and my subject the view of China presented in the writings of Victorian travelers, I place the writings as much as possible in the context of both Victorian Britain and "colonial" China. To some readers this may occasionally seem to exaggerate Britain's influence in China or to neglect the Chinese perspective. Obviously, the Chinese view of history and the West may be somewhat different from my own, as well as from that of the foreigners who wrote about it in the nineteenth century.

My examination of the six travelers in this study is also influenced by the concept of orientalism as described by Said in his book *Orientalism.* Said's work has had a dramatic impact on the reading of Western texts on the "Orient," a word that has come to symbolize just about all (former) colonial and Third World nations.[42] For to Said, the Orient is not so much— or, rather, not only—a discrete place, but also an entity over which the West can exert power. The orientalist "makes the Orient speak" rather than listens to it. By "representing it or speaking in its behalf" the orientalist, by which Said means the Westerner, projects the Orient as weak or decadent, a topos of the exotic, cruel, and barbarous, or whatever is considered to be non-Western.[43]

In speaking for China, Victorian travelers reflect such orientalist representations while simultaneously expressing consciousness of and respect for China's once-glorious civilization.[44] Discussing the alteration in China's status during their era, travelers treat the nation as a backward child who must be coached and patronized. This happens even when travelers criticize the West for its role in China, as Bird does in introducing *The Yangtze Valley and Beyond*, the subject of chapter 5. She begins by chiding the "talk about 'open doors' and 'spheres of influence' and 'interest' [and] much greed for ourselves," but ends by connecting compassion for the Chinese with Western covetousness when she worries about the risk of "ignoring the men who, for two thousand years, have been making China worth scrambling for" (YVB, 11). Such sympathy drowns out the voice of China.

Some Victorian accounts of China, particularly those of the globetrotters, present the colonizer and colonized as opposites. Knollys, whose tour of China is discussed in chapter 4, has a powerful "us and them" mentality. He would make it fairly easy to take the line of anticolonialist interpretations in describing the Westerner as heartless exploiter and the Asian as hapless victim.[45] However, travel writing about China, like China itself, does not lend itself to easy categorizing because most travelers fall under the spell of "Cathay," as Knollys regrets. Even when they go to China as conquerors bent on altering centuries of mercantile and religious customs, Victorians often come away of two minds about their efforts.

An explanation of this phenomenon lies in the paradoxical lure of

China's legendary xenophobia. Zhang Longxi writes that "while the Westerners tend to see the Chinese as fundamentally Other, sometimes the Chinese would think the Westerners eager to become like the Chinese themselves, that is, if they want to become civilized at all."[46] If the Western travelers do not necessarily see themselves as becoming "civilized" by their experience in China, some do "become like the Chinese" in adapting to life in China, or attacking the depredations of the West for corrupting traditional Chinese culture, or undertaking a humanitarian project to benefit the Chinese.

From another point of view, becoming "like the Chinese themselves" represents a literary colonization project when writers attempt to explain and interpret Chinese customs and beliefs by reconstructing Chinese reality in relation to Western values and perspectives. Novels, perhaps culminating in Pearl Buck's *The Good Earth* (1931), often represent the extreme of such literary colonization. Earlier examples are Payn's *By Proxy* (1878), which reproves the Englishman's affront to Chinese sensibilities, from eroticizing Chinese women to defacing religious shrines, and Ready's *Ch'un-Kwang* (1905), which aims to give an accurate picture of Chinese domestic life in a sentimental romance showing that "'All the world's akin.'" The chapter on Mrs. Little makes extensive use of nineteenth-century fictional representations of China that complement the travel writing of English residents.

Although most Victorian travelers demonstrate an appreciation for certain aspects of Chinese culture, they do so with a sense of superiority. They deploy race to essentialize China's dissimilarity from the West, commonly featuring subjects that sensationalize cultural difference. In broaching the subject of cultural difference, I am made self-conscious by Bhabha's argument in "The Other Question" that stereotype or "'fixity' in the ideological construction of otherness" is used even in anticolonialist argument so as to support the colonialist point of view.[47] Bhabha explains that the discussion of stereotype aligns the colonizer with the positive and the colonized with the negative. Similarly, Mohanty observes, the occidental judging of colonialist texts "amount[s] to a kind of colonialism all over again, a paternalistic desire to interpret the other's interests for her or him."[48] The Chinese themselves seem to offset this tendency, however, by "othering" or racializing those who are describing them, even if their voice is filtered through the account of the traveler.

The Chinese racializing of the foreign visitor demonstrates the reverse of Pratt's findings on the "gaze"—her interpretation of the tropes used in the explorer's observation of landscape and people. In discussing Barrow's travel account of southern Africa, Pratt argues convincingly that "seeing as an inherently passive and innocent act cannot be sustained."[49] Seeing is the antecedent of appropriation and exploitation; thus the act of seeing is itself highly charged with the imperialist project. But transferring this kind of analysis to travel writing about China can take us only so far, for Victorians did not go to China as to an empty land that yields to the monarchical gaze Pratt ascribes to the explorer. Travelers in China constantly faced, not to say were harassed by, the nuanced response of those gazed upon. The "foreign devil" meeting the "celestial" and the "barbarian" meeting the "barbarous" represents a unique combat between counter-stereotypes, a simultaneous orientalizing and occidentalizing—a subject that I take up mainly in chapter 5.

Victorian travelers struggled to find a professional voice in their presentation of information about Chinese life and culture. Porter writes that Victorian ethnography is the "province of amateurs," but science and personal journal may be found layered and interwoven in many substantive works.[50] In books as different and separated by time as Darwin's *Voyage of the Beagle* (1845) and Lévi-Strauss's *Tristes Tropiques* (1955), for example, the voice of both the traveler and the scientist, diarist and professional may be heard.[51] The different voices of the traveler prompt Frawley in *A Wider Range* to link women travel writers to the professions as sociologists, art historians, and so on. The Victorians who write about China similarly speak with several voices, toggling their role as traveler with that of ethnographer, naturalist, and geographer. Added to those voices are those of the actual professionals—of Fortune as horticulturist, Knollys as military officer, Archibald Little as merchant, and Alicia Little as novelist. As travelers write in multiple voices, their texts often reveal inconsistent and conflicting views of Chinese culture as well as of their own government and its role in China. My investigation of the travelers' texts considers the impact of these multiple voices.

The unselfconsciousness with which Victorians combine their different voices is of special interest in view of the recent discussions about the problems of representational authority in ethnographical writing. In this specialized kind of writing, as Victorian amateurism gave way to the professionalism of the field-worker–theorist and empirical researcher in the twentieth century, the autobiographical self lay sequestered under a layer of objectivity. However, modern ethnologists have come to understand that autobiography and ethnology are inseparable.[52] The reestablishment of the autobiographical self in ethnographical writing is often attributed to the discovery of a personal diary kept by Malinowski while he did the research published as *Argonauts of the Western Pacific*.[53] The discrepancy between the "life-among-the-savages" persona of the *Diary* and the "objective" anthropologist who describes the Trobiand Islanders has led ethnographers to ask not just which version is accurate, but whether any ethnographical account can be separated from the ideology and personality of its author. Malinowski's fashioning of a "divided self" inevitably invites others to reconstitute the unsplintered original. The process is reversed in Victorian travel writers. They celebrated wholeness, so to speak—allowing prejudice and personality to color their observations and daring the reader to detach ethnography from autobiography. How autobiography and ethnographical description intersect is taken into account in my study of Victorians in China.

Beyond the desire to be informative, individual travelers had personal economic goals for "Opening China." Chapters 1 and 2 consider the "business" of empire as represented by two men whose stay in China was directly related to the commercial interests that drove Britain's China policy in the nineteenth century. Travel writing was also part of the "business of empire," however. Victorian travel writing enjoyed the benefits of an age in which emigration continued apace and mass tourism emerged.[54] Numerous people went abroad, and many others found pleasure in the travelers' accounts of foreign countries, apparently agreeing with Emily Dickinson that "there is no frigate like a book." Possibly those who traveled were also consumers of travel books, but in any case, tales of adventurous travel beyond the reach of most sold well.

Most of the China books of the travelers included in this study saw more than one edition. Fortune realized a sizable profit from his book sales. The financial return of his years in China is discussed in chapter 1. Cumming, who came home from her years of travel to find her income lost to bad investments, was driven "by sheer necessity" to turn to travel writing to earn a living.[55] Her sales appear to have been assisted by her aristocratic background. Bird was not only an inveterate traveler but a traveler who, encouraged by her publisher John Murray, sometimes chose her itinerary with a view toward producing a book about the journey. The popularity of Bird's books is indicated by the size of her estate at her death (1904): £33,408.[56]

Besides hoping to write a popular book, most travel writers are also interested in the art of writing itself, and they often employ the methods found in contemporary essays and novels to color the account of their sojourn. Percy Adams has shown with a mass of evidence in *Travel Literature and the Evolution of the Novel* how fiction may be seen as an outgrowth of travel writing.[57] But Victorian travel writing about China reflects the crossover of this phenomenon in enhancing—or fictionalizing—experience with sensational details and what Behdad calls "'self-exoticism.'"[58] How presentation affects substance is therefore another topic I consider in the following chapters.

Ever since Lady Eastlake's comments on travel writers in 1845, criticism of travelers has tended to fall along gender lines. Women's travel writing is superior to men's, Lady Eastlake writes, in its attention to "close and lively details" and its style, "all ease, animation, vivacity," in contrast to the "gentleman's either dull and matter-of-fact, or off-hand and superficial" writing.[59] Subsequent criticism of women's travel writing privileges adventurousness, as in Blaikie's "Women Traveler's" and Middleton's *Victorian Lady Travelers.*[60] More recently, studies of women travelers such as those of Birkett, Mills, Morgan, and Pratt focus on feminine discourse as it relates to or is in conflict with the discourse of imperialism.[61] The gender division in discussing travel writing is also continued by Fussell, who virtually ignores women travelers because they do not fit his masculinist idea of travel. Porter apologizes for excluding women since the father-son relation is essential to his analysis.[62] Leed (with "Women's Mediations") and Buzard (on women and family touring parties) compartmentalize women travelers as a small part of a large study.[63]

By dividing my attention between men and women and between globetrotters and long-term residents of China, I deliberately look for the ways gender, length of stay, and purpose or occupation in China structure the dialogue between the traveler and place. Gender clearly shapes the experience of Victorians in China. Both Western and Eastern patriarchal forms influence the mechanics of travel, sightseeing, and the traveler's relation with the Chinese. The division between globetrotters and those who lived and worked in China is marked but subtle. While the accounts of longtime residents of China reflect a greater depth of understanding of the culture, history, and language than those of short-term travelers, globetrotters compensate by research: Cumming and Bird feel compelled to be encyclopedic. Globetrotters focus on difference more than longtimers do; they also pay more attention to describing the Chinese national character. But along with commitment to China comes cynicism about its present and future that often blurs the lines between the "twenty-years-in-the-country" people and the globetrotters. After giving a close reading in the earlier chapters to the texts Victorians produced about China, in the conclusion I draw together the inferences on gender, time, and travel in a semicolonial China.

part one

Travel and the Business of Empire

Tea Plantations. Frontispiece in Robert Fortune, *The Tea Districts of China*.

one

Gathering in China

Robert Fortune

As EXCITEMENT about the end of the Opium War mounted in London after the decisive battle at Ningpo in August 1842, a popular Chinese Exhibition opened in Hyde Park. A two-story pagoda constructed especially for the purpose housed "Ten Thousand Chinese Things," actually 1,341 items, displaying the "Genius, Government, History, Literature, Agriculture, Arts, Traditions, Manners, Customs, and Social Life of the People of the Celestial Empire." This "gorgeous exhibition" seemed to herald British victory over this fabled land.[1] When details of the Nanking Treaty were publicized in the *Times* in December 1842, the popular press made the end of the war less noteworthy than its treaty provisions—the opening of five new ports and the "splendid advantages . . . of opening a mighty empire and its resources to ourselves."[2] Even an organization seemingly distanced from mercantile politics, the Royal Horticultural Society (RHS), joined the rush to capitalize on the drubbing of the Celestial Empire and decided to send Robert Fortune on a botanical collection mission to China.

At age thirty, Fortune had already demonstrated the intelligence, ambition, and adaptability that made him particularly suitable for the RHS expedition. From humble origins as a garden boy at a country estate in Berwickshire, he rose to prominence at the Royal Botanic Garden in Edinburgh before becoming a superintendent at the botanic gardens in Chiswick in 1842. In the next twenty years, he would be employed by the RHS, the East India Company, and the United States, make five journeys and spend nearly fifteen years in China, and visit Java, Manila, Formosa, India, and Japan. With a utilitarian usefulness, he gathered observations on not only horticulture but Chinese aesthetics and social customs to produce four books of travels: *Three Years' Wanderings* (1847), *A Journey to the Tea Countries* (1852), *A Residence among the Chinese* (1857), and *Yedo and Peking* (1863).[3] These books help chart the story of China between the two Opium Wars and the evolution of Victorian views of China.

Fortune's initial mission in China was to collect plants for the enrichment of British gardens and the RHS. The kind of financial return the organization hoped to make on Fortune's work is suggested by the fact that the Duke of Devonshire paid a hundred guineas for the first imported specimen of *Phaloenopsis Amablis,* a rare, spectacular orchid found in the Philippines.[4] To insure that Fortune's venture turned a profit, the RHS attempted to prevent him from taking private commissions, laying claim to all plants he would collect. In a letter from 1846 marked Private, Fortune worries about patents and sale of plants propagated from his collections and shows a shrewd calculation of the value of certain plants.[5] Fortune's fear of being deprived of personal profit by the RHS draws attention to the mutual interests underwriting the mission.

Although his employers had an imprecise idea of what Fortune might find, they were certain of its value. Their instructions imply a belief in the superiority of both Chinese produce and the horticultural practices that the RHS expected to appropriate. Fortune was ordered to collect twenty-two specific plants, some of them rather fanciful, such as the "peaches of Pekin, cultivated in the Emperor's Garden and weighing 2 lbs."[6] He was also instructed to gather information on more mundane topics such as the management of manure. Once in China, he at first approached his assignment with the imagination of a lazy schoolboy and happily took advantage of the knowledge accumulated by a Dr. Maxwell, "an ardent lover of botanical pursuits," thus saving himself "some months" of personal research (TYW 63). Soon, though, his collecting activities took him to the gardens and nurseries of the Chinese, and his representation of plant collection becomes less personal and more political.

Fortune's plant collecting follows in the wake of voyages of discovery and scientific collecting that from the eighteenth century on set out to find, classify, and ultimately lay claim to natural resources, plants, and animals from all parts of the globe. This work is associated with what Pratt has described as the "project of natural history," in itself an "utterly benign and abstract appropriation of the planet," though it also provided a means of "territorial surveillance, appropriation of resources, and administrative control."[7] Fortune's successive missions in China follow this scenario as his work becomes enmeshed in the British imperial project. At the same time, his plant gathering engages him in a benevolent effort to "gather in" Chinese culture. In Fortune's case, occupation and acculturation collude in the business of empire.

Signaling the essential role he plays in China, Fortune begins his first book with an appropriation trope. He says that by keeping the world at bay for so long, the Chinese perpetuated "the false colouring which has been given to every picture by authors who have written on this country, and who have extolled to the skies her perfection in the arts, in agriculture, in horticulture, the fertility of the soil, the industry of the people, and the excellence of her government and laws" (TYW 4). Now the curtain is "rent asunder" by men like himself living among the Chinese, and "we find, after all, that China is just like other countries." Echoing the nature of his plant gathering, Fortune's comment is on the one hand benign in that he means to depict China as part of the family of nations, and not as unapproachable or fantastic. On the other hand, he means to rob it of its aura even as he aims to collect China's assets for the enrichment of the West.

Before he can collect China's riches, Fortune must first learn to negotiate Chinese culture. He shows this in anecdotes that demonstrate his transition from naïve traveler to street-smart operative, for example in his pursuit of a yellow camellia he was ordered to collect by the RHS. The abundance and variety in Chinese nursery gardens attract him as an easy means of fulfilling his instructions, but this means of collecting allows him to be duped by a "rogue" who tricks him into buying what turns out to be a common camellia instead of the prized plant he sought (TYW 93). The episode suggests that the Victorian stereotype of the Chinese as greedy and crafty arose at least in part by the Europeans' desire to see the Chinese as simple rustics. Fortune says he had fancied himself as cunning as the Chinese, but he had really imagined they were too innocent to accept his money fraudulently.[8] Moreover, his desire to obtain inexpensive items to sell at great price in England sets up the conditions for his entrapment. Although he loses some money, Fortune learns some lessons in basic business sense that show China is indeed "just like other countries."

Mingling occupation and acculturation, Fortune generates a collection of practical suggestions that usually show him trying to adapt to Chinese manners rather than force a Western style on the Chinese. This is evidenced in the collecting anecdotes he tells most animatedly—not those about discovery of plants in the wild, but those in which he must outwit the Chinese in order to purchase a specimen. In an early episode, he explains his method of gradually winning the trust of wary Chinese: "A few months wrought a great change upon these diffident and timid people, and, at length, they . . . begged me to bring my friends and acquaintances to see their flowers" (TYW 133–34). Plant collectors have scoffed at Fortune's unoriginality in finding "new" plants in nursery gardens, but from the point of view of cultural politics his method is astute. It proves invaluable in later journeys, when the ante in collecting the plants of China is raised. Connecting with the Chinese psychologically and overcoming their legendary suspicion of foreigners gives Fortune a pleasing ambassadorial quality, though put to use in a business context, his attainment manipulates trust.

Thoroughly professional in his work, Fortune served his employers well. In the places he explored, he gathered data on climate, rainfall, temperature, and composition of soil—the habitat of the plants he collected. He nurtured plant specimens by potting them or planting them in the gardens of English friends in Shanghai and Canton where they would remain until ready for shipping home in what amounted to a miniature greenhouse, called the Wardian case. As insurance against catastrophe, he sent duplicates home on different ships. Altogether, Fortune introduced to England about 250 species of plants, 190 previously unknown there, including the windflower, bleeding heart, and his personal favorites *weigela rosea* and Japanese anemone. Others were the fan palm and species of rhododendron and spirea bearing his name, and varieties of roses, camellias, azaleas, and peonies. He also sent about 450 herbarium specimens to England, most during his first stay in China.[9]

After returning to England in May 1846, Fortune wrote his first volume of travels and took a new position as curator for the botanic gardens of the Royal Society of Apothecaries. His stay in China had brought him fame and success that must have gratified him as much as it irritated his employers at the RHS. In 1845, his request for a salary increase had been refused with a stinging reminder of his social class: "The mere pecuniary returns of your mission ought to be but a secondary consideration" because of the "distinction and *status* which you could not have attained in any other way."[10] For agents of empire such as Fortune, it was held, the surveillance and appropriation of resources is work of the lower classes, accomplished for the empowerment and economic gain of the privileged classes.

However, competence had its rewards. The "distinction and status" Fortune gained from his first sojourn in China attracted the attention of the East India Company, and in 1848 he again set out for China, this time to study tea propagation and manufacture. During his first journey, he had made pertinent discoveries, such as that black and green tea come from the same plant, differing merely in their processing.[11] Fortune's boast that "even those who have had the best means of judging have been deceived" (TYW 198) emphasizes his ability to ferret out information that China had always jealously guarded. That was the ability on which the East India Company hoped to capitalize. While the RHS had selected Fortune for its China mission based on his horticultural skills, the new position added those of a commercial traveler, with proportionally higher stakes. The RHS had merely wanted to enhance its collections and earn money from its nursery stock; the East India Company wanted to appropriate the tea trade.

The East India Company, a mercantile empire founded on the tea trade and whose propaganda had turned Britain into a tea-drinking nation, lost its monopoly on the tea trade with China in 1834, due to acts passed by the British Parliament.[12] In the aftermath of the Opium War and the competition created by free trade, the East India Company was looking for new ways to increase its revenues. For that reason, and on the pretext that internal strife in China might disrupt the tea trade, the East India Company treasured the prospect of establishing tea plantations in India. All attempts by Europeans to develop tea plantations had failed. The Chinese themselves were blamed for this failure, for they were accused of boiling the tea seeds they sold foreigners so as to prevent germination; however, failure of early tea plantations was partly due to the horticultural challenge presented by the tea plant itself. The East India Company hoped that Fortune would be able to overcome these difficulties. He was commissioned to buy tea seeds and utensils needed in the processing of tea and to help establish a plantation in India.

Fortune's tea-collecting work may not be the earliest case of commercial espionage, but its success makes it significant. In 1736, the East India Company had sent an orphan named James Flint to China to learn the language as a prelude to his becoming an advocate for the company. Flint lived in China for years and became fluent in Chinese, but his mission for the East India Company, to protest the taxation of tea, ended with his imprisonment.[13] In contrast, Fortune's success may be credited to a simpler plan and more adroit execution in that it avoided government officials and dealt directly with farmers and tea merchants. In order to make his discoveries, Fortune had to overcome both cultural and practical problems, including China's distrust of foreigners and the treaty regulations keeping foreigners in coastal compounds. Success, Fortune believed, lay in disguise. During his first tour of China, he had used disguise to visit Soochow, a city fabled for its beauty but off limits to foreigners. Fortune's motive was curiosity and adventure; his secret weapon was stealth. Although in Chinese costume, he had to trick the boatmen in order to reach the city. The thrill he feels in breaching many rules and passing as Chinese makes his account arresting:

> As I was crossing the bridge, which is built over the moat or canal on the outside of the city walls, numbers of the Chinese were loitering on it, leaning over its sides, and looking down upon the boats which were plying to and fro. I stopped too, and looked down upon the gay and happy throng, with a feeling of secret triumph when I remembered that I was now in the most fashionable city of the Celestial Empire, where no Englishman, as far as I knew, had ever been before. None of the loiterers on the bridge appeared to pay the slightest attention to me, by which I concluded that I must be very much like one of themselves. (TYW 258)

Fortune's "transvestism" is a kind of traveler's game with a number of implications, including an abhorrence of being a "typical tourist" and a desire to deceive the "natives" by appearing to be one of them. As a method of controlling unfamiliar situations, disguise provides the traveler with a sense of security. Fortune's thrill in passing as someone else is linked to his sense that it privileges him to go "where no Englishman" has ever been; his delight is doubled when later his British friends fail to recognize him through the disguise. Such success encourages him to use disguise again in his second tour when he sets out for the tea-producing areas to buy seeds and tea-manufacturing implements.

The purpose of his second trip is to "procure the true plants which produce the finest green teas of commerce" (JTC 21)—literally, to buy twenty thousand seeds to start a plantation in India. For such an important venture, Fortune decides he has to oversee the purchases himself rather than entrust them to an agent because "no dependence can be placed upon the veracity of the Chinese" (JTC 22). Although Fortune means to deprive the Chinese of their monopoly on tea production, his guile is mixed with the naïveté and superiority he showed during his first tour of China. First he apologizes for discrediting Chinese veracity: "I may seem uncharitable, but such is really the case." Then, attiring himself in Chinese dress, shaving his head (rather painfully scraped, it seems), and donning a false queue he goes without a meal because he believes his awkwardness with chopsticks will give away his disguise. He even manages to make himself appear a victim when he realizes that his servant Wang loses no time in telling everyone "in confidence" that his employer is a foreigner. Fortune believes this betrayal places him in great danger, but foreigners were such rare sights outside the treaty ports in the 1840s that they were likely to be treated as curiosities rather than threats. Several examples of Fortune's own experience during his first tour prove this. Besides, the missionary W. H. Medhurst had traveled into the same area before him, so it was not quite as daring an escapade as he makes out. Fortune appears to embellish a travel experience already replete with novelty and risk.[14]

Fortune's fear of discovery on this particular journey is grounded in his duplicity as much as in its risks. He relished his pose as a "mandarin from beyond the Great Wall," as his servants describe him, signaling his desire to meet the Chinese on their terms—as an equal so to speak, rather than as a conquering outsider—and he appears scrupulous in paying a fair price for all his purchases. At the same time, his gambit aims to undermine one of China's main industries. In two separate missions, 1848 to 1851 and 1852 to 1856, he traveled to the Bohea mountains and other important tea districts in the eastern provinces, all in areas sealed to Europeans at that time.[15] In the green-tea district of Hwuy-chow, more than two hundred miles inland from Shanghai, he bought manufacturing implements and about forty thousand tea seeds, and hired supervisors and laborers to work in tea plantations in India. The seeds germinated and the seedlings were transplanted. It took the "enterprise of the practical Scottish gardener" to prove that tea plants could be cultivated outside of China.[16] Fortune succeeded at what numerous others had failed in.

During his first two tours of China, Fortune's tea quest gathered information from the mundane to the esoteric: details about the soil and climate requirements for tea plants; propagation methods; when and how the leaves are picked, dried, and sorted. The effect of disseminating this information to the West was to demystify tea, inevitably moving it from the realm of Eastern exotica to just so much trade goods, sold by the hundred-weight. However, Fortune's various discoveries about tea went further to devalue tea itself.

First, when he writes in *Three Years' Wanderings* that some export teas are "scented" with gypsum and indigo, a caustic reviewer takes offense, suggesting that the "deleterious compounds are employed in adulterating the tea of commerce for the American and European markets."[17] In *Journey to the Tea Countries,* Fortune adds to the process of depreciating tea by undervaluing Chinese labor. He gives a lengthy calculation of the cost of transporting tea from its site of origin to the seaport towns in order to show that "we may still hope to drink our favourite beverage, at least the middling and finer qualities of it, at a price much below that which we now pay" (JTC 270). Finally, on his third tour he observes that in the processing of "caper" tea, it is periodically sprinkled with water of "a yellow, dirty appearance." Inquiring about the ingredients, he is informed "'there was nothing in the water, it was quite clean, but that the workmen were in the habit of washing their hands in it!'" (RaC 209). This singular discovery about a "specialty" tea serves to drive the consumer from the product altogether. Fortune's unraveling of the mysteries of China tea first moves it to the realm of the ordinary, then transforms it into a rather shabby and undelectable substance. Psychologically, he prepares the way to replace the British taste for China tea with the Assam teas that were being produced in India, Ceylon, and Java by the 1880s.[18]

The development of tea plantations outside of China is not solely due to Fortune's seedlings, but is, rather, a long story involving the discovery of a native tea tree in Assam in the early part of the nineteenth century; however, Fortune's pioneering work proved the possibility of tea culture in India. By the end of the Victorian period, China's tea trade had dwindled to one-tenth of what it once held as a monopoly. The legendary Chinese fear of foreigners, which Fortune managed to overcome, appears well grounded. Fortune, on the other hand, became for a brief time England's foremost expert on tea.

Fortune's story, in its way a heroic and canny anecdote in the history of British imperialism, is also one of betrayal and loss to the Chinese—something that Fortune's compatriots often allude to with both triumph and regret. At the end of the Victorian era, Michie calls what happened to the China tea trade "a victory of race over race, of progress over stagnation, of the spirit of innovation and experiment over that of conservative contentment." Ernest Wilson, one of Fortune's successors at the Royal Botanic Garden at Kew in the early twentieth century, blames China's "antiquated" agriculture, "conservative methods," and "heavy taxation" as well as the changing taste of tea drinkers for China's loss of the tea trade.[19] Once the wall surrounding the mythic empire was scaled, its icons fell one by one. Fortune himself recognizes this process when in his second tea-seed buying mission (1852–56) he deems himself familiar enough to the Chinese and reasonably proficient in the language so that he dispenses with disguise and makes all his purchases without incident. Fortune coaxed Chinese farmers to relax their vigilance against foreigners. Men of business like Fortune "opened China" with a mixture of humanity, integrity, and cunning.

While Fortune could exult in his professional success in China, the last chapter in his tea-collecting career serves as poetic justice for his role in decimating China's tea trade. He had returned to China a fourth time, in 1858–59, now in the employment of the U.S. Patent Office (which managed agricultural affairs before the establishment of the Department of Agriculture).[20] He wrote excitedly about superintending the development of a tea plantation in South Carolina and of becoming a sort of Johnny-Teaseed who would render the tea plant "common in every garden of America."[21] To his enormous disappointment, however, after shipping his seed collections to the United States, he was "terminated prematurely, and without notice."[22] He had been so eager to take on this new challenge that he had brushed aside the dangers invoked by the Taiping Rebellion, writing to Mr. Holt at the Patent Office, that "the unsettled state of the country does not interfere with my plans in the slightest degree. Everywhere the people receive me kindly and welcome me back amongst them."[23] Gardener notes in the *Arnoldia* that the looming civil war in the United States may have been responsible for aborting the project. However, the final correspondence between Fortune and the Patent Office indicates that money was an immediate issue. The United States appears to have balked at Fortune's expense account in addition to a six-months salary, and Fortune's demand for payment "by the next mail" was met by a counterdemand for detailed information on the cultivation of tea plants.[24] Fortune had devoted fifteen years to acquiring his expertise on tea production but was unable to parlay it to a postcolonial country. To be fired by the United States at the height of his fame made him bitter.[25] The result of this failed plantation scheme

places Fortune as the unhappy token of a symbolic rebellion against imperialism: Britain's former colony, the United States, using the production of
the semicolony, China, to reprove the "colonizer," Robert Fortune.

The poetic justice in the final chapter of Fortune's tea collecting has a
share of irony, for horticulture rather than imperialist ventures was always
the conscious level of his work for the RHS and East India Company. He
never allowed himself to speculate on what the consequence of developing
tea plantations outside of China might be on China itself, instead seeing
the country simply as a treasure trove to be gathered up by the West, a view
he expresses as late as 1857 about the prospects of extending the opening of
China to its interior: "The riches of the country will be largely developed,
and articles useful as food, in the arts, or as luxuries, at present unknown,
will be brought into the market. It cannot be true that a vast country like
China, where the soil is rich and fertile, the climate favourable, and the
teeming population industrious and ingenious, can produce only two or
three articles of importance, such as silk and tea, for exportation. There
must be many more, and these will be brought to light when the country
is fairly and fully opened to the nations of the west" (RaC 439). The depth
and naïveté of this belief in as-yet-unfound riches in China must have allowed Fortune to overlook the possible harm in his collecting activities; it
is also an oversight basic to the larger goals of empire.

The narrowness of Fortune's vision is apparent also in the egregious er-
rors in his predictions for the future of newly opened territory. One of the
more glaring is his first reaction to Hong Kong, recorded in July 1843 after
a four-month passage from London: "Viewed as a place of trade, I fear
Hong-Kong will be a failure" (TYW 28).[26] Fortune's blunder may be forgiven in consideration of his horticulturist perspective, for in 1843 the fledgling colony was little more than a cluster of wooden buildings at the base
of a bare granite mountain. Behind his initial reaction to China, there are,
too, the concerns about what lies ahead and the wife and children he left
behind.[27] All the same, he never developed an ability to foresee the possibilities and dimensions of international trade. In *Yedo and Peking* he repeats
his singular misjudgment: "As a place of trade, Japan, with all its advantages, has been probably overrated" (YP 293). Clearly, Fortune's skill lay in

areas other than establishing imperial institutions. In his gathering activities, his observations are more dependable and attuned to the immediate setting.

When Fortune's gathering turns from the literal to the metaphoric, to collecting impressions, it entails a process of "naturalization" or acclimation to the oriental setting. Traveling from Hong Kong to the newly opened treaty ports, Fortune discovered the lovely seaside city of Amoy and the beautiful Chusan archipelago, where he is awed by the landscapes. Hillsides covered with blooming azaleas, clematis, wild roses, honeysuckles, "and a hundred others, make us confess that China is indeed the 'central flowery land'" (TYW 67). His original goal of stripping away the myth of China fades as he succumbs to the allure of the landscape: "I do not know anything more beautiful than the yellow bamboo with its clean and straight stem and graceful top and branches waving in the breeze: it always reminded me of our young larch forests at home" (TYW 68). Within months of his arrival in China, his appreciation for the beauty of Chinese flora leads to associating China with Scotland. His second arrival at Hong Kong (1848) shows this process of naturalization more complete:

> It was a clear moonlight night; such a night as one sees only in the sunny lands of the East. Those who have anchored in the bay of Hong-Kong by moonlight will agree with me that the scene at such a time is one of the grandest and most beautiful which can be imagined. On this evening the landlocked bay was smooth as glass, scarcely a breath of air fanned the water, and as the clear moonbeams played upon its surface it seemed covered with glittering gems. Numerous vessels, from all parts of the world, lay dotted around us, their dark hulls and tall masts looming large in the distance. The view was bounded on all sides by rugged and barren hills, and it required no great stretch of fancy to imagine oneself on a highland lake. (JTC 3)

In five years, Hong Kong had changed, but not so much as to obscure the "barren hills" he first saw in 1843. The mind of the traveler, however, had changed a great deal. Now the East is an inviting and romantic space, shifting dramatically from an exotic scene possible "only in the sunny lands of the East" to a place where one might "imagine oneself on a highland lake."

Fortune's description shows how nature itself affects representation: he is home.[28]

Feeling at home in China is for Fortune a kind of psychological transvestism that mirrors his earlier use of disguise. It is demonstrated in his appreciation of the aesthetics of famed Chinese gardens such as those in Soochow and Ningpo that combine ornamental plants with artificial rockwork to form miniature settings in which "the resemblance to nature is perfect" (TYW 98). One of his lengthiest displays of appreciative description appears in his second book (JTC ch. 19), with twenty-four consecutive pages on Shanghai gardens specializing in peonies and azaleas. These gardens stimulate a nonmaterial manifestation of Fortune's appropriative impulse. Assimilating Chinese taste, becoming "like the Chinese themselves," is an unforeseen effect of Fortune's gathering in China.

Such assimilation of Chinese taste is out of step with contemporary British attitudes, according to an angry retort to Fortune's garden descriptions. A review of *Three Years' Wanderings* becomes an occasion to refute the possibility that English gardening could have been influenced by Chinese taste and methods. The writer, Gilbert Lewis, takes the suggestion of such influence as a sort of racial slur and goes so far as to question the provenance of eighteenth-century descriptions of Chinese gardens, for they raise "an anomaly which it is not easy to explain": "A pleasure in beautiful scenery, and the power of wish to imitate or create it, we should have thought most unlikely to be found in a people so palpably deficient in taste on other occasions; and who, in everything connected with the fine arts, are incapable of reaching any elevation of sentiment, or of appreciating the merit even of resemblance."[29] That Fortune's appreciative description of Chinese gardening could arouse such a politicized response is an indication of the trend in the contemporary image of China.

The trend is shown also by William Orr, another reviewer who accuses Fortune of being "utterly at variance" with other writers when he ventures positive views on uncultivated land, warm winter clothing, and the comfortable life of the Chinese; instead, the irate reviewer insists, the Chinese have "long reached the point of starvation at which emigration becomes *necessary.*"[30] Writing on the eve of the Taiping Rebellion, Orr seems to have been more informed than Fortune of the stresses of overpopulation on China. Perhaps Fortune's boyhood in Scotland contributes to his optimistic view of rural life in China—shown, for example, when he contrasts the art of food preparation even among laborers and sailors to the poor fare of the Scots (RaC 43).

At any rate, Fortune appears to have noticed the criticism of his views. He demonstrates conformity to contemporary opinion in his second book by appending comments such as the following to descriptions of public monuments and religious temples: "[A]s works of art they are not to be compared with the buildings of the same class which one meets with at home" (JTC 36). Criticism provoked a self-consciousness in Fortune's judgments that resulted in a deliberate effort to be the conventional Englishman of his day. Interestingly, modern sketches of Fortune continue the patronizing tone of Lewis's indictment: he "shook his head over the heathen darkness"; he was "unemotional" even if "courageous in the face of danger"; it is "impossible to gauge just what sort of a man he was."[31] Such comments suggest that Fortune forever needs to be kept in his place as an overachieving Scots garden boy.

Apologies for being politically and socially incorrect notwithstanding, Fortune's assimilation of Chinese taste prompts him to "gather" and recommend for adoption Chinese burial customs that he believes would augment Victorian practice. At about the same time Fortune was discovering Chinese burial customs, Dickens was in Italy (1844–45), where in his many rambles he found cemeteries both "revolting" and "like a meadow."[32] Sentimental cemetery scenes figure in the early pages of *David Copperfield* and *Great Expectations;* the cemetery theme in Fortune's books may be said to be in fashion. Fortune, however, ventures beyond sentiment in his comments: "Much of the respect that is paid by the Chinese to the memory of their deceased relatives may doubtless be a mere matter of form, sanctioned and rendered necessary by the custom of ages, but I am inclined to think that a considerable portion springs from a higher source, and I have no doubt that when the Chinese periodically visit the tombs of their fathers to worship and pay respect to their memory, they indulge in the pleasing reflection, that when they themselves are no more, their graves will not be neglected and forgotten" (TYW 331–32). The passage has a subversive element in its use of Victorian sentiment to undermine conventional disapproval of burial customs that have ancestor worship as their underlying principle. One of the reasons for the rupture in the Jesuits' early presence in China had been the pope's rebuke of their desire to accommodate ancestor worship with Catholic beliefs. Victorian Protestants agreed in this one instance with the pope and rarely failed to ridicule both ancestor worship and Chinese burial customs as abhorrent. Although Fortune believes the "unrestricted dissemination of the Gospel of Christ" (RaC 440) to be desirable, his more liberal view of traditional Chinese customs reflects the eclecticism of one who is able to quarrel with conventionality.

The implications of Chinese burial customs are not all. Fortune is moved from his first to last journey in China by the tangible evidence of Chinese sentiment: "When the nations of Europe were crowding their dead in the dismal churchyards of populous towns, and polluting the air, the Chinese, whom we have been accustomed to look upon as only half-civilized, were forming pleasant cemeteries in country places, and planting them with trees and flowers" (YP 376). He makes these assertions even though he was well aware of burial customs in the south of China that sometimes resulted in above-ground placement of coffins and ghastly incidents. While out on a woodland walk, "more than once I have been entangled by getting my feet through the lid of a coffin" (TYW 326). However, he remains undeterred from praising the flowers on scattered graves he sees on these walks. Fortune's lack of the orientalist rancor displayed by later travelers who write about Chinese burial customs with disgust and horror may be attributed to the cause he advocates. His cemetery remarks address the movement to eliminate grotesque conditions in English cemeteries such as the "hemmed-in churchyard, pestiferous and obscene" in which Dickens's character Nemo is buried in *Bleak House*.[33]

Chinese cemeteries also appeal to Fortune's horticultural interests. Two of his favorite botanic collections are the anemone he discovers growing on graves and the weeping "Funereal cypress" *(Cupressus funebris)* that he thought would beautify English cemeteries (it did not prove hardy in England) (JTC 61–63). He describes the latter discovery in the grounds of a country inn with great animation. Fortune's strong view on the subject of beautifying cemeteries even leads him to reverse the colonial equation:

Laying out walks and planting willows and flowers in cemeteries "would raise us" in Chinese eyes (JTC 14; cf. TYW 330, RaC 57–58). In his eagerness to appropriate things Chinese for the benefit of Great Britain, Fortune at times displays a surprising willingness to see his own culture as the inferior of China's.

Although horticultural collecting leads Fortune to see China in advance of his own culture in some ways, his avocational interests have a more polarizing effect. It is only in his third book, the account of his 1852–56 sojourn in China, that Fortune discusses collecting anything other than plants. With a good deal of time on his hands during the growing season, he turns his hand to geology, entomology, and art collection. In these ventures beyond botany, Fortune displays a different persona—one who feels more superior to the Chinese than does the horticulturist. An example is when a rumor turns his insect collecting into the making of folk medicine and he is besieged by a clamoring mob with basketsful of smashed insects. He boasts of a deft handling of the crowd: "What with joking and reasoning with them, I got out of the business pretty well. . . . by showing some liberality in my donations of cash to the old women and very young children I gradually rose in their estimation" (RaC 62). As in many plant-collecting episodes, Fortune reveals a charm and pleasing ability to relate to simple people, but in this incident he is more patronizing. As a horticulturist he is willingly tutored by Chinese experts; as an amateur entomologist he assumes the air of the tutor.

When he turns to collecting cultural artifacts, the transformation in Fortune is more marked, for the activity ventures into aesthetic and mercenary issues.[34] Fortune writes for the first time about collecting art objects in *Residence among the Chinese,* though he must have pursued this interest already during his first tour. As a collector of valuable porcelains and bronzes, Fortune demonstrates how race in the colonial context replaces class background as a bestower of status, the gardener equating himself with mandarins. He describes a cultivated Chinese collector as "like myself" an "ardent admirer and collector of ancient works of art": "Neither of us collected what are commonly know as *curios* . . . such things as take the fancy of captains of ships and their crews of jolly tars when they visit the Celestial Empire. Above all things, our greatest horror was modern chinaware"

(RaC 78). Fortune's "horror" of items perhaps made expressly for the export trade reflects the fact that in these items "quality declined and decoration became gaudier" after midcentury.[35] All the same, Fortune sounds affected in describing his taste for the more valuable and authentic objects.

When his rival collector, "a man of considerable wealth" (RaC 79) invites him to his magnificent home, a veritable museum of rare and beautiful works of art, Fortune shows not the least bit of modesty. Instead, the experience excites his vanity: "On going round the different rooms, I observed more than one specimen I had been in treaty for myself, and I thought I could detect a good-humoured smile upon my friend's countenance, as the same idea was passing through his mind which was passing through my own" (RaC 82). Perhaps Fortune was the connoisseur and art expert he projects, capable of dickering over a thousand-year-old vase with a wealthy Chinese collector.[36] In any case, the situation allows him to ignore markers of class and achieve a kind of retaliation against the snobbery of his employers at the Royal Horticultural Society and Lewis, the chastiser of his Chinese-garden views. In his guise as a collector of art objects, Fortune substitutes race for class and adopts the attitude of the privileged.

When money matters are added to his art collecting activities, Fortune's cultivated taste appears compromised. The robust market for Chinese artifacts after the Opium War obviously encouraged Fortune to develop this side interest in collecting, and he must have learned something about collecting artifacts from monied friends, such as the Beales, who had lived in Macao for years. At any rate, Gardener has shown that Fortune earned £11,560 from Christie's auctions of his collections and also that he had substantial earnings on his travel books and commissions on plant sales.[37] A mercenary element detracts from his anecdotes about art collecting: Though "The Chinese as a people are first-rate physiognomists" who "can tell at a glance whether their wares take one's fancy," he brags about outwitting them, once knocking down the price of a vase from eighty to a mere nine dollars (RaC 296–97).[38] The sensibilities Fortune displays in praising China's gardens and cemetery beautification are overshadowed by this boasting about prowess in haggling. Now China, vaunted repository of an exquisite aesthetic, is downgraded to a mere flea market, handled and picked over by the bargain-hunting Fortune.

Some of Fortune's collecting activities portend disagreeable possibilities, though his years at the edge of the British empire also nurture what Tuan calls "topophilia"—the affective link between people and place.[39] Men like Fortune demonstrate that the experience of individuals cannot easily be generalized to fit a single ideological framework regarding the business of empire. Fortune's topophilia encourages him to give a panoramic view of the country and travelers' tales that do not necessarily correct "the false colouring which has been given to every picture drawn" of China. His admiring descriptions of gardens and wild flora do not achieve that purpose, and even an occasional anecdote of the ludicrous, such as beggars using unburied coffins to prop up their mosquito nets, accents China's image as the fantastic Other.

Similarly, his tales about thieves and pirates, confined mostly to his first book, have a way of ending anticlimactically that abates their negativism. At the end of his first book he tells an amazing tale of singlehandedly fending off piratical junks, raking "their decks fore and aft, with shot and ball from my double-barrelled gun," while his Chinese crew cowered in fear (TYW 393). Afterwards, "the captain, pilot, crew, and passengers . . . actually came and knelt before me, as to some superior being, and expressed their deep and lasting gratitude" (TYW 396). Horticulture does not often afford opportunities for such heroics. In the face of real danger, Fortune remained cool, outfeinting the pirates and parenthetically proving to the RHS the value of the guns he had argued he needed; the society had felt that the weapons were a gentlemanly prerogative beyond his claim. The story provides a dramatic ending for his first book, but it has no sequel; moreover, the harrowing experience has an unexceptional conclusion: he has a reunion with his friends and tends his plant collections in Shanghai. Fortune is thus unable to sustain his complaints for long. The dominant image he gives of China and the Chinese is positive.

The images of rural life that Fortune collects are the ones that go furthest in depicting China in a positive way. In the book on his second tour of China (1848–51), he praises the ingenuity of practical contrivances, especially the "simplicity and utility" of such things as the waterwheel used for irrigation, icehouses that he thinks should be copied in England, and the simple plow used in rice paddies (JTC 66). Writing in the era of the

Crystal Palace Exhibition, in which Britain displayed its technology and progressiveness, Fortune seems to embrace an alternative attitude, rather like that advocated by the *Tao Te Ching:*

> Even when they have ships and carts, they will have no use for them; and even when they have armour and weapons, they will have no occasion to make a show of them.

> Bring it about that the people will return to the use of the knotted rope,
> Will find relish in their food
> And beauty in their clothes,
> Will be content in their abode
> And happy in the way they live.

> Though adjoining states are within sight of one another, and the sound of dogs barking and cocks crowing in one state can be heard in another, yet the people of one state will grow old and die without having had any dealings with those of another. (LXXX)[40]

Fortune never indicates any intimate knowledge of Chinese philosophy or religions, yet his own view of life often seems to coincide with them, a fact that helps explain his level of comfort in China. The simplicity, inaction, and isolationism celebrated in the above passage from the *Tao Te Ching* fits a man like Fortune who is happiest in horticultural pursuits.

After his third tour (1852–56), Fortune goes further in extolling a philosophy consistent with Taoism in his description of country life as an Arcadian idyll: "Here is no apparent want, and certainly no oppression; the labourer is strong, healthy, and willing to work, but independent, and feels that he is 'worthy of his hire'" (RaC 38). Each farm is "a little colony" where three generations of farmers "live in peace and harmony together" with their hired hands. "They live well, dress plainly, and are industrious, without being in any way oppressed" (RaC 98–99). It is a common phenomenon of world tourism in modern times for travelers from the industrial world to romanticize "the simple life" of Third World societies. In this respect Fortune's views are unexceptional, but in the context of mid-Victorian England, his idealization of a peasant society flies in the face of empire.[41]

Fortune's idealization of a simple, unchanging way of life is also reflected in his description of manners and customs. Unlike many traders and travelers who argue for rapid Westernization of China, Fortune shows a remarkable objectivity and acceptance of the Chinese as they are. Even when a custom seems silly—for example, the search for "hairs" that rise from the ground after an earthquake (RaC 4)—he good-heartedly joins in and applies common sense to explain the "phenomenon" to the Chinese. This, like his willingness to accept traditional Chinese medicine and to "see" an invisible relic of the Buddha (RaC 34), illustrates his basic rule of encounter with the Chinese: "In the course of my travels I have ever found it unwise to laugh at what I conceived to be the prejudices of a people simply because I could not understand them" (RaC 4). This is a rare humility for a European in circumstances such as those in which Fortune often finds himself.

This humility also marks situations in which race plays a direct role. In a parallel of the class division he had experienced in England, in China Fortune shows empathy for those akin to his own class background. On his rambles, he is pleased that rural people "never failed to offer a draught of the national beverage—tea" (JTC 116). During his first tour, Fortune is often delighted by the curiosity stirred by racial difference, when his presence draws a rapidly accumulating crowd "with wonder painted in every countenance" (TYW 54). His smoked eyeglasses and Turkish-style hat contribute to his novelty, and when one young man offers to buy his neck scarf, Fortune teasingly offers to buy the man's queue. He also takes it in stride when he finds that an enterprising boatman "used to make a good deal of money" by charging admission to see the barbarian's possessions (TYW 249–50).

By his third tour, a similar event elicits even greater tolerance and understanding. Fortune decides to "gratify them even in this" and eats and readies himself for bed with an audience of oglers (RaC 270). When villagers think he "might be a cannibal" or a "like a tiger," he takes it as a kind of patriotic duty to still their fear: "I trust when I left them their opinion of the character of foreigners had somewhat changed" (RaC 280). This is a reversal of the colonial mentality that is also seen in Fortune's argument, given above, that Britain should adopt certain Chinese cultural customs. Fortune's response to China and his acceptance of the way it responds to

View on the Grand Canal. Drawing in Robert Fortune, *A Residence among the Chinese.*

him approaches the idea about cultural exchange avowed in "The Myth of the Other": To "know the Other is a process of Bildung, of learning and self-cultivation, which is neither projecting the Self onto the Other nor erasing the Self with what belongs to the Other. It is rather a moment when Self and Other meet and join together, in which both are changed and enriched in what Gadamer calls 'the fusion of horizons.'"[42] Such fusion is the ideal result of gathering in China, whether of gathering horticultural specimens and impressions or of the gathering of Europeans there.

Though Fortune approaches this ideal connection with Chinese culture, when removed from people analogous to his own class background, he is much more likely to take note of dirt and cultural difference. He often expresses disgust with Buddhist priests, characterizing them as lazy and degenerate, and he has "a great horror of being touched by a Chinese beggar, who is generally filthy beyond description" (JTC 200). Fortune's usual calm demeanor is also disturbed when he is in unfamiliar roles. He can be an overbearing master when he is being carried in a chair or in forcing bearers to carry heavy burdens for long hours while he rides a pony. He is scathing about the apparent dishonesty of his interpreter-servant Wang,

Robert Fortune.
Photo, courtesy Royal
Horticultural Society.

and furious that another servant, Sing-hoo, takes advantage of him. The parsimonious Fortune presents an ironic self-portrait when the avid shopper Sing-Hoo makes purchases that he, Fortune, will have to pay bearers to carry. When money is involved or when dealing with people representing social conditions much above or below his own in Britain, Fortune affects the arrogant tone of a colonial master.

Fortune's collecting activities and portrait of Chinese life seem curiously detached from events of the time, even as they cover the period of Britain's most bellicose intrusion on Chinese territory, and yet he has a good deal to say about this. Some of his treatment of the opium issue is unique in that his role as an uninitiated observer leads him to give rather precise information about the opium trade on its basic level. In 1843 he spent a few days on Namoa, an opium station on an island about halfway between Hong Kong and Amoy, and he later saw Woosung, one of the main opium stations near Shanghai. His perception of the European and Chinese smugglers and traders, the opium clippers, and the silver and barter items exchanged for opium all lead him to conclude that "the trade is conducted by men of the highest respectability . . . esteemed as merchants of the first class in every part of the civilised world" (TYW 235). Striking in Fortune's assertions about the whole opium issue is its reversal of his gathering-in idea about China. As buyers and users of "foreign mud," as it was called, the Chinese are seen as a reprehensible lot that somehow justifies their exploitation as a market for European traders.

There is no more vivid illustration of the racism inherent in the opium trade than when Fortune contrasts the images of the traders with those of the users. In Fortune's description of a "dead-house," at the rear of an opium den, the cold contempt he expresses for the smoker passed into "the long sleep to which he is blindly hurrying" (TYW 241) grows more profound in comments during his later tours. During his second journey, for example, he describes an opium smoker as "a pitiable depraved specimen of man" lost to the beauties of "creation itself," unredeemed and presumably unredeemable (JTC 343); Fortune, on the other hand, can go outdoors to drink in a fresh new day. Fortune unfailingly represents opium smoking as the difference between the British and the Chinese, the saved and the damned. Remarkably, though, he compartmentalizes the opium trade and use so that in other ways China remains a field of riches for the gathering.

Fortune's third book is bracketed by accounts of the Taiping Rebellion, the Small-Sword Society, and the Lorcha *Arrow* incident—events that would ultimately contribute to his disillusion about China. The Taiping Rebellion was a lengthy, bloody period of strife, claiming twenty million—or perhaps thirty million—victims from 1850 to 1864; it was accompanied by more than a hundred unrelated uprisings of various factions and ethnic minorities that extended the area of internal upheaval to most of the provinces and the period up to 1868. When it all ended, the Manchu dynasty still formally claimed rule, though politically the power of the government had shifted to the Chinese. Karl Marx, who had been disappointed in the outcome of the 1848 revolution in Europe, found hope in the Taiping Rebellion as a prototype of peasant revolutions, and later Maoist China proclaimed it the first socialist revolution. Both internal and external stresses contributed to the Taiping Rebellion: there was the ineptitude of the Chinese leaders, plus famine and the suffering brought on by heavy taxes to pay for the war with Britain, compounded by the disappearance of native handicrafts due to the competition from imported goods—a vast field that, trumpeted as an opening to British merchants, looked very different to the Chinese.[43]

Contemporary Western accounts of the Taiping Rebellion focus on two factors: the leader who claimed to be a son of the Christian god and the Western military assistance that was given the Chinese emperor to quell the rebellion. Fortune's account of the Taipings, "the Kingdom of Heavenly Peace," is interesting for its on-the-spot perspective. At one point, he says, the movement was seen by some Europeans as a miracle "performed by the Almighty" to rescue a country "for ages sunk in idolatry" (RaC 16). Western governments dithered between acknowledging the insurgents and supporting the emperor, and Fortune decides to suspend his judgment of the rebels until he can "admit them to be Christians" (RaC 20–21). Later he decides to adopt the view of the "respectable Chinese in this part of the country"— that the "Kwang-si rebels" are "nothing more than thieves and robbers" (RaC 127). When Britain's "splendid opening" of China looks more like a torturous closing down of the past, Fortune seems to abandon his usual empathy for the lower classes and takes the conservative view of mandarins and landlords against the "rabble."

On the other hand, stories of atrocities and looting both by the Small Sword Society and the Western forces putting it down in Shanghai prompt him to support the "masses": "China is a big country, and those parts disturbed by rebellion bear but a small proportion to the remainder, which is perfectly undisturbed" (RaC 141). Fortune's desire to minimize the seriousness of the upheaval at its outset reflects his own nature as well as his desire to see China as peaceful, Arcadian. His response seems reminiscent of the philosophy suggested by the lines of the *Tao Te Ching* cited earlier: "Though adjoining states are within sight of one another, and the sound of dogs barking and cocks crowing in one state can be heard in another, yet the people of one state will grow old and die without having had any dealings with those of another." His actions support this sentiment, to ignore the sound of trouble, when, as mentioned previously, he insists that the civil strife in China will not interfere with his purchase of tea seeds.

Fortune's view of the Taipings provides a roundness to his representation of his experience in China, but just as he was preparing his third book for the press, the flap over the Lorcha *Arrow* prompted him to add a chapter that complicates closure for him. In a sense, the *Arrow* incident in 1856 reprises the immediate cause of the first Opium War in that it involved a dispute over British property and Chinese authority in coastal waters. The situation again led to military action—the so-called Second Opium War. Fortune scolds the Chinese for breaking earlier treaty agreements: "In making treaties with a nation like the Chinese we ought not to look upon them as we do the more civilized nations of the West" (RaC 429), although in adding that the Chinese "must be taught to look upon us as a nation as highly civilized and powerful as themselves" (RaC 430), he seems ambivalent about which country exemplifies a more estimable ethic.

Just a year after Fortune's American venture fell through, Japan was opened to foreign travel, and he set out for an eighteen-month trip to the East to compensate for the frustration of his abortive 1858–59 journey.[44] He first stopped in China for one of his former interpreters to help him with collecting plants, insects, shells, and art objects. In Japan, new sights like the freeness of tea-house ladies and "promiscuous bathing" in the public baths elicit his usual tolerance: "All I can say is it is the custom of the country" (YP 94). China, however, receives his final attention. Before embarking for England at the end of 1861, he visited Tientsin and Peking, the latter with its new foreign "legations" near the Forbidden City.

A dominant view of China during the second half of the nineteenth century was of a decaying culture deserving to be reconstructed with Western values. Fortune half-heartedly joins this chorus in his first book when he mourns ancient temples that "are crumbling to pieces": "It is very true that these are heathen temples, and the good in every land will hail with delight the day when these shall give way to others which shall be erected to the true God: but nevertheless such is the fact, that these places are not supported as they used to be" (TYW 9). Such valuing of China's cultural treasures and feeble support of Western hegemony over China is reversed in Fortune's last book, his account of his visit to Japan and China in *Yedo and Peking*. The progressiveness and cleanliness of Japan startle him and result in frequent disparagement of China. Touring Peking in the aftermath of the Arrow War and the treaties of 1858–60 that left China thoroughly humiliated, Fortune expresses a chauvinism far beyond that which marks the early chapters of his first book: "Having received a good flogging, these children had now become very good boys; and if they did not love us, which we could scarcely expect, we were certainly feared and respected" (YP 326).

Fortune's remark may be seen in light of the wanton destruction served on Peking. In a bitter blow to China's pride, French and English soldiers destroyed Yüan Ming Yüan, the fabulous Summer Palace, to the Chinese symbolic of their cultural heritage. "Chinese" Gordon, who took a throne as his personal booty, regretted the destruction: "You can scarcely imagine the beauty and magnificence of the buildings we burnt. It made one's heart sore to burn them. . . . It was wretchedly demoralizing work for an army. Everyone was wild for plunder." Queen Victoria received a Pekingese dog from the spoils. Mirroring the sensibility of the whole operation, she named it Looty.[45] Numerous writers mention the dispersal of the treasures from the Summer Palace. Constance Cumming, for example, writes that she saw the emperor's ancestral tablets in New Zealand in 1874, and Kipling adds a fictional desecration in *Kim:* "The Sahibs prayed to their god; . . . a golden bull fashioned from old-time loot of the Summer Palace at Pekin."[46] Fortune's arrogance about the most recent beating of China reflects the spirit of the time.

China having endured such a routing, it may be expected that when Fortune sees the ancient observatory straddling the city wall in Peking, he is confused about this evidence of the civilization of a now-humbled people. He conjectures that the "beautifully cast" astronomical instruments "were evidently the work of foreign missionaries, and had probably been imported from Europe. If cast in China during Father Ricci's time, they are well calculated to excite our wonder, but this I think can hardly have been the case" (YP 353). It is unclear whether Fortune saw the instruments cast by the Chinese in the thirteenth century or only those cast in China in 1669 under the direction of the Jesuit Verbiest and those added in the eighteenth century.[47] But in any case, he seems eager to deprive China of credit for any of these objects.

Once a shining new opportunity for increasing the wealth and power of Britain, the China defeated by military might and forced to legalize the opium to which millions became addicted had to be revaluated as semi-barbaric or hovering in a state of suspended animation. For the Fortune of 1861, Britain's conquest made it difficult to accommodate the idea of China as a civilization with numerous "articles of importance" to export to the West, or one in possession of the craftsmanship signified by the ancient ob-servatory. With nothing more to gather, he traveled abroad no more. His collection of impressions and experiences in China must have helped fill his eighteen years of retirement, divided between his home in Brompton and his son's farm in East Lothian, Scotland, even as the opening of China took on new meanings to successive merchants and travelers.[48]

Three Views of Trackers Towing Junks through the Yangtze Gorges.
Watercolors in *Illus. London News,* 25 Feb. 1899: 256.

two

Westward the Course of Empire[1]

Archibald John Little

MERCHANTS, MANUFACTURERS, and tradesmen often fare poorly in Victorian fiction and social commentary. The novels of Dickens and Trollope abound with such characters tainted by pursuit of wealth, while Arnold indicts the "Philistines" who "seasonably disconcert mankind in their worship of machinery."[2] In the colonial sphere, contemporary opinions could be equally sharp. Dilke, visiting China in 1875, a few years after the Tientsin Massacre during which a French consul and several missionaries were killed, has little sympathy for "the fire-eating merchants at the ports, who think that China should be forced to do what they desire."[3] Alternative views of the merchant are, of course, also found in novels, such as that of a philanthropist bent on helping China by developing steamboats, railroads, and coal mines there. This philanthropist appears in *A Millionaire's Courtship,* a novel in which Mrs. Archibald Little immortalizes her husband as the romantic developer. Archibald Little, who spent nearly fifty years in China, went there to take advantage of China's opening and ended up tugging the modern world into western Szechuan.

This advocate of Westernization in western China complements collector-traveler Robert Fortune as a representative of the business of empire. First, the years the two men spent in China span the period from the end of the Opium War to Britain's agreement to halt its opium trade in 1907. Fortune first arrived in China in 1843 and departed from it for the last time in 1861; Little arrived in 1859, leaving China finally in 1907. Thus the experience of these two men is played out against all the political and economic events that affected Britain's long opening of China in the nineteenth century. The work of these two men also overlaps. Little initially went to China as a tea taster for a German firm, an occupation that connects him to the tea-collecting Fortune. In a metaphoric crossing of their paths, Little observed the fruition of Fortune's mission to deliver the secrets of tea propagation and production to the West by witnessing the last great year of the tea trade in Hankow. In *Intimate China,* Mrs. Little describes the event in May 1887 when "pretty painted boxes" of tea "streamed past the house at the rate of eighty a minute." By 1898, she adds, only one steamer called to take tea to London.[4]

Tea tasting was seasonal work. Little returned to England frequently, but he also settled into the life of the established mercantile community in Shanghai, where he and his brother developed several businesses. He pursued gentleman's sports, like yachting in the Chusan Archipelago, and dabbled in journalism, publishing occasional essays on trade, politics, and current events, some of which his wife collected in *Gleanings from Fifty Years in China.*[5] These eclectic pursuits may be seen as a corollary of his class and education. The eldest son of a London physician of some consequence, Little "had the good fortune to be rescued from the purely classical education to which all public schools then condemned their scholars" and completed his education in Berlin.[6] Fortune, whose rise from garden boy at a Scottish estate indicates the possibilities open to an enterprising individual in mid-Victorian England, and Little, from the educated upper-middle class, represent the diversity of those who went out to the colonies to make their fortunes.

Little's books contain nothing about his work as a tea taster: the closest he comes to commenting on it is to remark on the quality of cups of tea he is served by hospitable country people and to describe the "brick tea" that is a staple in Tibet. However, his books and essays contain a good deal about his other work, as well as his views on trade between Britain and China. We can be grateful he wrote about such matters as much as he did, for few merchants have left memoirs about their work in China. Part of the credit for his literary effort must be given to his wife, novelist A. E. N. Bewicke, since she encouraged her husband to publish his writings. All his books appeared after he brought her out to China in 1887.

This merchant, traveler, and author was characterized by a friend as something of a renaissance man: a geographer by inclination, a humanist by temperament and education, and a "merchant by the accident of career" (GFY v)—qualities that earned him election as a fellow of the Royal Geographic Society. These qualities also characterize his writing about China, which combines geography, ethnography, and the politics of trade. *Through the Yang-tse Gorges,* of primary interest in this chapter, exemplifies this combination. The journal of an exciting and, for Little, adventurous journey, it combines discovery and trade reconnaissance.[7] Pure science gives way to applied science, applied science to self-interest; his investigations into geology turn into hunting for natural resources that may be useful to his mining-equipment business. To the merchant's eye, China sometimes appears either as a commodity or something to be commodified, and his travel becomes infused with the methods of business.

If "all business is war," as Little once wrote (GFY 49), his Yangtze River journey should be seen as preparation for battle, in that it allows him to assess his opportunities, his marketplace, and the role of the British in China. He harbored plans to develop trade in the city of Chungking, fourteen hundred miles inland, and to that end made his speculative journey there in 1886. At that time, steamboats plied the Yangtze River twice daily between Shanghai and Hankow, six hundred miles upriver, and somewhat less frequently to Ichang, nearly four hundred miles farther. The beautiful and treacherous gorges and rapids allowed farther travel on the great river only by native junks and wupans. Little took the first leg of this journey by steamboat, hiring a wupan from Hankow to Chungking. The journey proved enormously influential; Szechuan and the upper reaches of the Yangtze River were a revelation to him. With the discovery of this vast and rich part of China came the zeal of the recent convert. He devoted much of his next twenty years to western China.

Little's account of this journey up the Yangtze and into riverside villages shows how his professional life influences his sightseeing and ethnographical and geographical commentary. Appropriately, his travel account displays the methodical nature of the merchant: it often reads like a ledger, with credits and debits carefully lined up. Foremost in the credit line of the journey is the wild beauty of forest and mountains bordering the upper reaches of the Yangtze. Almost daily, Little enthuses over spectacular scenery. He also conscientiously documents the scenic with place-names in Chinese and English, and he includes an abundance of geographical detail: the speed of the river in knots; the height of cliffs, surrounding mountains, and high and low water; the width of gorges; distances between places in both Chinese and Western measures; geological formations, soil, flora, and agriculture of the area; types of housing and building materials; temples, pagodas, and even "luxurious ornamental *cabinets d'aisance*" placed by the "scientific agriculturists" (TYG 65). The precision, attention to detail, and quantity of his daily tabulations show Little to be conscientious and practical. The credit side of Little's ledger also contains his quibbles with and corrections of the Englishmen who first explored and mapped the area, Capt. Blakiston, Colborne Baber, and Alexander Hosie.[8] He is gratified to dispute their calculations of distances and to find a gorge Baber leaves unnamed.[9]

The merchant's eye for detail occasionally admits a wry comment on what free trade could mean for scenic Szechuan. He contemplates "a picturesque cliff, backed by wooded hills—such a spot as in the United States would be selected for an advertisement of 'Smith's Liver Pad' or 'Jones's Liniment'" (TYG 163), retaining a sense of irony despite his matter-of-fact tabulations. Besides the scenic, the river journey also introduces Little to the Szechuanese, about whom he is enthusiastic. Like Fortune before

A Farmhouse in Szechuan. Photo by Isabella Bird, *Yangtze Valley and Beyond.*

him, he is won over by the unaffected friendliness of rural people, the offer of tea, the "politeness common enough in the poor, though unusual in the rich, where a foreigner is concerned" (TYG 96). Travel encourages Little's characterization of the Chinese, formed over his many years in China, as law-abiding, easy-going, loyal to employers, and unselfish.

While the scenic, the scientific, and the human landscape all contribute to Little's Yangtze-journey credit list, a sense of helplessness against both natural and manmade evils, dangers, and miseries pervades his debit list. Especially painful is the evidence of ignorance and disease, "the sight of so much wretchedness, which is kept out of our sight in the Concessions, and which we can do so little to alleviate" (TYG 54). Little's humanitarian instincts are aroused by sights of human suffering, and, removed from the control and command of his usual workaday life, he often feels oppressed by his inability to combat such suffering. His being bitten in the leg by a dog—Chinese dogs "have a mad antipathy for the barbarian" (TYG 87)—seems a fitting trope for this sense of helplessness. What is most important, he feels the power of nature in the physical challenges of the river, the wearying, dangerous rapids to be struggled against day after day. The experience has a direct influence on his later obsession with steamboats on the Yangtze.

In this context, the merchant finds the sun, too, a natural enemy. Even during his early spring travel in February-April, he says he has "to avoid the sun" from "noon till four" (TYG 187). Complaints about the unhealthiness of the sun and climate are frequent in Victorian travel lore, but they seem inconsistent with Little's descriptions of strenuous hikes along the route. The implications of his fear of the sun may be better understood by noting an episode in Mrs. Little's novel *A Marriage in China,* in which she has a character scoff at Europeans in pith helmets on cool, deeply overcast, days in Hankow.[10] The character, recently arrived in China, overlooks the symbolic meaning of the pith helmet—that the Europeans' "uniform" betokens their control over native subordinates as well as being a practical defense against the sun. In Archibald Little's hiding from the sun, we see a man uncertain of his power and control in the present circumstances— a lone passenger on a frail boat in a barely known setting.

The hint of anxiety in Little's travel account accords with the fact that as a merchant-traveler he is acting out of character. As a rule, foreign merchants traveled little in China. They were notorious for not learning the language and avoiding the Chinese population. To some extent these patterns were a response to the treaty-port regulations in that foreign businesses and housing were confined to the concession areas. Like Fortune, Little ventured further into the Chinese countryside than did most foreigners, and he prided himself on his ability to converse with and meet the Chinese on their level. He traveled Chinese style, carrying his own bedding, staying with the Chinese in their homes, and spent evenings playing *morra,* a chess-like game, with them. But if Little proved his adventurousness in breaking free of the treaty-port mentality, he had given his travel a good deal of thought; when he made that exploratory journey in 1886, he had been in China for twenty-seven years.

Little's import business in 1886 included the sale of coal-mining equipment, a pursuit that may be said to have entries on both his credit and debit lists. In good utilitarian fashion, he called at river ports to tour coal mines and make sales of mining equipment, but this commercial interest is not

Archibald Little. Photo, Archibald Little, *Gleanings from Fifty Years in China*.

without benevolent concern, as his description reveals: "The reach above Kwei-Fu [in Hupeh Province] has a picturesque charm of its own, from the steep mountain sides being cultivated in patches to their summits, and studded with small villages embedded in trees and bamboo.... At one village I noticed a small stack of patent fuel ... and I traced the coal to a small burrow in the side of the hill, shored up with timber, not more than three feet high and less than two feet wide. Out of this miserable hole, women laden with baskets of coal-dust on their backs were painfully toiling" (TYG 126). In a later essay, he adds that mine workers were virtual slaves who often were kidnapped children (GFY 158). Such mining scenes cry out for modern equipment and foster the image of the merchant as one whose motivation includes both humanitarianism and practicality.

On the other hand, his visit in Szechuan to a thriving coal mine with an effective ventilation system and good compensation to workers (a daily warm bath and ten days' wages for nine days' work), gives him "a favorable impression of the exceptional well-being of this province" and appeals to his entrepreneurial spirit (TYG 281). He dreams of developing enormous deposits of coal and other natural resources similar to those in the United States: If "Western appliances" could be brought to work the mines, "and the coal, the iron, the precious metals, and the petroleum springs properly developed ... there [would] be such a trade, that junks and steamers would hardly be able to carry it all" (TYG 7).[11] Echoing the Robert Fortune of 1859 who thought there must be much more than just tea and silk to exploit in China, scenes of both misery and prosperity encourage Little's hope both to forward and profit from the modernization of Szechuan.

Occupation influences not only the way Little writes his travel journal but also what he looks at and how he sees it. He uses few figures of speech, but when he does they usually reflect his professional interests. In the following passage shortly after his arrival in Chungking, he manages to present a romantic view of a loading-dock scene. The passage gives an insight into his combination of pragmatism and dreaminess—his interest in the workaday world and the lure of what lies beyond the horizon:

> I stood a long time on one of the many rocky platforms by which the stream is broken up, watching the busy gangs of coolies loading and discharging the vast fleets of junks, laden with the mingled produce of the

east, north, and west. Conspicuous as they climbed up the long flights of steps, were files of porters toiling under huge bales of white unpressed cotton, looking in the distance like regiments of busy ants carrying their eggs. I gazed at leisure on the busy scene, enjoying the novelty of being allowed to look unmolested by the crowd, as well as the stillness of the natural scenery, amidst which so many long days had been spent. Here unfortunately, was the goal of my present journeyings, as business required me to be back in Hankow in the following month. The farther one travels the farther one wants to travel. (TYG 207–8)

The mood of the passage is influenced by Little's relief at momentarily escaping the crowds of curious onlookers attracted to the unusual sight of a lanky foreigner dressed in knickerbockers. He has stationed himself on a perch above and outside the busy scene, far enough away so as to perceive it as a silent, orderly mingling of the produce of three corners of the globe, moved by men likened to insects. The sense of detachment from the scene presents itself appealingly. No human hands are so far connected to the "eggs" of white cotton. Their "hatching," their dyeing and construction into items for human consumption, can only be imagined. It is a scene of trade at its purest, completely impersonal and with no visible consequences. That it urges him to continue traveling at first seems a non sequitur, although it fits his idealization of free trade as boundless prosperity.

Little's momentary idealization of trade seems innocent enough. It also suggests how he has accommodated himself to Chinese culture—how being a merchant not only influences his sightseeing but shapes his response to China. These qualities are demonstrated in a topic he returns to often, *feng-shui* (literally, wind-water), what Westerners typically derided as superstitious belief in the relationship between natural phenomena and human events. Little's presentation of this topic humanizes the merchant, depicting him as an inoffensive toiler in the work of empire.

Although he charges it with being "an obstacle to all works of progress in this benighted land" (TYG 224–25), he takes a hobbyist interest in *feng-shui,* the principles of which, he notes, are based on science. Fluency in the Chinese language enables him to indulge, not to say showcase, his commonsense interpretations of "wind-water" confluences: "[P]rofiting by the vague latitude allowed the seer in all ages, I am seldom at a loss when questioned" (TYG 118). Asked for his views on the *feng-shui* of two houses situated near the Ping-shu gorge, for example, Little suggests that the house with a view "seemed to draw in prosperity from the waters rolling towards it, while the other seemed to have its fortune wafted past its door by the up-river wind" (TYG 118). As his interlocutor was the underemployed owner of the ill-sited house that had been experiencing bad luck, Little followed up with practical advice: erect a wall to keep away the wind and seek employment on a trading junk. Little's quick wit allows him to find *feng-shui* an entertaining mental sport. It is easy to see that his good humor and practicality must have enabled him to do business with the Chinese. At the same time, he reveals the advantage he has in understanding the nature of his marketplace.

Little diverged from the Shanghai-merchant pattern in becoming fluent in both spoken and written Chinese, and he justly boasts that this explains the relative ease with which he travels and does business in China. He demonstrates his expertise in Chinese by translating several long Chinese documents in *Through the Yang-tse Gorges,* but whether he had command of the Szechuan dialect, he does not explicitly say; it seems likely that he did.[12] He contends that he is not a "'speechless' barbarian" in Szechuan, and as a result "the people are amiable, and their civility to the stranger is a delightful surprise, after the rude treatment he has been subjected to in the Coast and Central Provinces" (TYG 208–9). On a later journey with his wife, described in *Mount Omi and Beyond,* he again mentions that his ability to speak the language contributes to the safety of his travel, and he adds that being able to speak for himself rather than through an interpreter spares him a great deal of difficulty since "misunderstandings generally arise through the arrogance and greed of one's native servants" (MOB 240). Little understands that language is an essential for the traveler to hurdle difficulties caused by culture, character, and employment.

Little's comments about language and servants reflect both understanding of human nature and business sense. These qualities resonate in his understanding of Chinese culture, as shown in his comments on a suspiciousness that seems to be part of the national character. In Little's day, local authorities controlled travel as well as collected duty on goods passing through their province. Respecting local rule, Little registers at each river port, but he notices that on these occasions one of his guides gives a different birthplace to each magistrate. Asked why he does this, the man replies that "it was well not ɩo let the officials know too much." Little notes that on a practical level this cultural quirk makes it difficult for a Westerner "to gain an exact knowledge of the simplest fact," while on a metaphysical level, it implies the elusiveness of real understanding between East and West (TYG 237). For the merchant who wants to introduce western machines to China, it means overcoming deeply-rooted custom, not simply replacing local work methods.

The difficulty the merchant might experience in negotiating custom and local practice stems in no small part from the trade article to which he indirectly owes his presence in China: opium. Unsurprisingly, he is enormously defensive about the subject: "It is annoying to find the English name everywhere associated with the forcible introduction of this beneficent and at the same time pernicious drug" (TYG 283). However, he takes it as a matter of conscience when traveling in Szechuan to inspect opium fields (after legalization of the opium trade, increased addiction made home-grown opium desirable and profitable). Little's analysis focuses on agricultural and moral issues; the economic issues at the heart of the opium trade are apparently too disturbing for the merchant to address.

He visits the farmstead of a family named Lin and there sees poppies "just ripe for gathering." This leads him to try a plethora of rhetorical techniques to exonerate Britain's role in the opium trade. First he shifts the blame to the Portuguese for introducing the drug and to the Chinese for inventing the opium pipe. Next he diminishes the evils of the drug by insisting that it harms neither people nor land. He says he has never met anyone "seriously injured" by it, though in the next paragraph he blames "the system" for allowing addicted mandarins to keep their posts. As for agricultural issues, he refutes the arguments that opium leaches the soil and forestalls food crops by noting how Chinese agricultural methods alleviate those problems. Besides, he reasons, in his efficient businessman's style, as a winter crop opium "would pay" because of its by-products (oil from the seed, lye for dyes, ash from the stalk, leaves for pig fodder). In the end, though, Little undermines his argument when he notes that the prosperous farmer Lin is "himself a non-smoker" (TYG 285). Opium, an inescapable topic for Victorians in China, also inescapably stains their discourse on it.[13]

Beyond the opium field, Little's inspection of Szechuan's agriculture repeatedly leads him to exclaim about the wealth and populousness of the province, as yet unexploited by Western traders. Part of his attraction to the verdure of Szechuan is the aesthetic of its agriculture—the harmony between the man-made and the natural environment it exhibits. In Chungking, Little extends this principle to architecture: "[H]ere in the west of China, nothing has intervened to mar the accord between Man and Nature" (TYG 244). This aesthetic draws the merchant to Szechuan and Chungking in particular, but therein lies a dilemma. Once the foreigner with his trade and "western appliances" settles in, the old "accord between Man and Nature" is disturbed. In the midst of his initial attraction to the beauty of Szechuan and the possibilities for Western development in it, Little ignores these gnawing issues.

The beauty of Szechuan and the hopes he has for establishing business there encourage his optimistic interpretation of recent and past events that shaped the area. He praises the Chinese as a peace-loving people among whom convulsive rebellions are rare. He shares with Fortune, though to a lesser degree, the image of a pastoral China. As a result, Little compares the violence of the Taiping Rebellion to the indiscriminate slaughter that ushered in the Ch'ing dynasty (and depopulated Szechuan) as once-in-two-hundred-years occurrences. Little's view of the Taipings seems a deliberate attempt to ignore the rebellion's implications as a symptom of the chasm opening between the Chinese people and their leaders, a chasm that Britain and other Western powers were deepening through their wars and treaties and trade with China.[14] At the same time, Little's equivocal attitude toward the Taipings is apparently indebted to the great adventure of his life —a harrowing experience in Taiping territory in January 1861, involving a march through Nganhui to Kiukiang while on a mission to charter a steamer to transport troops for the Imperialists (those loyal to the Chinese emperor).

Little tells the story in "The Romance of Chinese Travel," presenting the experience as an illustration of an ironic thesis: "The charm of travel in China is the unexpected" (GFY 110–16). While looking at a temple near

Nanking, he is suddenly attacked by a dozen men loyal to the Chinese emperor. They strip him of his clothing, pelt him with mud and stones, and carry him to a filthy cellar, all the while yelling "Kill him!" As he contemplates whether he will succumb to assassination or hypothermia, his "faithful coolies" rescue him by convincing his captors that he is a "great British merchant" who is bringing them guns and ammunition. He later charms the general who wants to retain him as a bodyguard. The general had offered Little a pretty Chinese girl as bait, and the twenty-three-year-old Englishman seems to have considered the offer; however, he writes that "no self-respecting European could serve either side unless in a free command [,] which was never conceded" (GFY 116). Other Westerners did rise to such bait. The so-called Ever-Victorious Army—a band of mercenaries that was first commanded by the American Frederick Ward, and after his death in combat by Charles "Chinese" Gordon—played a role in suppressing the Taiping Rebellion.[15]

Little's ambivalence about a Westerner's role in the Chinese emperor's military operations is linked to his assumption that political and economic conditions are connected, and that any political disruption affects foreign trade. However, he and other free-trade, promodernization merchants did not necessarily recognize the reverse of this argument—that radically changing the economic system of China might need to be accompanied by political change. In this way the merchants agreed with the reformers within the Chinese government who hoped that "self-strengthening" could be effected by selective adoption of Western ideas while maintaining the Confucian state.

There is another reason for Little's equanimity about the Taipings in *Through the Yang-tse Gorges* that relates to his status as a merchant; namely, that the rebellion was an anomaly for which missionaries could be blamed. Discussing the Taipings with the captain of a local militia group, Little notes derisively that the Taiping leader, "Hung siu chuen, was one of the very few genuine Christian converts ever made in China" (TYG 136–37). Traveling in China's interior, Little adds to his itinerary a visit to British missionaries at the China Inland Mission in Chungking, but the courtesy call only confirms his prejudice. When he next links missionaries and the Taipings, it is as companions in delusion: the missionaries do not appear to be troubled by "the fact that there are few or no genuine Protestant converts in China," but the destruction of Nanking, the Taipings' capital "still desolate" years later, "remains a witness and a warning" of the risks, or folly, of Christian proselytizing among the Chinese (TYG 309).

Little's lack of sympathy for missionary work certainly is due in part to the deep rift between merchants and missionaries in China and much of the colonial world. He recognizes that the two groups are alike in that it is their goals that put each at odds with the Chinese: "We each have our gospel to preach to unwilling ears," free trade and Christianity, outside of which "there is no salvation" (TYG 3). Missionaries and merchants were alike in attempting to break down and alter institutions that developed long before Christianity and modern capitalism existed. While the two groups gamely enough accused each other of assaulting long-established Chinese cultural practices, they held themselves as couriers of enlightenment and competed against one another for credibility among the Chinese. The merchant's discourse is laden with self-righteous accusations against missionary goals: "Our relations with the Chinese would be far more cordial than they are, were we not suspected of an insidious design to wean them from such habits of filial piety and loyalty as they possess, to our own secret advantage" (TYG 234). Missionaries could turn the accusation on the merchants by accusing them of wanting "to wean" the Chinese of "sobriety" and "hand labor" in plying them with opium and Western factory goods.[16]

But Little's differences with missionaries go beyond those of occupational rivalry. He simply does not think that the moral doctrines of the Chinese need to be replaced: "That a people so generally well read as are the Chinese, and possessing in the teachings of Confucius a doctrine in no way inferior to Christianity, and which, unlike the latter, has survived unquestioned throughout all the wars and commotions of twenty-five centuries; to expect that a people so unemotional and so eminently practical . . . should ever pin their faith to . . . the Bible, seems to a layman, preposterous" (TYG 257–58). Change in China will be effected by secular agents, he adds. Such strong sentiments do not invite rapprochement between merchants and missionaries.

Whereas occupation influences Little's way of seeing China and British enterprise there, travel affects his work as a merchant. Little's journey confirmed his desire to establish himself in business in Chungking. With the exception of missionaries, few Englishmen had traveled in Szechuan. For Little, a large, blank space on the map had suddenly been filled in as populous and meticulously cultivated, brimming with untapped resources and with a commercial center that was an enchantment "of rock, river, wood, and temple, crenellated battlements, and uplifted roofs, crowded with bewildering detail" (TYG 243). To the merchant's eye it was El Dorado.[17] The one obstacle to opening it was the Chefoo Convention, a treaty that Little obsesses about in his books and essays.

The Chefoo Convention of 1876 was one of a series of treaties extracted from the Chinese that stipulated an indemnity far in excess of the cause. The Chinese had murdered the British consular officer Augustus Margary in Yunnan as he was returning from an expedition to set up a trade route through southwestern China to Burma. Little fully agreed with his countrymen's "horror and disgust" over this "coldblooded crime" (GFY 195). Some Britons beat the drums for war, but in the end they settled for £10,000 compensation from the Chinese for Margary's family, the opening of new ports to foreign trade, and limiting of *likin* (transit) duties in the treaty ports.[18] Although Little would like to represent the Chefoo Convention as a great benefit to China, he can sustain his argument only through part of a sentence: "The best means to enlighten the Chinese people and open the country to foreign enterprise and capital is the using of diplomatic pressure to remove the official obstructions to our free intercourse" (GFY 209). He cannot veil to whom the treaty is a boon, nor the means by which it should be gained and enforced.

The new treaty ports included Pakhoi, Wenchow, Wuhu, Ichang, and Chungking. The first four were opened unconditionally but did not prove profitable. Little complains that they give occupation to only five resident Europeans "and of these five three are Germans" (GFY 5). Ichang was a small town in the mountains barely accessible by foot or boat, but it was the westernmost port navigable to steamboats. The British believed that in Chungking they could create a Shanghai of the west, but starting that development was stymied by a condition that frustrated them for more than a decade: the inaccessibility of Chungking to steamers. Little's journey to Chungking convinced him of both the value and feasibility of extending steamboat service to that city fourteen hundred miles inland; however, the river itself presented a major obstacle to modern navigation.

In some ways, Little's journey up the Yangtze is no less allegorical than Huck Finn's rafting down the Mississippi, in that both must contend with the powers of nature and the wiles of man on the journey. The Yangtze River, the main artery between eastern and western China, has always been both a lifeline and a raging monster to central China. From Shanghai to Hankow, the river is wide and deep, in places more than a mile wide, and easily navigable in Little's time by "one of the many magnificent steamers of the American type" as well as traditional junks (TYG 42). Even so, the journey could be risky, as when the steamer Little traveled in got stuck for an hour on a sandbar above Kiukiang and later collided with a cargo junk. The next four hundred miles upstream from Hankow were also accessible to steamboats, and Little had pioneered a service to Ichang in winter when the water level is low. Beyond Ichang, the shallowness and boulder-strewn river bed thwarted steamboat travel. In some of the gorges, the river narrows to less than two hundred yards and the summer and winter water level may vary by one hundred and fifty feet or more. Native craft used sail when winds permitted, but otherwise the boats were poled and pulled upstream by men called trackers.

Traveling upstream in February 1886 was a long and complicated journey. It took Little four days and nights to steam the six hundred miles from Shanghai to Hankow. The four hundred miles from Hankow to Ichang took fourteen days by wupan and another twenty-one days for the next four hundred miles from Ichang to Chungking. The wupan in which Little made the latter part of his journey is a small, partially covered shallow-draft boat with one sail. In the larger junk, the journey took twice as long as in a wupan. Mrs. Little, feeling rather homesick, notes that one could sail from England to Shanghai in less than a month in the 1890s, then take two months to travel the last thousand miles to Chungking.[19] The downstream journey could be accomplished in a matter of days, of course.

Steamboats plying the river all the way to Chungking were the developer's dream, all the more because of the current state of China's transportation system. The country had no long-distance carriage roads. All overland cargo was carried on the backs and shoulders of human beings who often had to rely on footpaths that in some areas were only five or six inches wide, due to farmers begrudging any uncultivated land. In this situation, waterways were essential for transporting goods. Little also saw traditional cargo junks as inefficient. Not only did they take a long time to travel upstream, it was grueling work to get them there. His wupan needed some twenty men to tow it; a cargo junk used teams of two hundred or more men.

The work was dangerous. Two of Little's trackers fell to their death. Harnessed together, towing a rope as thick as a man's arm, sometimes crawling on all fours, at other times scrambling over sheer cliffs, the towing was accomplished with a pandemonium of drums and "howling and bellowing like cattle and surrounded by six or eight overseers walking erect and belabouring their men with split bamboos" (TYG 178).[20] At one particularly difficult passage, Little describes the gangmaster warming the men to their work by stripping off his clothing, rushing into the river, and there rolling in the sand. "Then, like a maniac, he danced, howled, tumbled, crawled on all fours through the ranks of the trackers, jumped at and struck at them" (TYG 178). The occupation of the trackers was a sort of theater, as orchestrated and choreographed as a Peking opera. Little, like every other traveler who has left accounts of the trackers, is full of admiration for them:

> [M]ost assuredly a more cruelly-worked or more poorly-paid, and withal a better-tempered set of fellows are not to be met with the whole world over. Dirty and ill-paid, mostly covered from head to foot with itch sores, and treated like dogs, they work with a will, and are always ready for a joke. During the whole of my trip, I, in my ridiculous foreign dress, never heard an uncivil word from one of them, and, as I have related in my account of the upward journey, on more than one occasion, when rambling along the shore I found myself unexpectedly caught in a tight place, they goodnaturedly came to my assistance. (TYG 331–32)

For Little, witnessing the trackers is a sort of primal experience. To a labor so arduous, laborers so distinctive bring harmony to water, earth, and man as they scramble over beach and bluff to pull their burden up the mighty Yangtze. Little does not harness himself to the towrope, but he feels initiated into a rare society.

All the same, he wants to bring it to an end. Being progressive, a modern man, a businessman, he wants machines to do man's labor, to conquer nature. Although labor was cheap—trackers were paid two dollars and food for two months' work—and the losses due to junk mishaps amounted to only about 2.5 percent, he is persuaded that steamers would be welcomed by merchants. To Little, the irrevocable change that steamboats would bring promises nothing but prosperity: "The uninsurable junks would be quickly abandoned; then, with reduced freights, and the regularity of steam, the Szechuen [*sic*] people would ship to the east their varied and inexhaustible supplies of produce in greatly increased quantity, thus enabling them materially to augment their purchases of foreign manufactures in return" (TYG 351). Like the loading-dock scene mentioned earlier, Little's scheme tries to transcend real concerns. He brushes aside the inherent problems of dismantling an entrenched system and overlooks the possibility that the efficiency, regularity, and "purchase of foreign manufacture" that he advocates as replacements for traditional methods are, for many Chinese, unappreciated Western values.

Also disregarded in Little's vision of the economic benefits of rapid river travel are the concerns of his Chinese competitors. He complains about the self-interest of provincial officers who commanded a "gauntlet of customhouses" along the river route to Chungking, without ever acknowledging his own self-interest in the project (TYG 5–6).[21] The *likin* system meant that excise taxes had to be paid on cargo at each station. The system slowed transport and was vulnerable to corruption. Little hoped that steamboats would be able to bypass this system, to the economic advantage of merchants. In his best captain-of-industry stance, he also rationalizes Chinese concerns about the displacement of junkmen and trackers: "The few thousand trackers thrown out of employment would not suffice to supply one-tenth of the labour required" by new methods and industries, and salaries would increase. Little's arguments reveal a basic lesson of history: the failure to learn from the past. There was, first of all, a parallel in Britain earlier in the century when "stage-coach drivers, the gentry of Leicestershire, and the literati of Cambridge" joined forces to reject "with doctrinaire contempt" the idea that railways would not diminish employment.[22] The

Luddite action against China's first railroad, a ten-mile span from Shanghai to Woosung built in 1874, might have been a sobering reminder to Little: when turned over to the Chinese, he says it was "pulled up and thrown into the sea" (TYG 356).[23] Late-Victorian progressiveness naturally enough interpreted such antimachine fury as a throwback to a bygone era. The Chinese, on the other hand, saw it as a rebuke to foreign business.

Cultural problems aside, the stipulation of the Chefoo Convention making the opening of Chungking dependent on its availability to steamboats baffled Little. He, like other European merchants in China, maintains that the condition delaying the opening was simply another instance of the Chinese refusal to live up to their end of a treaty. China's failure to modernize in a timely fashion is today fully acknowledged, but abandoning a centuries-old system and local institutions was not easily accomplished. From his perspective, Little believes that if the Chinese could only be persuaded of the economic advantages for themselves, they would gladly adopt Western machines and methods.

Being of that frame of mind, he decided to vanquish Chinese fears by steaming into Chungking himself. He formed a company and built a sternwheeler, the *Kuling,* but it never got beyond Ichang: the Chinese "exerted every artifice for a delay that a crafty people could devise, or a British Minister over anxious to stand well in their good graces would submit to" (GFY 7). The "over anxious" British authorities who according to Little gave him insufficient support, were concerned throughout much of the 1880s that several outbreaks of hostilities, such as the one in Canton in 1883, could flare into full-scale war. The British administrative officers attempted to balance the legitimate claims of the Chinese with the interests of the merchants, reining in the aggressive merchants of the treaty ports.

Little's frustration with his steamboat plan was also exacerbated by his having to deal with the Tsungli Yamen, the Chinese foreign office created in 1861. Late-Victorian merchants thought the institution was about as efficient as Dickens's Circumlocution Office. Reflecting that view as late as the 1930s, a British historian jokes: "The Tsungli Yamen was a place where mandarins watched their beards grow longer, amidst the crafty and unchanging race of spiders."[24] Originally, the Tsungli Yamen had represented a considerable bureaucratic innovation in China, the first significant one since 1729. Of course, such a rate of change was not very inspiring to pragmatic Victorian merchants. Prince Kung, a champion of modernization, presided over the Tsungli Yamen, but when he crossed swords with the empress dowager and lost, the effectiveness of the foreign office withered away.[25] Thus bureaucracy and tradition proved a stolid team against Little.

Another impediment the Chinese raised to Little's steamboat project sounds like protoenvironmentalism. The Chinese argued that the monkeys on the precipices would "resent the intrusion of the strange apparition" and hurl rocks on the steamboat decks (GFY 8). The claim represents an alliance between Chinese conservatism and cunning that calls to mind the sentiment expressed in the lines from the *Tao Te Ching* cited in the preceding chapter: "Even when they have ships and carts, they will have no use for them." Fortune admired the pastoral life these lines extol. To Little, half a century later, they represent quixotism—a fable, monkeys battling steamboats. The merchant comes down firmly on the side of machines and modern development.

After enduring nearly a year of bureaucratic obstructionism, Little sold the *Kuling* in defeat to the Chinese in December 1889. However, the 1894 Japanese war with China cleared the way for another attempt to get a steamboat to Chungking. This time Little succeeded in bringing the *Leechuen* through the rapids from Ichang to Chungking in the spring of 1898. In *Intimate China*, Mrs. Little describes the journey as harrowing but accompanied by the kind of excitement that the first railway journeys and early groups of Cookites—Cook's tourists—created in provincial England: "That voyage will for ever rank among the most exciting experiences of my life; for all the population of the river turned out to see the steamer" (52). Sometimes five Chinese lifeboats with pennants and burgees flying, sometimes firing their cannon, vied to be towed by the little steamboat that was something of a model for "the little engine that could." At one point, a team of three hundred trackers had to help her over the rapids, the towrope snapped, and the *Leechuen* foundered. Little proved his point, however. In 1900, he launched the *Pioneer*, a more powerful boat he had manufactured in England at his own expense and assembled in Shanghai. Steamboats have plied the Yangtze from Shanghai to Chungking ever since the *Pioneer*

The S.S. *Pioneer.* Photo by Mrs. Archibald (Alicia) Little, *Intimate China.*

tugged Szechuan into the twentieth century.[26] Little's pioneering work eventually proved more valuable to the Chinese than to him, as the Boxer Rebellion caused the *Pioneer* to be almost immediately turned into a gunship and forced the Littles to flee Szechuan.[27]

Little's difficulty with developing steamboat transportation on the upper Yangtze presents a specific example of a problem with increasingly serious consequences in nineteenth-century China—its resistance to change. The Western view of an "unchanging China" was originally based on observations of similarities in the government and court structure in the Ming and Ch'ing dynasties.[28] Within China, ancient custom and an economy that had been stagnant for centuries stymied attempts to modernize. As the nineteenth century wore on, the combined effects of outdated methods and Western imperialism, and by the 1890s, of Japanese imperialism, took their toll. China's economy became troubled by declining exports, the importation of opium and foreign manufactured goods, and heavy indemnities after the Opium Wars. In the 1890s, the trade imbalance was exactly the reverse of that which existed in the 1830s before the Opium War: "nearly three-quarters of China's trade was with Britain, forming a sixth of Britain's total commerce."[29]

For Archibald Little, who as a foreign merchant perhaps contributed to China's economic problems, stagnation is understood more as a cultural than an economic phenomenon. On this point, China's cultural stagnation, Little can seem rather prescient, as when he anticipates the ideology on which a later era was fixated. For example, he notices a "properly constructed towing-path" that eases the trackers' work; however, like "all the public works" in China, it is "ancient and out of repair" because "the old public spirit of the many wealthy grandees seems totally to have died out" (TYG 181–82). The traveling merchant seems well informed of the collapse of public works dating back at least to the period of the White Lotus Rebellion (1796–1804). At the same time, his blaming the "gentry and so-called Literati" foreshadows the social upheaval of three or four generations hence, when these groups would be held responsible for various societal problems.[30] Little's vocabulary even suggests that future era, characterized by interclass strife: "This is the class opposed to all progress, and which stirs up the otherwise indifferent masses against the foreigner" (TYG 182). Little's image of reactionary elements causing trouble, though played out differently in the incendiary class warfare of the Cultural Revolution, reveals a shrewd assessment of Chinese culture.

Though Little is at times forward looking, he also reflects the thinking of his era when he places cultural stagnation in a racial context: The Chinese "never invent anything new, and while doubtless they are thus spared many of the pains that a superior development of this faculty afflicts us with, they lose nearly all the highest pleasures which our more sensitive organization affords us." They "follow instinct, or hereditary tendencies rather than reason, and their ambition seems limited to the gratification of their senses"; they lack courage, are "apathetic in the presence of sickness and death," and therefore are cowardly in situations where "energetic resistance" would be appropriate (TYG 220–21). This rather terrifying appraisal of the Chinese character is a response to the refusal of the crew of his small boat to accept an ointment he offered them for "itch-sores"—an affliction with which he says every man was covered. In this case, "stagnation" says more about Little than the Chinese. His petulant tirade is quite in excess of the fact. The trackers seem to need some skin ointment, but not many people would accept an unknown medication from a stranger. When the Chinese act in ways like those of people anywhere, they are faulted with a host of negative qualities. The incident serves as a trope for the ongoing attempt of the Chinese to retain their cultural identity and the Europeans' insistence that they should become Westernized.

Finally, Little's travel in the west of China leads him to identify stagnation as a crucial difference between Chinese and European civilization. After returning to the comforts and amenities of English life in Shanghai, he says the most striking thing about his tour was the view it gave him of "the total absence of change" and "the intense stagnation of this peculiar people" (TYG 358). The tone of the passage suggests the inherent paradox in Little's view of China: while he criticizes the country for being unlike the progressive West, he romanticizes the timelessness of Chinese civilization. He then appeals to the authority of antiquity for support of his analysis of China's nature, first mentioning the descriptions of Marco Polo, then reaching back ten more centuries to Pliny:

> "The Chinese, though of mild disposition, yet having something of the brute nature, avoid intercourse with other mortals, but yet are ready to trade and barter.
>
> "The Chinese live quietly, always keeping clear of arms and warfare, and as peaceful and quiet men are fond of repose, they cause their neighbours no trouble." (TYG 359)

Little's contribution to the construction of the Victorian view of China codes it as a country passively awaiting foreign intrusion that will push it to modernize.[31]

Almost as a rebuke to a stagnant China, Little's travel in Szechuan inspired him to make a bold fresh start in his own life. He married and took his wife out to China, and then as if to rebuke Shanghai cosmopolitanism, the Littles moved to Chungking, where Archibald established himself in business some years before it was officially opened to foreign trade after the war with Japan in 1894. While the Littles did not exactly "go native," they lived in a Chinese house, had endless dinner parties with their Chinese associates, and replaced their British dress with Chinese costume.

The Littles' sensitivity to the Chinese view that Western clothes are indecent takes a stand on an important ideological faultline. In the treaty ports, Westerners had always maintained that adherence to Western dress was a sign of power—that the Chinese cowered before them for refusing the metaphoric kowtow of donning Chinese gowns. The China Inland Missionaries, who began arriving in large numbers in the 1870s, aroused the ire of the Western establishment, religious and secular, by arguing that missionaries' success was linked to their ability to conform to Chinese custom, dressing like the Chinese, and living in Chinese houses. As a lay person, Mrs. Little found little comfort in missionary zealotry and found the clothing transition difficult: upon the symbolic shedding of her Englishness and donning loose-fitting Chinese clothes, she develops a severe stomach illness.[32] Mr. Little's altered dress may have been more successful. His Chungking Trading Company appears to have thrived while he lived in Chungking, *habillé en chinois,* but whether his success with steamboats involved the power of clothing is left to speculation.

Little's vision of China diverges from the "I am the monarch of all that I survey" approach ascribed by Pratt to early explorer-travelers in Africa.[33] The late-Victorian imperialist is more complex, more evocative of the anxieties of modernity, if no less grounded in the goals of profit. Exploitation in China is not a matter of grabbing riches lying about or seizing "empty" territory, as indicated in Little's explanation: "It is not as though one were living with savages: the Chinaman has all the outward manifestations of a refined civilization" (TYG 319). This patronizing bow to Chinese civilization is coupled with his claim that Western imperialism is an advantage to China: "The Chinese were the real gainers" by the Nanking Treaty, for "the golden touch of foreign capital and energy" led to rapid increase in wealth and importance of the treaty ports" (GFY 57).[34] These beliefs no doubt enabled Little to achieve the economic success so euphorically predicted for merchants in the opening of China to British trade in 1842.

This success coupled with his many years in China makes him a good representative of the merchants who participated in the business of empire. His travel account is colored by his professional interests: geological features betray valuable natural resources; abundant agricultural production invites foreign trade; ancient modes of transportation portend modern makeover. To the merchant, what is unexploited is wasted, but he does not think of this merely in terms of personal gain. He believes—as did most contemporary Westerners—that railroads, telegraphs, and the other paraphernalia of industrialized countries would be good for China.[35]

Complementing the pragmatic merchant was the romantic dreamer, a man who trekked the Himalayas with the hopes of establishing sanatoriums there. As a merchant, he remained committed to the idea of change, modernization, and the metaphysics of prosperity, yet an occasional doubt nags at him. Contemplating the legacy of the West, he predicts catastrophic cultural loss on the basis of an ostensibly minor trade item. As natural dyes are replaced by foreign imports, he asks "whether all the good we have given to Asia by our intercourse is not counterbalanced by the destruction of the old artistic feeling, which permeated all its productions" (GFY 21). Wealth gained but culture lost is part of the legacy of modernization.

Archibald Little and Robert Fortune, both idealists in spite of their capitalist singlemindedness, have an affinity for each other. Little writes admiringly that "the Kew botanist, who first brought to light the wealth of the Chinese flora, has left us a charming account of his life amidst the people in the interior of Che-kiang and of his kindly feeling towards them" (GFY 289). Little, too, feels kindly to the Chinese, but in a more impersonal way. Fortune felt more involved with the Chinese than Little: he names his Chinese friends; he brags about his negotiations with specific people. The Chinese are crafty and the Scotsman feels ebullient at outwitting them. Little, on the other hand, recounts specific conversations with the Chinese but rarely individualizes them. After a European companion leaves, he once admits, "I was alone (for the Chinaman can never be a sympathetic companion to the European)" (TYG 105). His wife's photographs show him towering above his Chinese comrades, looking embarrassed and sorrowful. There is a tragic element in this man who spent most of his life in China, yet to whom the Chinese remain generic: he remains alien. It is a personal tragedy that may be said to represent the business of empire itself.

The different goals of the horticulturist and merchant also distinguish the two men and their ultimate impact on China—one for ill, one for good, it would seem. Fortune wanted to take things away from it—its plants, its cultural artifacts, its tea trade—while Little wanted to sell things to it and develop its resources, for its own good as well as his own profit. Fortune never entertained a grand scheme for China and never envisioned what became Little's goal—altering China—yet both held the paradoxical view that China should retain its essential culture in spite of whatever might be taken away or done to it. Mrs. Little acknowledges the cost of supporting this view in the semi-happy ending of her novel *A Millionaire's Courtship*. Trevor Lawrence, the millionaire modeled after her husband, succeeds in building the railroad that pierces mountains and connects cities and countries, but it nearly kills him.

part two

Globetrotters in China

Constance Gordon Cumming in 1887. Photo, Constance Cumming, *Wanderings in China*.

three

An Unbiased Stranger

Constance Gordon Cumming

WHEN CONSTANCE FREDERIKA ("Eka") Gordon Cumming arrived in China at Christmas 1878, she had been traveling continuously for four years. She had spent two years in Fiji, with brief visits to Australia and New Zealand, and another two years touring Tonga, Samoa, Tahiti, and California; she then sailed back to Asia.[1] Her letters, journals, sketches, and watercolors record her luxuriating in balmy places. As pleasant autumn months in Japan turned to winter, Cumming felt "nearly frozen, living in paper houses, without fires," and sought refuge in the mild climate and English social life in Hong Kong. This aristocrat with a Rousseauistic bias would find pleasant winter quarters in China, but she would also find herself absorbed by the private and political dimensions of colonial efforts there. Claiming a tourist's privilege, Cumming writes in *Wanderings in China* that "an unbiased stranger like myself, continually receiving kindness from all ranks and conditions of my fellow countrymen," is particularly suited to giving an accurate account of colonial and native life.[2] More accurately, her social position, wealth, and detachment from the work of empire grant her an independence that permeates her celebration of travel in China.

The breadth of her itinerary and her aristocratic background have worked to both the benefit and bane of Cumming, daughter of the Scots baronet Sir William Gordon Cumming. She achieved prominence as a travel writer among her contemporaries: Blaikie writes, "As a writer Miss Gordon Cumming is undoubtedly the most popular of our lady travellers."[3] Her books were cited by travelers and historians into the 1930s. In more recent times, however, she has been excluded from representations of adventurous travelers, and critical studies of women travelers by those such as Birkett, Frawley, and Melman pay her only fleeting tribute.[4] No explorer, enjoying the hospitality of well-placed Westerners in the colonial world, Cumming's contribution lies in turning distant places on the globe into sites of tourism, in normalizing the exotic, and sketching colonial life.[5]

This perspective of the privileged tourist complements the picture of China given by others taking advantage of its opening. Cumming is nearly the opposite of her fellow Scotsman Robert Fortune in terms of class, and far more interested in creature comforts in her travel than Isabella Bird. The bent of her humanitarianism is more passive than that of Alicia Little, and her utterances on religion and morality often contradict those of Knollys. She is plainly hostile to merchants such as Archibald Little for being unsupportive of missionaries. Cumming locates her response to China in her touristic impulse and noblesse oblige, which cooperate to depict China as a cultural backwater in need of British-influenced renewal. Her progress from south to north, from Hong Kong to the treaty ports and mission stations, and finally to the heart of imperial China presents a falling trajectory, starting with enthusiasm and then becoming anguished and inconsistent as her sense of distance from Western culture increases.

Anticipating Hastrup's suggestion that "fieldwork has revealed to the

City of Victoria, Hong Kong. Watercolor by Cumming in *Wanderings in China.*

ethnographer parts of his own hidden nature," Cumming's interest in Asian and South Sea cultures is accompanied by an irritation at the effort of "field-work," and she has to be wooed by each new environment.[6] As a result, her initial response to a country is typically characterized by disappointment and complaint. The landscape of Fiji seems boring to her; in California she is chagrined at having to carry her own luggage; and the cold drizzle of a December day makes her flee Shanghai almost as soon as she lands. The sensual appeal of Hong Kong, however, seduces the newcomer instantly: "I had not the remotest conception that I was coming to anything so beautiful; so, when with the earliest light of dawn, we slowly—very slowly—steamed into this exquisite harbour, its beauty, so suddenly revealed, left me mute with delight" (WiC 7). In this arrival trope, the traveler falls in love at first sight with the colony.

What consummates the seduction by Hong Kong is its development. By the end of the century, the colony would take on a more sinister quality in the fiction of writers like William Carlton Dawe, in *Yellow and White,* but in 1878 it was burgeoning.[7] The natural beauty of the setting awes

Cumming, as it had Robert Fortune in 1848; however, in Cumming's description the emphasis is on the natural landscape succumbing to human manipulation. Hewing a city out of a granite mountain dazzles her. The colonial enterprise responsible for this feat is imagined as a godly power that makes stone appear "gilded by the mellow sunlight," fashioning an Eden out of land "reclaimed artificially": "And in the midst of it all is the loveliest Botanical Garden, beautifully laid out, and where all rich and rare forms of foliage, from tropical to temperate climes, combine to produce a garden of delight, whence you look down upon the emerald green and dazzling blue of this beautiful harbour, where a thousand vessels, and boats and junks without number, can ride in absolute safety." Cumming's landscape description asserts European presence as beneficent; the work of the (British) human hand has fashioned a paradise. Moreover, this image supports a patriarchal view of colonial authority in representing it as an omnipotent caretaker of "boats and junks without number." Implied though unseen is the presence of those colonized who might disturb the image of Edenic perfection.

With typical independence, though, Cumming's beneficent image of colonization is soon tempered by a more mundane view of the colonizing process—one that combines "masculine" professionalism with "feminine" domestic concerns. Building a colony included establishing an English infrastructure in a preindustrial country, something Cumming had witnessed firsthand in its earliest stages in Fiji, where she watched the construction of a capital from a few beachfront buildings. In Hong Kong she reveals a practiced eye for matters of city planning when she worries about how a good water supply and sanitation system can be arranged for a population of 130,000 (the population in 1881). Later, the horror she expresses about the polluted water used by the boat people in Canton shows a heightened awareness of water-borne disease, a scourge that had recently been addressed in Britain's sanitation laws. Cumming is sensitive to the inequities in living conditions of the colonizers and colonized. She imagines the misery in "the densely packed houses" of the Chinese inhabitants (WiC 22). Adding that life is pleasant for those with "no call to look below the surface," she exercises the tourist's prerogative of criticizing the colonial establishment for ignoring the plight of colonized people while exonerating herself from complicity in it.

Cumming's brief but dualistic representation of colonization is soon supplanted by images of the luxury and sociability experienced by the foreign residents in China. Enjoying the spoils of empire requires that worrisome details about the health and welfare of the Chinese community be dismissed; indeed at times both the colonizer and the traveler need to look without seeing at all. Thus, in Canton, Cumming greatly admires the island of English self-sufficiency, literally joined to the Chinese city only by two closely guarded footbridges: "Here is transplanted an English social life so completely fulfilling all English requirements, that the majority of the inhabitants rarely enter the city!" (WiC 27). Without pausing to think of the implications of her praise, the traveler's delight with novelty and the unexpected carries her away. Cumming's representation of the colonial world here puts her in league with the women who, according to Stevenson in *Victorian Travel Writers in Africa,* were "benign" agents of empire seeking adventure, freedom, improved health, and "'the excitement of the unpredictable'" rather than the mastery sought by men.[8] But in the colonial world what is malignant and what is benign often depends on point of view. Such is the case of a privileged traveler who endorses an English enclave thoroughly isolated from the sovereign nation on which it is built.

Cumming's embracing of colonial life puts her at odds with other celebrated women travelers such as Mary Kingsley, Marianne North, and Isabella Bird, all well known to have taken an adversarial position toward European life abroad, though like Cumming they also took advantage of the hospitality and amenities it offered.[9] Women travelers' disdain toward colonists was partly a defensive gesture for the travelers' sense of breaching at-home decorum in their solitariness and unconventional activities. On the other hand, travelers tended to view the replication of English life in the colonies as antiquated or anachronistic. In India, ten years earlier, Cumming herself had complained of the rounds of social calls and "worst of all the deadly-dull races."[10] In Hong Kong, however, she is uncritical of colonial amusements, even coordinating her travel so as not to miss the great event of the year—the races. Perhaps her years of traveling had mellowed her and made her less attuned to manners and customs in England and more appreciative of colonial sociability. Moreover, she never lost her girlhood love of parties nor the tourist's savoring of a holiday mood.

But Cumming's appreciation of colonial life is also more complex, combining the demeanor of those to the manner born with the ingratiating politeness of the adventuress trying not to outwear her welcome (which, however, she seems to have done on occasion). If Cumming is on the whole an exemplar of good breeding, as Jane Austen would say—a guest who praises her hosts; who is grateful for entertainments, parties, good food, and varied and interesting sightseeing trips; who so enjoys Hong Kong and her side trips to Canton and Macao that she rather makes the reader want to visit that old colonial world—she is also self-centered. If she were a character in an Austen novel, Cumming would be satirized for unselfconscious acceptance of privilege and luxury: she is one who, in deference to her social position, always gets the best accommodation, and though rather sturdy in build and six feet in height, she has herself carried in a chair while others walk.[11] Enjoying the spoils of empire often makes Cumming appear obtuse about the feelings of others, even as she is attentive to form.

The most spectacular event during Cumming's entire sojourn in China —the fire that devastated the fledgling city of Victoria at Christmas 1878— serves as a trope for this obtuseness. Cumming leaves a lengthy, vivid account of the conflagration that typifies her detached point of view. From the veranda of an Englishman's home on a hillside above the town, she spent the "livelong night . . . watching this appallingly magnificent scene— the flames rising and falling, leaping and dancing" (WiC 11). If this aesthetic reaction to witnessing the city go up in flames has shades of Nero watching Rome burning, touring the disaster area the next day takes an imperial approach. Cumming is at a loss to explain that the offer of help from "kindly Britons" arouses a "curiously suspicious and by no means flattering feeling" toward them by the Chinese. That the Chinese victims of the catastrophe might not be grateful for assistance by the foreigners who are treating them as objects of sightseeing is beyond Cumming's analysis. It comes as an afterthought to her that "of course" the losses of the poor Chinese are "more pathetic" than those of the fully insured rich.

The overwhelming impression given by her description is the pictorial quality of the fire and the Olympian perch of the British onlookers. There is even the hint of Zeus-like complaint that mortals have only themselves to blame in her accusation that "there is little doubt that the fire was the work of an incendiary" in the general store of an absent Englishman (WiC 10). Cumming's treatment of the fire and its traumatized victims primarily as spectacle is not unusual, in the sense that natural disasters and human catastrophes often attract curious onlookers; in that way, her description anticipates the type of modern reportage that exploits victims and grief-stricken relatives. In another way, however, her treatment of the fire displays Hong Kong and China as contested sites, battlegrounds on which to exercise Western power.

Besides serving its purpose as a touristic phenomenon, the Hong Kong fire becomes a professional prop in the contest between rival travelers Cumming and Bird. To appreciate the dimensions of this contest, it is first necessary to understand the relationship between the two women. Cumming and Bird first met, in Scotland, in 1870 at the home of Cumming's niece, Lady Middleton, after Cumming returned from India and Bird had already found success with her *Englishwoman in America* (1856). They were of a similar age—Bird was born in 1831, Cumming in 1837—and they formed a cordial friendship based on their mutual love of Scotland and travel. However, the relationship became strained after Bird read proofs of Cumming's *From the Hebrides to the Himalaya* while Cumming was in Fiji. Bird embedded criticism of Cumming's work in the explanation of her emendations and a lifelong rivalry ensued. Their paths crossed frequently, both at home and abroad, and they were inevitably compared by reviewers. Cumming envied both the fame Bird achieved and the fearlessness she demonstrated in her *The Hawaiian Archipelago: Six Months in the Sandwich Islands* (1875) and *A Lady's Life in the Rocky Mountains* (1879). Cumming's sojourn in Yosemite Park and Hawaii, as well as her books about these places, were pale imitations of her friend's travels and writing.[12] Bird, for her part, begrudged Cumming's personal likability and professional popularity. She wrote uncharitably to her publisher, John Murray, on 28 July 1883 of her surprise that Cumming's books were doing so well, and she accused Cumming of plagiarizing her description of Mauna Loa.

Both women were in Japan in 1878 when Bird made her celebrated foray into the homeland of the aboriginal Ainu, a feat for which she is generally credited with a "first." Unadventurously, Cumming stayed with friends in Tokyo and Nagasaki. Bird wrote to Lady Middleton that she had seen Eka, adding ruefully that she "is beautifully dressed, and is strong and well."[13] The rivalry between Cumming and Bird emphasizes the distinction between a "tourist" and a "traveler," between conventionality and originality, and between "tourist" and "anti-tourist"—terms that have been used to explain opposing attitudes toward travel.[14] "Anti-tourists" regard the activities of the "tourist" as banal or based on ignorance, their own as unique and authentic. In this regard, Bird believed herself far superior to Cumming.

After Japan, Hong Kong served as the next bout between the rivals. When Cumming "fled south with the swallows," Bird followed a few days later, complaining about winter gales and her ailments. Bird's ship arrived nearly a day after the Christmas fire had begun. She gives a melodramatic self-portrait of struggling to get ashore while Hong Kongese are putting out to sea to flee the flames. The fire was still smoldering, and with an air of self-importance she immediately hires a chair to have herself carried to the home of Bishop Burdon, with whom she "at once went down to the fire." She may have feared Cumming had scooped her. Her seeming heroics veil the fact that she was witness only to the disaster's aftermath; however, her shifting attention away from victims as spectacle to herself as traveler-participant has the humane effect of reducing the exploitation of the victims.

The contest between the two travelers appears in their account of southern China in Bird's *The Golden Chersonese* (1883) and Cumming's *Wanderings in China* (1886).[15] Somewhat disingenuously, Bird refuses to describe colonial Hong Kong beyond mentioning "its boundless hospitalities, its extravagances in living, its quarrels, its gaieties, its picnics, balls, [and] regattas" to explain "the facts concerning this very remarkable settlement" (GC 37–38). Cumming strikes a more personal note: Bird might go to Canton to inspect hospitals, but Cumming goes to enjoy herself. However, in *The Yangtze Valley and Beyond* (1899), Bird follows Cumming's lead in plying the reader with factual information. Then Cumming answered with a new edition of *Wanderings in China,* adding details influenced by Bird, such as a long note on the Yangtze River. It hardly seems a coincidence that Cumming published her memoir in 1904, the year of Bird's death.[16] A published account of a journey exploits distant people, customs, and places to enhance the fame and fortune of the author. In the quest of these two travelers to establish representational authority, China becomes a pawn.

Cumming's claim to authority is encumbered by the fact that because she is a tourist, her ethnographic description tends to be slighted. Her contemporaries patronized her for covering "ground more or less familiar" and, as another reviewer implies in his choice of metaphor, for presenting an insubstantial commentary: she "was able to touch, as it were, but the hem of the empire."[17] Modern analyses may also characterize the tourist as superficial, or, in Culler's terms, as "interested in everything as a sign of itself, an instance of a typical cultural practice."[18] Such views repudiate the voice of the tourist by privileging that of explorers and discoverers. However, the tourist has power in personal response, subjectivity, and literariness. Cumming makes the most of these resources in her portrayal of China and her informal report on the progress of empire.

Her comments on aesthetics demonstrate this progress. More than three decades earlier, her fellow Scotsman Robert Fortune was reprimanded for his appreciation of Chinese gardens. Cumming's pronouncements on the subject not only illustrate the distance between her and her countryman but also show a hardening of the view expressed by Fortune's critics. What Fortune particularly admired—training plants on a wirework form— Cumming faults for the "grotesqueness of the figures." Fortune also was intrigued by the horticultural feat represented by bonsai, which Cumming finds merely "grotesquely distorted and dwarfed shrubs and trees" (WiC 63).[19] Some of Cumming's preposterous assertions result from incomplete knowledge of Chinese culture, as when she insists that the Chinese lack "appreciation of beautiful scenery" and "in building their houses seem deliberately to place them so as not to see the view" (WiC 305). Such assertions simply assume an inferior or absent sensibility of the Chinese and the superiority of her own (British) aesthetic.

The political dimensions of personal taste also appear in Cumming's pronouncements on oriental art: "Neither in China nor Japan need you look for beauty of architecture in the sense we generally imply" (WiC 63). Victorians rather liked the baroque, which might have made Cumming susceptible to Buddhist art. Moreover, although the fad for chinoiserie had faded by the time Cumming visited the Far East, japonserie was increasingly popular in Britain. Her rejection of various forms of oriental artistic creation may thus be seen as a corollary of her sense of the expanding distance between the powerful British empire and the shrinking power of China.

There is a word of caution to be added to this explanation of Cumming's negative pronouncements on cultural productions, because she often expresses appreciation for many things Chinese, even sometimes inveighing against herself, as when, after ridiculing Buddhist art, she cautions that "it does not do to judge hastily" on the effect of Buddhist religious practice on believers (WiC 64). Her view of China is not only conflicted but often a mixture of objective description and spontaneous outpouring on a specific experience, a common enough feature of Victorian travel writing. The competing demands of ethnography and autobiography are magnified when the travel account consists of letters and diaries tailored for a specific audience of family and friends, as in Cumming's case.

Cumming's problems with thematic consistency may also be seen to place her in good company, for they are shared by professional ethnographers, some of whom have suffered from suggestions that their writing style dilutes the content of their work. Margaret Mead's writing, for example, has been criticized as "too feminine" because she incorporates the techniques of creative writing in her scientific writing. For example: "Mead oscillated, as Clifford Geertz says most ethnographers do, between rhetorical intentions. These include the subjective stylist, or anthropologist as author, and those of privileged expert, the anthropologist as social scientist."[20] Cumming, too, oscillates between rhetorical intentions in her representation of China, as seen in her comments on aesthetics and religion mentioned above, and in her attitude toward Chinese culture, which betrays a Rousseauistic bias or nativism even as she argues for Westernization.

Cumming's nativism, expressed in her regret of the destruction of native culture by outsiders, whether in the Hebrides, Fiji, or California, appears in all her travel accounts. In China she often demonstrates an appreciative

fascination for local culture. One example is in the exuberance and comprehensiveness of her four-page list of Chinese customs that "are diamet-
rically the reverse of ours" (WiC 347). This list marks an accumulation of
observations that started with her visit to Canton. Cumming enthuses over
the English enclave in Canton, but once she discovers the native city, she is
ebullient. The hubbub and the "Chineseness" of it enrapture her: "What
really fascinates the eye and bewilders the mind is simply the common
street-life, which, from morning to night, as you move slowly through the
streets, presents a succession of pictures, each of intense interest and novelty. In all this there is life—the real life of a great busy people—and one
feels that it is really an effort to turn aside from these to see any recognized
'sight'" (WiC 29). Of course, the function of this "real life" for the tourist
is its spectacle, its entertainment value. Even its disagreeable elements such
as the bad smells, squalor, and teams of beggars serve their purpose as material for the letter home that will enhance the writer's image.[21]

One way the nativist-traveler can show appreciation for native culture
is in that rite of tourism—shopping. Typically, shopping is mentioned, if
at all, in discussions of travel writing as a vaguely embarrassing activity. As
noted earlier, humbly-born Fortune wrote disdainfully of curios as evidence
of low taste; the middle-class Bird refers to souvenir buying only once—
involving an ancient axehead in Szechuan—though she had a large collection of items from the East that she sold to raise money for the medical
missions she established. The aristocratic Cumming, however, shamelessly
reveals a taste for souvenir hunting; she devotes many pages to describing
shops and cataloguing her purchases, which include silver nail protectors,
jade, toys, an ancient compass, and painted snuff bottles. She admits, "When
satiated with temples, there still remained the interest of the fascinating
little shops" (WiC 132). Cumming's image as a forerunner of the shopping
mall *flâneur* is also bolstered by her regret that in the Christmas fire in
Victoria "some of the best curio shops . . . burned" (WiC 17). Tourist shopping, however, also has anthropological interest in that it signifies a symbolic bonding with local people, allowing the visitor to connect, however
slightly, with another culture. Conversely, finding nothing to buy signifies
an inability to empathize with local culture. The dirt of Tientsin and the

flat alluvial plain on which it sits appall Cumming. That she "could not find a redeeming feature even in the shops, which to me are usually so tempting," is a manifestation of her response to that city (WiC 362).

The ability of this traveler from a background of aristocratic privilege to respond positively to native culture is one of her attractive qualities. It may derive from the conventional gentlewoman's charity work, but also from particulars of her own life. A younger daughter in a family of fifteen, whose mother died when Constance was an infant (she was raised by her grandmother until she was eight years old), Cumming never fully disengaged herself from the role of dependent daughter. Even when thirty-nine years old, Cumming sought permission—which she got grudgingly—from her cousin, the governor of Fiji, to accompany a French bishop touring his South Seas island diocese, a story she tells in *A Lady's Cruise in a French Man-of-War.*[22] Along with her lifelong dependency is the fact that though she often traveled alone with men, she leaves few hints of involvement with them—unlike Bird, who mentions would-be suitors in accounts of several voyages. Cumming's silence on this subject may be related to what Valerie Sanders has noted: "Repeatedly in writing by Victorian women, the intimate is marginalized, pushed to the very edge of the text, or restricted to incidental or fragmented expression in works purporting to be about something else."[23] In any case, Cumming prefers to write about her observation of life and people in the countries she visits.

Notable in these observations is her sympathy for women and children, which also gives evidence of her feminism. As a tourist, she sees upper-class Chinese women only in a few formal encounters, but she is impressed by the female laborers she see more frequently—lively boat women and strong tea coolies, many of whom "are really pretty" (WiC 17). Her lurid tales of female slavery, for example, are not just conventional travel lore, but matters for (feminist) humanitarianism to take up. She addresses that idea after visiting schools and orphanages for girls, urging Englishwomen to train for and staff medical missions in order to serve the needs of Chinese women whom custom denied tending by male doctors. Although her pride is a bit ruffled by her observation that American women doctors were already at work in China, she would have applauded the two Chinese mission-school

graduates who, with their American university degrees, set up practice in
China in 1896.[24]

Cumming's feminist leanings are evident in her concern for women's
health and education, but when class and race are of consequence, she is
unable to sustain her sympathies for Chinese women. She finds the richly
dressed, highly made up wives and daughters of the wealthy to be tedious,
and like Bird she unkindly refers to the bound foot as a "hoof." Overtly,
the appellation places these Englishwomen on the sidelines of the "discourse of philanthropy" that, according to Mills, distinguishes the travel
writing of women.[25] From another point of view, however, the dehumanizing term for the bound foot expresses the travelers' rebellion against the
limitations placed on Chinese women: the bound foot symbolizes their situation. When Cumming admits she prefers the company of men to that of
these women, she is making a pitch for freedom.

Class and race also conspire to nullify Cumming's nativism and feminism in her response to that distinctive cultural ritual, the mandarin's dinner party. The dinner party, a set piece of China travel books, elicits a special
kind of orientalism. Ludicrously mocked by Knollys (see my chapter 4),
regarded as a kind of labor by Fortune and the Littles, Cumming politely
criticizes it even though the forty-course meal appeals to her gourmand's
appetite. For the mandarin, the invitation allows a display of wealth and
luxury, heightened by the approach to his home as the foreign guests are
carried through impoverished neighborhoods to his lavish, walled compound, his wives and daughters appearing for inspection dressed in costly
clothing and jewelry. The British guests are disdainful: "Of course we admired everything, but the position was oppressively dull, and as soon as we
could venture we took leave with all possible courtesy" (WiC 177). In fact,
the wealthy mandarin can never succeed in leaving a positive impression
on his guests, whose home standards of class and wealth have been displaced in the colonial world by race. They rebuke the display as a pre-
sumptuous assertion of equality. When native culture is represented by a
distinctly premodern way of life, Cumming can romanticize it, but when
it is an oriental version of a British earldom, it is a travail.

When Cumming leaves the pleasure-filled colonial world of Hong Kong and Canton for Amoy, Ningpo, and Shanghai, it is primarily the world of missionaries that she encounters and a very different view of China that she relates. It is foremost a fallen world, signified by her view of the physical surroundings as repellent: paddy fields are "that most hateful form of agriculture" in which the "fresh young rice is growing in deep mud" (WiC 179); the Yangtze River is "hideous" and has "dead level shores" that barely separate it from the "dead-flat surroundings of Shanghai" (WiC 266). Shanghai, though favored by foreigners for its social life, has a native city that "may claim the palm for dirt and bad smells," although later Tientsin and Peking elicit much stronger condemnation from Cumming (WiC 268).[26] In these polluted environments, meeting Chinese face to face exacerbates Cumming's fear of contamination by the "common herd" (WiC 25). For example, on an excursion with Mrs. DeLano, wife of the American consul in Amoy, Cumming comes upon a back entrance to a home and is invited in by the occupants, but she is frightened by the unexpected contact and hurries away. She is blunter about the fear of contamination on a sketching expedition during which her opera glasses attract the interest of the girls who gather around her. Reluctantly allowing the glasses to be inspected, Cumming "need scarcely say" that she gives the glasses "a severe rubbing" before using them again herself (WiC 108–9).

In *The Politics and Poetics of Transgression,* Stallybrass and White have explained cleanliness as a class issue—the middle-class fear of contamination by the immorality and anarchical social conditions they perceived among the lower classes.[27] Translated to the colonial world, cleanliness and dirt take on racial significance as a paradigm for the power relation between colonizer and colonized.[28] It is a pattern that comes easily to hand as a method of defining and separating self and other, and consequently appears in various cross-cultural and interracial contexts. Within China, for example, dirtiness is associated with long-standing stereotypes of its minorities. Bird recounts the story that the aboriginal Man-tze bathe only twice in their life, at birth and death. Edgar Snow in *Red Star over China* presents this as a joke about the peasants of northern Shaanxi, and modern urban Chinese turn it into an epithet describing Mongolians and Tibetans. Using "dirty" as a modifier for race, class, and cultural difference also appears in intra-occidental stereotyping, as when the modern English travelers Spender and Hockney favorably compare Chinese cities to dirty American cities.[29] Cumming's rhetorical use of dirt conforms to this general practice and significance.

For Cumming, dirt and bad smells also become involved in a religious interpretation of culture. They are associated with a disorderly and sinful world that the missionary must root out: class gives way to religion as a discursive approach to China. Cumming dramatizes the vast field of work for missionaries by enumerating images of "heathen" China that incidentally indulge the Victorian penchant for the grotesque. Her tally includes traditional Chinese medicine, which she sensationalizes with an inventory of disgusting ingredients and strange practices. Lacking a proper geographical and historical perspective, she relates tales of flood and famine mainly to emphasize horrible side effects, such as instances of cannibalism. Overpopulation, infanticide, superstition, and gambling are among other topics Cumming dwells on to characterize the field for missionary work.

To complete her picture of a culture that can only be salvaged by outside forces—Christianity, British culture—Cumming argues that China's own religion and culture are its foes. Although she rightly enough blames ancestor worship as a cause of political stagnation in China, she cannot resist finding evidence of decline even in China's ancient achievements, as in this odd passage on the *Peking Gazette:* "This strange, stunted little gazette, which has thus survived seven centuries of dwarfed existence, is a characteristic example of many a Chinese institution, fairly commenced ere the rest of the world had emerged from barbarism, but then remaining spellbound, never developing" (WiC 337). Cumming's conclusions have a certain historical validity, but her cavalier rejection of past accomplishments allows little hope for Chinese-inspired reform. Instead, her images of China as sunk in a Bunyanesque Slough of Despond imply that, as in *Pilgrim's Progress,* only Christian can help it climb out.

In keeping with this allegorical interpretation of China, Cumming's image of the British empire as Eden-maker in Hong Kong is replaced by one closer to Mr. Worldly-Wiseman in the treaty ports, where she sees Britain's image compromised first by the opium trade and second by the hostility shown toward the work of missionaries. For nineteenth-century China proved Marx wrong: religion was not "the opium of the people";

opium was the opium of the people. As Cumming becomes increasingly aware of the impact of Britain's role in China's opium scourge, she undertakes a more serious mission than previously shown. She tries to show that missionaries must fight on two fronts—one a pitched battle to convert the Chinese and the other desultory skirmishes with their own irreligious countrymen—but this requires some sleight of hand. Her repugnance at the opium trade is compounded by the fact that it lies at the heart of Britain's economic and political interests, which she supports. To deal with these competing aims, she resorts to methods that de-center the opium trade and foreground humanitarian efforts aimed at bettering the lives of the Chinese.

To this end, Cumming places her opium material in the latter half of a chapter titled "Medical Missions," then uses several strategies that dissociate opium from British respectability. One strategy is to relate opium to non-Western beliefs about death by citing sensational data, adding exclamation points for emphasis: "[O]pium suicides throughout China now average 160,000 annually!!" (WiC 478). Cumming acknowledges that opium use is widespread (estimates of the number of users varied according to the attitude of the writer toward the opium trade, from less than 10 percent of the population to 80 percent).[30] However, she associates it with the lowest classes, whom she likens to the "abyss" in England—those at the edge of society for whom institutions can do little: "As with gin in Britain, so with opium here, the hungry poor are the most inveterate smokers" (WiC 480).

Cumming also attempts to de-Anglicize opium by appealing to conventional British disdain for America. Writing of San Francisco, she excoriates opium use not only among thousands of Chinese living there, but also among "a large number of college students and literary men" and "fashionable Ladies' Club" members (WiC 487). Finally, she fears contamination from across the Atlantic, as opium smoking may "gain a footing in England," where, she says, it has been discovered not only in public houses visited by "the low population of the shipping quarters" (WiC 488–89), but in several public houses elsewhere. The inspiration for her fears may be partly attributed to Gustave Doré, an artist and East End social explorer to whom she refers at the end of her China book.[31]

Nevertheless, it is difficult for Cumming to maintain her argument relegating opium use to non-Britons and British lowlife in the face of widespread use of laudanum and other opium-based medicines in Britain (where recognition of the dangers of opium led to the 1868 Pharmacy Act, which required it to be sold in bottles marked "Poison") and the rather public addiction of famous writers, including Coleridge, De Quincey, and a host of other Victorian luminaries.[32] Dickens's use of East End opium dens for settings in *The Mystery of Edwin Drood* suggests the extent to which opium lore was part of popular knowledge by 1870, and in a sense this verifies Cumming's fear of a worldwide opium culture. Further verification of her fear may be said to appear in a short story about American opium addicts, Willa Cather's "A Son of the Celestial" (1893), in which opium-smoking philosopher-linguists in San Francisco castigate China as a dead culture.

Cumming does her best to place opium use in opposition to British respectability because of her commitment to the anti-opium debate, even though this requires the accommodation of contradictory views. She portrays China as the victim of British villainy on the one hand, and on the other argues that China the unredeemed should surrender to the savior, Britain. Humanitarianism addressed this latter argument in that the opium refuges established by medical missionaries transferred the moral onus from the British as suppliers to the Chinese as users. The irony in the introduction of rescue efforts for addicts by the people who helped create a need for them goes without mention by Cumming. Instead, she offers a description of a twenty-one-day cure that only Pangloss could believe in: "Some have been known to continue steadfast for years" (WiC 478).[33] In a particularly cruel twist, the medical missionaries attributed the failure of the cure to the religious shortcomings of the addicted: when the Chinese complain that the refuge provides only temporary respite, "the preacher tells them that though they sought the Christian's medicine, they must have neglected to seek the help of God" (WiC 479). Blaming the victim is an embarrassing tactic, but Cumming finds opium a problem with no graceful resolution.

In the end, Cumming resorts to shifting the focus in order to extricate herself from the discourse. With a deft use of moral indignation, she returns to the root of the opium issue: trade. "The British official conscience has lulled itself, Cain-like, with the assurance of having no responsibility in the destruction of Chinamen, while gaining a solid advantage in the

revenue of about nine million pounds sterling a year," she writes (WiC
482). Having condemned economic issues that are snarled with moral ones,
Cumming confuses her argument by ending with a discussion of the competition from new opium-producing countries in East Africa: "So between
foreign and native competition, there is every prospect that British opium-
dealers may continue still further to lower their prices, this iniquitous source
of revenue will fail, and England will realise too late that in compelling
China to legalize opium, she has poisoned the goose which might have
supplied a never-failing store of golden eggs, in the form of legitimate
commerce" (WiC 486). Her moral outrage spent, Cumming sets the opium
debate back into the economic niche that it always occupied and joins the
imperialists.

It may be added that Cumming's anti-opium argument is in line with a
contemporary movement, the Society for the Suppression of the Opium
Trade, founded in 1874. However, it was not until 1907 that Britain formally agreed to gradually end its opium trade. The Shanghai Conference
of 1909 pledged international cooperation in the control of drugs, but it
was World War I that did most to curtail the opium importation in China.
The last official importation of Indian opium was in 1917.[34] It was left to
the later Communist government to eradicate opium addiction among the
Chinese people.

For Victorians writing about China, the companion issue to that of
opium was missionaries. The rationalization of the Opium War as a means
of Christianizing China, mentioned in the introduction, haunted the debate about the opium trade throughout the Victorian era. In 1884, C. R.
Haines was still defending opium as "the means indirectly of opening the
gate of the empire for the admission of Western ideas, and . . . the Gospel
of Christ." In 1909, J. B. Eames, on the other hand, argued the reverse—
that the intimate connection among "opium, missionaries, men-of-war" is a
good reason for "gradually diminishing the influx of foreign Evangelists."[35]
As an indication of the opium-missionary quagmire, Donald Matheson, a
defector from the family firm of Jardine & Matheson, whose business empire was based on the opium trade, supported the missionaries, who, he
wrote, complained that "so far as the Chinese were able to discern, it was

but one party—British Christians—presenting the Bible with one hand, and opium to enslave them with the other."[36] The opium-missionary conjunction is such that Bird establishes her credibility on the subject of opium by noting that none of her material was obtained from missionaries (YVB 503).

In being the purported good coming out of evil, missionaries faced a moral dilemma mirrored by their relative lack of success, despite the fact that the number of Protestant missions had soared from fewer than two hundred before 1864 to nearly thirteen hundred by the end of the century.[37] The Chinese language, culture, and the deeply inbred Confucian ethic made it difficult for them to integrate themselves into the community, much less convert people.[38] Cumming's support of missionaries stems from her conventionality, religion, and a sense of duty. Her strategy for bolstering mission work is to attack its critics and provide hagiographical accounts of missionaries and converts, often registering a surprising credulity in repeating stories such as those about a miraculous cure, an exorcism, and the heroic fortitude of Christian converts enduring "one outrage after another" during antiforeign riots (WiC 237–41). Her patronage of the Scottish missionary Rev. W. H. Murray, whom she memorializes in several publications for his work among the blind, goes furthest in this regard. These writings have earned her an enduring association with missions in China.[39]

As mentioned above, Cumming's support of missionary work also leads to her antagonistic approach toward British merchants. She berates British authorities in China for viewing "missionaries and their work as altogether a mistake—an annoying effort to bring undesirable and unprofitable changes" (WiC 243). This attitude puts her in sharp conflict with a merchant such as Archibald Little, who has little patience for missionaries: "'I come not to bring peace, but a sword,' has been but too truly exemplified in this country, and nothing but the weakness of the Chinese enables them to tolerate missionaries as they do" (TYG 214).[40] Intramural conflict in the foreign community evidences the ambiguous moral stand of both missionaries and merchants. A stronger sense of irony might have enabled Cumming to see the comic element in some of the squabbles among the Chinese, missionaries, and foreign merchants over such things as the

Chinese offering swampland for a mission site. Instead, the violation of China by both merchants and missionaries overwhelms her, and she retreats from the battleground to make a final foray into tourism.

The last leg of Cumming's travel in China was the only time she was on her own, so to speak, and this solo travel worried her. The trip to Peking was an arduous one that she forced herself to take because she "was told on all hands" that she could not form a proper judgment of China without seeing some of its northern part (WiC 351). Earlier in her sojourn, she had enjoyed a leisurely boat trip on the Min, when she boasted that she and Mrs. DeLano were served by a staff of fourteen men. Traveling to Peking entailed little such luxury, and aristocratic privilege actually landed her transport that was very uncomfortable, if showy: on one part of the journey she was given a large, ornate, springless Peking cart to travel in by land, while a missionary family was crammed into a small native boat to traverse the same distance more comfortably by water. The journey to Peking included sailing from Shanghai to Chefoo, changing to a native boat and sailing up the Pei-ho to Tientsin, switching to another native craft and continuing to Tung-Chow, and finally enduring the aforementioned bruising ride to Peking by wooden cart over the imperial highway—a road seemingly unrepaired since its construction in 1260 A.D. Although Cumming does not make the comparison, in California a teamster had given her and two Englishmen a very punishing buckboard ride to Yosemite. The Chinese carter seems to have had a similar object in mind. At the dawn of the age of tourism, those in the "service industries" felt no need to mask their resentments toward the holidaymakers.

The object of Cumming's travel was to pay homage to the cultural artifacts and faded glory of the Celestial Empire, and by comparison to the superiority of victorious, modern Britain. Cumming visited Peking's city wall, ancient observatory, and temples, turning her travelogue into a guidebook with long, detailed information explaining the history and significance of each sight. Her personal reactions to these sights often reveal a shallow understanding of their historical and cultural importance, and she adds a good deal of subjective commentary in support of the "China in decay" theme. Dirt, dust, and dilapidation are dominant images, more oppressively frequent than in her descriptions of sights in southern China.

Peking Cart. Drawing in Eliza Scidmore, *China: The Long-Lived Empire.*

For example, at a visit to the Lama temple, she notes that the two gigantic prayer wheels are "thickly coated with dust" (WiC 394).

The temple tour leads her, by a series of associations, to an essay on Chinese literature and an ancient library of 173,000 volumes that ends in condemnation of the present: "It is, however, necessary to add that the majority of the books are little more than mere commentaries, by intellectual pigmies of modern days, on the writings of men possessed of a far wider range of thought and freer imagination than these, their cramped descendants" (WiC 402). In Cumming's depiction of China, time is an anti-Darwinian phenomenon, illustrating deterioration rather than progress, as she relegates the intellectual efforts of centuries to the dust heap of history. She makes no explicit comparison to the contents of British libraries or contemporary British intellectual efforts, making a blanket discrediting of Chinese civilization suffice.

Cumming also uses droll humor to criticize Chinese civilization. Confucianism is a frequent target of her barbs. She jokes that an early emperor who attempted to destroy the Confucian classics might have been motivated by being forced to memorize "these wearisome volumes" as a boy (WiC 398). Perhaps remembering her days at boarding school in London during her visit to the examination hall, she ponders the imperial examinations, a triennial, three-day ordeal for students camped in cells only three feet by five feet in size: "I scarcely know which to pity most—the students or the examiners. . . . On the whole I think the examiners have the worst of it; for though a student is occasionally found dead in his cell, he has only one set of essays to produce . . . whereas the luckless examiners have to wade through, and carefully weigh the merits of, perhaps 8000 of these dreary sets of papers" (WiC 405–6). Although lighthearted, Cumming's satiric comments on the imperial examination system fit a pattern of disparagement of Chinese institutions that pervade Victorian views of China.

When China's cultural artifacts seem above reproach, Cumming shifts attention to the Chinese character, as on a sightseeing trip to the Temple of Heaven. In describing the flights of stairs on one structure, for example, she alludes to the stereotype that the Chinese defy Western logic: "These somehow represent a mystic figure known as the Eight Diagrams, the symbolism of which only a born Chinaman can fully grasp!" (WiC 380). Next, a view of the Imperial City (entrance was forbidden) offers an opening for ridicule of China's aristocracy. Although "the scene certainly does not lack enchantment," stories about the nefarious deeds of the empress dowager and mocking details about distinctions in rank and dress in China deflect Cumming's admiration of the sight (WiC 440).

Even personal laziness serves the purpose of deprecating China. Cumming complains unfailingly about every discomfort of the journey to Peking, as well as of her subsequent sightseeing, which often begins with a four-in-the-morning ride in the hated springless cart. In fact, she weighs the benefits, bother, and gratification of such effort. She tires of ancient temples and bickering with guides, of curtailing an expedition only to regret missing something she would never again have an opportunity to see: "But truly, in the matter of sight-seeing, flesh is sometimes weak!" (WiC 396). When the object of interest presents an obstacle to being seen, she questions its intrinsic value. In the end, China itself is blamed for preventing the tourist from appreciating her.

One sightseeing trip, however, falls into a special category, combining the idiosyncrasies of Victorian tourism in China and class privilege. In 1878, the Temple of Heaven was still a sacred precinct that only a few, select foreigners—men only—were permitted to see. Cumming, unaware of the restrictions, she says, rose early and appeared at the temple gate on the very day that Ulysses S. Grant, making his postpresidential world tour, was to be shown the temple. When Cumming arrived, the temple retainers confused her with the honored Grant. As well she might, she makes the most of the episode in her book. Both the Chinese and Grant's American staff were furious with her, but she deploys hauteur to defend her self-confident enterprise: "Like certain Pharisaical Christians, they seemed to think that the gates of heaven should open to them alone, and that the admission of others was an injury to themselves! I only congratulate myself the more on the advantages of early rising" (WiC 388). Celebrity and serendipity combine to give Cumming a touristic coup in which social rank takes precedence over gender and professional stature. Or she perhaps was exhibiting the brazenness of one with nothing at stake.

Peking also gives Cumming an opportunity to use her aristocratic connections to bask in reflected glory. She makes up to the Grants by calling on Mrs. Grant (who had not been permitted to see the Temple of Heaven) and attends a farewell reception for them in Peking. She seems to have quite charmed the president—perhaps the hard-drinking old general appreciated the lady's taste for a glass of Chartreuse with her breakfast.[41] At any rate, she deemed it "wise" to refuse his invitation to sail onto Japan with him and Mrs. Grant, though she later agreed to sail with them to San Francisco. In the first chapter of *Fire Fountains,* Cumming describes the Grants' fantastic send-off in Tokyo, then boasts of dining at the same table with them on board ship and details their triumphal reception in San Francisco in October 1879.[42]

The Temple of Heaven episode is a high point in an increasingly difficult visit for Cumming. Until she traveled to Peking, she had very little contact with individual Chinese and had seen China essentially through the eyes of the Westerners with whom she stayed. Her nativism was slightly tattered by meeting Chinese from the wealthy classes, but still intact.

Peking, however, affects Cumming much as it did Fortune. The crowded capital made it impossible not to rub shoulders with its teeming humanity, but it is a humanity different from that she observed in India and the South Sea islands. In those places she had learned to look on nakedness as natural —bronzed bodies as part of the landscape, and sensually appealing. In China, however, Cumming is clearly embarrassed by naked children "basking in the warm wet mud along the edge of the river" (WiC 354). Only a few years earlier in Fiji and Tahiti, Cumming could sleep in primitive huts and swim nude in forest pools, but in Peking the absence of European accommodations causes her "some anxiety" (WiC 372). Peking makes Cumming uncomfortable because it isn't primitive enough; it is civilized, and if it is not exactly on a level with European civilization, it is a place where European amenities are noticeable for their absence.

The longer Cumming stays in Peking, the more trenchant her description of it. It suffers from "neglect and decay," is "sickening," "appalling," and "pestilential" (WiC 371, 461). The grand compounds once belonging to members of the imperial family and now housing the foreign legations are valued for what they negate: "a privilege in this horrid land of exile" (WiC 371). Even her sketching expeditions turn into crowd-gathering torments. Under the weight of these images of defilement, the ideological framework for Cumming's interpretation of China collapses. Rather than envisioning Western civilization and Christianity grafted onto Chinese culture, redeeming the people, she turns even admirable qualities into something negative, imagining an enormous oriental diaspora threatening the West: "Everywhere they work their way by gentlest but dogged force of will, by imperturbable good-nature, by a frugality. . . . That they will continue more and more to overrun the earth is certain" (436). The evidence of former glory and current degradation of China, and in particular the role of the West in contributing to that degradation, provokes her inchoate fear of China.[43]

Visiting the site of China's capitulation in 1860, the wreck of the old Summer Palace, Cumming feels ashamed of her country's destruction of what had been the central symbol of Chinese culture. She observes that the destroying armies had "the best possible intention" but that their "destruction of an Imperial glory" convinced the Chinese "that all foreigners are

barbarous Vandals, that it is generally coupled with their determined pushing of the opium trade, these two crimes forming the double-barrelled
weapon of reproach wherewith Christian missionaries in all parts of the
empire are assailed, and their work grievously hindered" (WiC 497). Cumming feels collective guilt as an oppressive burden. Politics and ideology
make a mockery of her tourism. Her response is to flee to Japan.

Traveler and Chairbearers. Drawing in Robert Fortune, *Three Years' Wanderings*.

four

The Pen and the Sword

Major Henry Knollys

> Had he but spar'd his Tongue and Pen,
> He might have rose like other men.
>
> —JONATHAN SWIFT, "Verses on the
> Death of Dr. Swift, D.S.P.D."

"A COURTIER TO HIS FINGERTIPS, an accomplished gentleman of the old school" is the way a friend describes Henry Knollys[1] in an obituary.[2] An impressive résumé accompanies this characterization. Knollys served the military from 1860 to 1897, commanding the Royal Artillery in South Africa from 1889 to 1891. Earlier he had served on the staff of General Sir Hope Grant, who saw duty both in the Indian Mutiny of 1857 and the Second Opium War in China. Knollys collaborated with Hope Grant on books about these military actions and later wrote a biography of the general. Knollys also wrote on other military subjects.[3] He ended his career as private secretary and controller to the Queen of Norway (formerly Princess Maud of Wales). His family connections are equally formidable. Henry was the third son of a general; his elder brother, Viscount Knollys, was private secretary to King Edward VII and King George V, and his sister Charlotte served as secretary to Queen Alexandra for more than fifty years.

Social position, career, and authorial style lend interest to Knollys's account of his several months in China in 1884. As a military officer and historian of sorts, he possesses professional qualifications that give him distinction among the six travel writers under consideration in this book. Interestingly, though, this background seems to have prejudiced him, for he arrives in China with a full baggage of preconceptions about it. As a result, his book, *English Life in China,* has more extreme views than the others I discuss, and his assessment of Chinese culture and colonial life is more often flawed than theirs.[4] At the same time, *English Life in China* is arguably the most literary of the travel accounts here considered, in that it is strongly influenced by creative literature, particularly eighteenth- and nineteenth-century satire, and these influences need to be taken into account in evaluating Knollys's rhetorical presentation of China. A further interest in his book is his masculinist perspective, which balances the feminine/feminist views of globetrotters Cumming and Bird. Finally, Knollys's decision to present his material as an on-the-spot journal gives it a subjectivity that turns him into a text himself.

Knollys begins with unconscious self-satire in describing his first days in Hong Kong. Many of his comments seem shaped by the wit and repartee of a gentleman's club—he lists Arthur's Club as his address in his preface —or a character in Thackeray's *Book of Snobs.* The harbor may be beautiful, but the hotel is "terribly stifling—second rate as to comfort and equipment, first rate in point of cooking" (ELC 4). A few more lines show Knollys directing his snobbery toward the "English life" in the colony: "Steer clear of the rank and file of the civilian community." Knollys is soon rescued from the "rank and file" by a fellow officer and gentleman who offers him luxurious accommodations in his home, but "best of all, he avoids that fatal error of hounding you with amusements and occupations" (ELC

A Temple Theater. Watercolor by Cumming in *Wanderings in China*.

5). Knollys shows none of Cumming's delight in the social whirl of colonial Hong Kong and Canton nor Bird's stuffiness in writing only about serious matters. On the other hand, he complements the women's images of colonial life with domestic details they never mention, such as a vivid description of laundry drying on the hillside, which he apparently regarded as a novelty.[5] Perhaps in their quest for authority, the women travelers ignore such details.

Both personal taste and his officer's perspective shape Knollys's depiction of colonial life. He admits that the fresh flowers, rattan, and punkahs have their charm, but they are offset by "enough revoltingly ugly china to satisfy the most vitiated taste of a depraved virtuoso" (ELC 5). He is also plainly embarrassed by certain colonial rituals and the emotion they arouse, such as the weekly arrival of the mail boat, "which thrills with the effect of magic" and results in moments of silent anticipation and emotional reading of letters from home. Expressions of homesickness provoke his mockery again in Shanghai, when "open-handed hospitality" ends with sentimental toasts to "'Old Folks at Home'" (ELC 42, 93–94). He prefers the races and a solitary look at local sights. Knollys's penchant for satire tends to put colonial life in an unfavorable light, and it shows his misanthropic streak, discussed more fully later in this chapter.

His position as a military officer afforded Knollys some experiences not available to ordinary travelers, such as his inspection of Hong Kong's military installation. But an unfortunate incident at the garrison early in his tour seems to color the rest of his stay in China. Knollys was dining with the officers when an enormous flying cockroach landed on the tablecloth (ELC 32). The English officers were incensed by this unwelcome disruption of their meal and called in their "coolies" to remove the creature. That the officers' squeamishness is revealed to the Chinese, the colonized people, is an added embarrassment. To Knollys, China is at fault for presenting such a disagreeable happening, and, in a sense, the greater part of his account of China is a "getting even" for the discomforts and irritations arising during his travel there. This idea of the narrative as retaliation can further be seen as an adaptation of Knollys's military background in that he depicts himself and China as antagonists, opponents in battle. China "fights" him by alienating and frightening him. He in turn makes his pen his sword, using a variety of methods to represent China negatively.

Climate provides one of the noticeable ways China defines itself as an enemy to Knollys. The timing of his visit, the summer months, compared with Cumming's from December to June, disposes him to find China a topos of heat and unhealthiness: "The majority of the men, nearly all the women and the children without exception, succumb more or less, sooner or later, to the enervating effects of severe heat combined with extreme steamy humidity" (ELC 29). Certainly, tropical climates and the swiftness of infectious disease—Knollys lists "dysentery, fever, liver or a general break down" —were a serious cause of concern to Victorians. In Hong Kong, evidence of such health problems is the high fatality rate for British soldiers in the first years after the Opium War, an issue to which Fortune calls attention in his first book. However, by 1884, when Knollys visited, living conditions in the colony had greatly improved, so that his comments represent a conservative point of view. He himself notes that a large proportion of the graves in the English cemetery date from forty years back. To avoid concluding that the "remarkably low death rate" in Hong Kong could indicate it was a generally healthy place, however, Knollys adds that "all whose circumstances admit fly to other climes as soon as they sicken" (ELC 29).

Knollys's impatience with the climate leads him to furnish striking details about colonial life. He notes the health precautions and regimen followed by soldiers in the barracks at Hong Kong—a routine that must have made boredom a serious problem. They were served a cup of cocoa in bed at 5:15 and a half pound of beefsteak for breakfast; were confined to the barracks from nine to five in the hot months (with nothing to do because of the ubiquitous "coolie"); protected by the pith helmet and cholera belt when outdoors; and fanned by punkahs all night long (ELC 56). Concern for the men operating the punkahs is reduced to callous jokes about their falling asleep on the job. On the theme of climate a few months later, however, Knollys observes that the English merchants in China are more forgiving about the summer heat: "The hot, stifling, enervating, and sickly" climate of Foochow makes "it not surprising that intimacy is close, that hospitality is unsurpassed" (ELC 280). In this final comment on climate, Knollys shifts attention away from China to praise the resilience of Britons living there.

Perhaps his hosts in Hong Kong found his jousting with China a bit trying, for Knollys soon was assigned a courtesy post in Shanghai. He says he was selected by "British Imperial Hong Kong" to "inspect the volunteers, horse, foot, and artillery" of "British Republican Shanghai" (ELC 66). To this official duty he added visits to Foochow (one of the coastal treaty ports) and Hankow (six hundred miles up the Yangtze River), where he seems to have met Archibald Little. Treating sightseeing as an extension of his inspection tour, Major Knollys appears to look for faults and infractions, delineating them with his satirist's pen and often turning his travelogue into a species of military operation.

Such a purpose occurs even in Knollys's landscape description. The countryside, he says, might have been beautiful had it not been disturbed by "man's grotesqueness," "ugly, childish-looking pagodas," and "squalid dwellings" (ELC 136). He has none of Fortune's admiration of Chinese skill in manipulating nature, the engineering and construction projects that shape, adjust, and alter the natural landscape. Nor does Knollys have Archibald Little's appreciation of the way the Chinese can harmonize nature and architecture, nor Cumming's romantic fondness for primitive life. Instead, the evidence of human life and habitation on the landscape provokes Knollys. His description is nearly the opposite of what Coetzee calls the antipastoral, the "white writing" about South Africa in which the labor of the black man who creates an idealized landscape goes unmentioned.[6] The antipastoral and Knollys's image of a disfigured landscape have a similar effect, however, in that they justify colonialism/imperialism as a means of improving a country.

It follows, then, that an unpeopled landscape ought to be attractive to Knollys. In fact, vistas of astonishing fecundity on the Yangtze River salvage his view of China and stimulate his sportsman's goodwill that spills over into favorable descriptions of the "sprouting riches" of agriculture on its shores. Steaming up the Yangtze River near Wuhu, Knollys is awed by the spectacular number and variety of water fowl: "Well, as we ploughed our way, several acres on either side were crowded with wild geese, teal, and mallard as thickly as in a feeding pond. But what inspired me most was that, whereas their American congeners take flight at the approach of any craft, these Chinese wild-fowl with national sagacity allowed us to steam up to within a few yards of them, tumbling, quacking, and flapping out of our way, making by successive lengths a lane which sometimes extended over a mile" (ELC 137). The glorious bounty of China is here connected with conquest in what Pratt describes as an "explicit interaction between esthetics and ideology."[7] The trade agreements Britain wanted from China and the subsequent wars waged to secure them were predicated on a belief in China's fabulous wealth and placid insularity. This seductive scenario is echoed in Knollys's description of the "acres" of wild fowl that, "with national sagacity"—like their human counterparts—offer only nominal resistance to the intruders; their very passivity invites trespass.

If the hunter's paradise offers a parable of imperialism, it also quite literally inspires Knollys's paean to hunting that makes "sport" an outgrowth of military conquest, specifically glamorizing the massive destruction of wildlife by Victorians in Asia, Africa, and North America. Constance Gordon Cumming's older brother Roualeyn rather famously exemplifies these goals, as revealed in his *Five Years of a Hunter's Life in the Far Interior of South Africa* (1850).[8] The sense of license with which the Westerner exploited flora and fauna in newly opened territories is trumpeted by Knollys. Part of the joy of hunting in China is that you "land when and where you please . . . for the natives view with perfect indifference your trampling even through high standing crops" (ELC 138). The reader can imagine the seething helplessness with which the Chinese farmer observed the well-armed Western hunter march through his fields. Two decades later, Oliver Ready in *Life and Sport in China* turns Knollys's arrogant claim into an entitlement: "Here is my ground, here I can take my gun and my dogs and go just wherever, and do whatever, I please, without let or hindrance, shoot what I will, stay as long as I like without asking anyone's leave" (46). These hunters serve as a powerful trope for Western imperialism. The benign scientific project of an earlier age to classify and collect the flora and fauna of the world is transformed by late Victorians into a covetous "killing for sport."[9]

Knollys's implacability toward China partly derives from vicarious experience gained when he edited the papers of Sir Hope Grant, published as *Incidents in the China War of 1860.*[10] Hope Grant was the general who served under the command of Lord Elgin during the onslaught of Peking in 1860.[11] Some of the incidents described in this book have a Chaplinesque quality, particularly those detailing the advance of the French and English forces on Peking. Moreover, the flight of the Chinese emperor to his palace in Jehol (in Manchuria), leaving Lord Elgin no one with whom to negotiate, makes the idea of imperial conquest seem almost accidental. The infamous looting and burning of Yüan Ming Yüan (in which Chinese villagers participated) Knollys insists was instigated by the French. Of Hope Grant's Homeric share-and-share-alike handling of his troops' plunder, which he rounded up from the looters and sold at auction, Knollys says that the English officers would have liked the whole affair "to sink into oblivion."[12] Embarrassing as these "incidents" were to Knollys, they might have been worse. Lord Elgin was persuaded by French and Russian diplomats to settle for the burning of the Summer Palace rather than carry out his more ambitious thought of destroying the Forbidden City and replacing the Manchu dynasty with a Chinese one.

Clearly resisting a conclusion to the opposite, Knollys declares the war of 1860 a great victory of three months' work: "We procured for the civilized world protection from the oppression and barbarous outrages which the nation had been previously wont to inflict upon strangers."[13] The "outrages" Knollys refers to are the loss of four ships and hundreds of British troops at the hands of the Chinese in 1859 in the repulse at the Taku Forts, an installation near the mouth of the Pei-ho River leading from the Gulf of Chihli to Tientsin, and the murder by the Chinese of Harry Parkes, the British official at Canton who was "probably the most hated foreigner in China."[14] Knollys's work on *Incidents in the China War of 1860* clearly predisposed him to find fault with China during his 1884 tour.

Knollys's work on recent military history and his background as an officer obviously influence his way of seeing China and his way of writing about it as well. His rather consistent use of an attack mode may be seen as related to these influences. When he turns to writing about Chinese culture, he mobilizes his literary interests to assist in his presentation and uses devices more typically found in creative writing than travel accounts. The result is a pastiche of vignettes that display orientalism as entertainment. One device Knollys uses is to intrude into the text as interrogator, and he uses dialogue to convey both factual information and opinion. For example, once he asks an anonymous "boy" about the queue (his parody of pidgin English is the lesser evil in this exchange):

> "Boy, why do you submit to such bother with your hair? Why do you not wear it like mine?"
> "No savvy. Every Chinaman do same ting; old-o custom."
> "Well, I savvy; 300 years ago, the Tartars conquered you and compelled you to wear ... pigtails, and you have continued the custom without comprehending the meaning." (ELC 232)

To Knollys, the queue exemplifies a fatal attachment to custom and the rejection of progress. Dialogue affords him an economical method of ridiculing both the hair style and Chinese men, while representing himself as informed Westerner teaching the Oriental a lesson. Dialogue has the added advantage for him in using the reader's inference rather than his own direct statement to convey his opinions—not that the ploy saves him from tarring himself. However, the novelistic devices allow Knollys to present outrageously racist and gendered views more openly than is usual in a prose narrative.

More idiosyncratic than this use of dialogue in ethnographic reportage is the interior monologue of an imagined informant, a device Knollys employs to make the Chinese condemn themselves. This occurs in a vignette about a Chinese opera. Knollys, like many Westerners, has difficulty appreciating traditional Chinese music. After attending a Chinese opera, he mocks the performance by imputing to a Chinese gentleman a view that he scorns: "In all the sciences and in most departments of civilisation you greatly surpass us," the imaginary Chinese gentleman says, "but in one respect we are undoubtedly far ahead. We alone understand true harmony: you are ignorant of its first principles" (ELC 111). This method of attributing ideas to the Chinese as a way of deriding the culture may be the mark of a frustrated novelist. If there is a positive side to the method, it is that the attributions show a thinking, responsive populace. From another point of view, assigning fairly light-hearted thoughts to the Chinese is a way of demonstrating that Chinese culture is not to be taken seriously.

Knollys uses this tactic to inscribe the Chinese with his own point of view with great verve and frequency. Other subjects besides music include the Chinese understanding of world geography, food, funerals, and religion. In one long vignette, he fantasizes the Chinese interpretation of the Englishman's love of sport, Knollys's passion: "The sight of the apparently purposeless, exhausting, and dangerous run quite confirms the natives in their opinion that these 'Fung Yang' (foreign devils), who hold over them such a mysterious and lordly sway, are the maddest lunatics the world ever produced" (ELC 102). The monologue that follows attempts an ironic assessment of English sportsmen: "You will spend hours, you will face cold ... of all your insane occupations that which you call athletics is surely the most insane." This supposed Chinese understanding of the Englishman's psychology allows Knollys to express his own view that *the Chinese* believe in the cultural superiority of the English. On the other hand, Knollys's purpose here may fail entirely for the reason that the reader may indeed find the Englishman's love of sport "insane."

In some situations in which race and gender are an issue, Knollys is unable to novelize his thoughts and loses all control of his narrative, addressing the Chinese directly. Observing a barber at work, for example, he is moved to disgust: "What a feminine brushing and plaiting and finishing up of the pigtail with ribbon. . . . You nasty creatures! every single one of your actions has an element of dirt in it and here you wind up with a filthy operation on the ears" (ELC 232). The sudden lurch into second person, the leap from barbering to a generalized comment on culture, from grooming to "dirt," bespeaks Knollys's confusion and terror of cultural difference. He falls back on gender, seizing on the stereotype of the effeminate Chinese man to defend his reaction.

Adding these gendered stereotypes to his arsenal in describing Chinese manners and customs corresponds to a historical process set in motion by an alteration in power structures. To re-image the proud Chinese as a people subjugated by the West, Chinese men became "effeminate" and adult men became "boys" and "coolies." Even the derogatory terms used by the Chinese for non-Chinese, "barbarian" and "devil," were turned into a joke by Westerners. These stereotypes began appearing in travel literature around 1850, according to Mason, suggesting the rapidity of the image makeover after the Opium War.[15]

Yet many travelers in China show discomfort with the evolving stereotypes, as exemplified by their feeling compelled to explain why they call their servants "boy." Knollys states apologetically that it is what servants are "invariably called" (ELC 43). Others feel a need to explain the genealogy of the term. Dilke, who visited China in 1875, imputes "boy" to the Dutch term for "slave," while Capt. Gill, who explored China in 1876, suggests that the usage of "boy" is an importation from colonial India.[16] Arthur Smith (1894) and Oliver Ready (1904) put the term in their glossaries, indicating that the usage belies common sense.[17] For all the overt racism of Westerners in China, the country retained a special aura that made the usage of "boy" embarrassing, and even Knollys, who can seem intolerably belligerent to the Chinese, adds an occasional patronizing compliment to compensate. For example, in a passage very like one expressed by Robert Fortune, Archibald Little, and just about every other Victorian traveler in China, he admits the intellectual and cultural astuteness of the Chinese when commenting on the probability of Christianizing China: "To consider the Chinese, with so much intelligence and industrious foresight, in the light of untutored savages whose minds may be easily moulded to a new creed, would clearly be the height of absurdity" (ELC 199). Following this reasoning, the Chinese may be "boy," but they are not boys.

When confronted with cultural difference, Knollys resorts to gendered stereotyping in situations involving women also, and again combines methods of creative and expository writing. Describing a banquet that is somewhat different from the mandarin's dinner party Cumming attended, his narrative falls back on a satiric style, and he uses techniques similar to those in the barber scene mentioned above. Hardly a positive word appears in the long account of the banquet, an invitation to which he "obtained, not without difficulty," and that was apparently one of the highlights of his tour. After a strange assessment of what he supposes to be the moral stature of the women attendees, to show the reader he is not "indiscriminately mixing up demi-monde and family life," he suddenly switches to second person: "Now what physical beauties has nature bestowed on you? Few indeed." He ends an insulting analysis with "I can only find you distortions of nature" (ELC 286). The misogynistic tone of this description balances the misanthropic spirit of the barber scene. At the same time, the emotional energy expended in each scene seems out of proportion with the context, suggesting that incidents involving sensuality of any kind make Knollys uncomfortable. He discloses his offense as defense, answering a feeling of vulnerability aroused by the oriental demimonde with an unpleasant description of it.

It should be added, however, that describing the women at the banquet at all separates Knollys from other men, who, as a rule, keep a discreet silence about Chinese women in their travel books. Both Fortune and Archibald Little mention women and social contacts with the Chinese only in general terms. In contrast to these men, the globetrotting Knollys remarks candidly on the English merchants of Foochow who live a sybaritic life in enormous, well-fitted houses: "Their gambling is considerable both in cards and racing, their immorality in many cases more than considerable, and it would be well if that homage which vice pays to virtue, sometimes termed hypocrisy, were exercised to throw a cloak over their dealings with Chinese women" (ELC 281). Knollys's reproach of these men looks forward to Alicia Little's writings about the double life of Englishmen in the colonial world, discussed in chapter 6.

From his gendering of Chinese culture to his moralizing on English life in China, Knollys displays a certain consistency in style and point of view. This consistency extends to his representation of race. As a military officer trained to see people in terms of friend or foe, Knollys was perhaps destined to view the Chinese as racially inferior. At the same time, his fixation on the implications of Darwinism indicate that he is troubled both philosophically and affectively by race.[18] Knollys's consciousness of Darwinian thought is reflected in his several attacks on "Darwinites" and in his sentiments on race that have the tone of Gulliver recognizing his affinity to the Yahoos: Knollys remarks on the "novelty" of this "strange population, which only resembles ourselves—apart from the theological point of view—in being two-footed, unfeathered, grinning mammals" (ELC 63). This recognition of shared humanity of the races is all the more troubling to Knollys because it makes him conscious of the relation between humans and animals.[19]

He conveys this consciousness in a plethora of animal imagery to represent a dehumanized subject. The allusion to Swift's style and themes in the passage above is indicative of the range and direction of this imagery. Many of Knollys's descriptions of the Chinese use terms that echo the misanthropy in the Houyhnhnm section of *Gulliver's Travels,* and a long passage on "Bouquet de Chinois" echoes Swift's coarse humor (ELC 91).[20] Knollys describes a widow's lamentations in extravagant terms as resembling the "howling of a jackal and the miauling of a cat" (15). His metaphors for the Chinese also include "spaniel nature" (48), partridges and sheep (67), salmon and smelt (70), hares and "snaky" (86), civet cat (91), cat-like (89), baboon (99), bulldog, beetle, and cockroach (286); in addition, women with bound feet have difficulty walking "a few yards on their own hind legs" (73). Chinese food is likened to "childhood's dirt pies" and "carrion" (73), "semi-putrid viscera of their unhealthy swine" (120), "a tallow candle stuck thickly full of bristles" and "eyeballs of a rat" (233). One of Knollys's preferred verbs to describe the movements of people is "swarm." He also employs pejorative synecdoche to dehumanize his subject: the Chinese are "pigtails" and "naked hides" (21), "specimens of flesh" (72), and "carcasses" (116).

Beyond the racism, consciousness of Darwinism, and sheer puerility of the insults, Knollys's imagery shows an obsessive attention to bodies and physicality that, metaphorically, alludes to the eroticization of and ultimately transgression against, China. When Foucault says in *The History of Sexuality* that "deployments of power are directly connected to the body,"[21] it is not sexuality as such that he means is the axis of power, but the way in which sexuality inscribes the power relation between people; and Pratt expands on this idea in her analysis of precolonial travel literature with a provocative argument: encounters between European and native peoples begin "with the body as seen/scene."[22] The metaphoric language Knollys uses similarly represents the Chinese body as "seen/scene," and it is a scene he tries to exert power over by ridiculing it or representing it as inferior or dehumanized, which thereby justifies exploiting it.

A parallel to this representation of the body as an expression of power occurs in Knollys's landscape description. Here "the Yang-tsze-kiang— the River of Golden Sand" with its "inexhaustible fertility" is eroticized and mastered: "Then as we ascend one hundred miles after another, how wayward it is in its currents and wanderings! Not stormingly aggressive, but with quiet caprice upsetting, womanlike, all the calculations of experience, and entirely altering the face of its domain" (ELC 145). Capricious, unpredictable, the mighty river is assigned the stereotypical behavior of a woman, but dominated, in Knollys's thinking, by the masculine British, the victors in war, the captains of industry, the sovereigns of trade. What role does this leave for the Chinese, particularly Chinese men? As represented by Europeans such as Knollys, they are displaced, made into "boy" servants and effete opium addicts, or dehumanized as "coolies," beasts of burden.

On a more personal level, the frequent excesses of Knollys's language argue a high level of fear—fear of the latent power of those naked bodies. The clothed Westerner is synonymous with control—self-control and political dominance. Sensuality, a threat to control, announces itself in the semiclothed laborers. As a result, proximity to large numbers of Chinese

Opium Smokers in an Opium Shop. Drawing in *Tien shih chai hua pao* (Illustrated Magazine), Taipei, circa 1884.

often elicits feelings of vulnerability from Knollys, a fear of the oppressed seeking reprisal against the oppressor. One instance is during his journey to Hankow. On the river steamer, he is one of a handful of European crew and passengers ensconced in luxurious quarters; below decks are jammed 250 Chinese. Observing them, Knollys flinches at the specter of Chinese vengeance: "Why should not these 250 wretches, whose sole principle is that of gain, without the common tie of civilisation which is the common tie of brotherhood, select one day or night out of the three we are to spend on board with them, far from other human aid, cut the throats of the five or six Europeans, plunder the ship at leisure, and disappear into the wide adjacent country? I really feel grateful to them for their forbearance" (ELC 117). In his feeling of vulnerability, Knollys personalizes the relation between colonizer and colonized, though he cannot address his own insecurity satisfactorily. If the Chinese are bereft of civilized behavior, as Knollys claims, then what prevents them from savagery? The alternative seems equally troubling to him: If "the common tie of brotherhood" is what influences Chinese "forbearance," what justifies his own hostility toward them? One more voice needs be added to resolve the dilemma, the voice Houston Baker describes as "Caliban's triple play," a "guerrilla action carried out *within* linguistic territories of the erstwhile masters, bringing forth *sounds* that have been taken for crude hooting, but which are, in reality, racial poetry."[23]

Officially, the voice of the Chinese was that of the Ch'ing government, edging toward extinction but about to begin the third phase (1885–1894) of the not-entirely-successful Self-strengthening Movement. The "crude hooting," to use Baker's term, of the Chinese people could be heard in their attacks on foreigners in the last decades of the century (see chapter 5), actions that were signs of frustration with their own government as much as with the foreigners themselves. The humiliation felt by foreign encroachment on China for more than half a century found outlet in the Boxer Uprising in 1900. Educated and astute in his way, Knollys senses the rumblings of the people, and he is on edge during most of his tour.

A self-consciousness about his metaphoric silencing of the Chinese by speaking for them in his often blistering descriptions is evident in Knollys's comments on language itself. He repeatedly complains about the sounds and difficulty of the Chinese language and the "incessant inconvenience" of not knowing it. He gives extravagant excuses for not learning a few phrases, shifting responsibility for his own sloth to the Chinese language and culture. First is the danger of contamination: "Great as is the difficulty of adults in acquiring Chinese, greater still is the difficulty in preventing English children in picking it up from their *amas*" (ELC 325). Second is the subject matter of its written record: Chinese is "destitute of the literature of science and art, possessing only compilations of so-called philosophy" (ELC 326). Third is its structure, "a language without a grammar" or alphabet (ELC 329). That is to say, Chinese is contemptible because it is not Western. Not being Western, it has nothing to communicate. The foolishness of the syllogism is sufficient commentary on Knollys's charges against the Chinese language.

On one level, travel writing is predicated on a silencing of and speaking for the people and places visited, and travelers may develop rhetorical strategies that justify their explaining and analyzing a country and culture. One strategy Knollys uses quite early in his account is to credit the British for what is in reality traditional Chinese cultural practice. The Hong Kong Botanical Gardens, Knollys writes, prove that the British educated the Chinese, "in whom appreciation of nature's beauties is strangely nonexistent," in horticulture (ELC 28).[24] Capt. Gill, a fellow officer-turnedglobetrotter, uses the same strategy, declaring that the British had succeeded in teaching the Chinese "how to buy and sell without their aid."[25] The image of subjugated people as deprived of adult intellectual and emotional powers is a staple of colonialist writing. It leads to a metaphoric appropriation of native culture, what "we" have done for "them," and thus is a device for giving the traveler authority to speak for, to interpret, another people.

In Victorian travel writing about China, this desire to interpret the culture approaches being a compulsion in the attempt to define the national character, paying particular attention to ethics. In this pursuit, Knollys employs some devices already well established by earlier travelers, but he adds his characteristic satiric style that gives his definition of the Chinese character a sharp edge. Most Westerners in China found much to praise. If the Chinese ethic at times seemed antithetic to Western morality, it also had its admirable points that could put the Westerners to shame for a weak adherence to their own values. Thus, commentators developed several methods to deal with such conflicting views of ethics. One is to vitiate positive qualities with disclaimers. Accordingly, the Chinese are peace loving, but they "acquiesce in the infamous national misgovernment"; they are impeccable servants, but are apt to be overzealous, submissive but crafty, enjoy longevity but lack hygiene, are quick to learn and mimic but lack originality, have a reverence for learning but learn by rote without thinking or receive education based on superstition.[26]

Although Knollys sometimes follows established patterns in explaining the Chinese character, he also adds his idiosyncratic twist in depicting Chinese behavior as beyond the grasp of Western civilization. For example, he describes caged prisoners as "gleefully chattering with their fellow inmates," then reacts to the spectacle with an interpretive non sequitur: "They have no sense of shame at this public exposure, because Chinamen have no sense of distinction between virtue and vice otherwise than as it affects profit and loss" (ELC 92). According to this reasoning, the prisoners could be guilty of any crime other than something affecting "profit and loss"; they are shameless because they are amoral. What the actual crimes or feelings of these prisoners are Knollys has no way of knowing; nor does he try to make some up, based on what might be his own feelings in such a situation; instead of sympathizing with men treated as beasts, he declares them devoid of moral sensitivity; he sees them not as fellow-travelers on the road of life, but as soulless.

Another strategy Knollys uses to describe the Chinese character is to portray it as displaying feelings that are the reverse of those esteemed by the English or Western world. The humanitarianism demonstrated in medical missions and Britain's moderate justice system in the Shanghai concession is understood by Knollys as the opposite of Chinese indifference to human suffering: "Compassion is an unknown factor in their unamiable hearts" (ELC 240). Smith's influential *Chinese Characteristics* appears to lend support to Knollys's view. In a chapter entitled "The Absence of Sympathy," Smith attributes a lack of "fellow-feeling" among the Chinese to a combination of deep poverty among the masses, marriage customs, and the "sickening effects" on those "too accustomed" to constant "social war."[27] Bird tried to do her part to refute the view of the Chinese as uncaring by including a chapter in *Yangtze Valley and Beyond* on Chinese benevolent societies, addressing the needs of the poor and hungry. Smith also takes on this topic in his chapter "Benevolence," saying that the motive for Chinese charity is "retributive bookkeeping," the "reflex benefit which such acts are inspected to insure," "practised without heart."[28] None of these three writers see possible similarities in Chinese practice and British institutions such as the mean-spirited poorhouse system, nor the mutual belief that a good deed might be rewarded in the hereafter.

Another method Knollys employs to characterize the Chinese is to invoke the enduring stereotype of the inscrutable Oriental. Inscrutability is typically used in Victorian travel books, as it is today, in a mocking way, rather than to explain something truly mysterious. Knollys growls, "For some occult reason—certainly not veneration, for they are incapable of that—advanced age is considered a great merit" (ELC 233). Is it really "occult" to venerate long life? Do not "venerate" and "consider a great merit" mean the same in this case? Uncovering examples of inscrutability is a game many travelers find irresistible. Bird's entry is to invoke the "mysteries" of the "Oriental intellect" when describing a simple and reasonable system for counting small coins based on weight.[29] Coding an action as inscrutable proves to be a gratuitous disparagement of the Chinese.

Inscrutability is often treated with a spirit of levity that is capitalized on in many depictions of the Chinese, such as Ernest Bramah's comic Chinese storyteller in *The Wallet of Kai Lung* (1900), and, later, Hollywood's Charlie Chan. However, characteristics of the Chinese that are also characteristics greatly admired in the English themselves bring out a much darker response by Victorian observers. For example, though the Victorians admired industriousness and the economic rewards it might earn, they condemn similar traits in the Chinese. As mentioned above, Knollys sarcastically reproves "getting and spending" as the supposed prime motivation of the Chinese, an astonishing accusation in view of the vastly greater "getting and spending" motives that made Britain wage war against and extract trade treaties from China.

Observing that the Chinese possess traits similar to those in his own culture antagonizes Knollys, and like many of his compatriots he reacts by depicting the traits as dehumanizing when they are exhibited by the Chinese. This is the case when he sees the stamina of men pulling away at heavy oars during a storm and they "begin to lift up their voices in a chorus of unearthly yells, which apparently affords them immeasurable ease and delight" (ELC 318). More frequently, he has the opportunity to marvel at the ability of Chinese men to carry heavy weights long distances for many hours. When the burden is Knollys himself and a companion borne in chairs by men two-thirds their size, "we almost feel a sensation of shameful sloth at thus taking our ease, while four human beings are slaving under our weight"—"almost," but not quite (ELC 35). The flicker of shame is put out by denying the men their humanity: "They are indifferent to heat and fatigue" (ELC 35).[30] An attitude toward labor that Knollys might have admired in an Englishman, in the Chinese only prompts him to distance himself from their toil and their shared humanity.

Another case of a shared value being devalued or denied by Knollys relates to parental affection for children. While Victorians had not returned to the eighteenth-century emotionalism of Mackenzie's *Man of Feeling,* sentimentalism was having a resurgence, particularly in relation to "family values" topics, of which the emergence of a new genre, children's fiction, may be seen as a result. In fact, an example drawn from this genre provides a striking conflation of Victorian sentimentality and images of China that put Knollys's views into relief. Mrs. Molesworth's *The Cuckoo Clock* portrays the lonely orphan Griselda in one fantasy sequence being charmingly entertained in Mandarin-land by various silent, nodding figures.[31] Connecting such sentimentality with the Chinese would be anathema to Knollys, for a crucial element in his assessment of the national character is that the Chinese lack feelings. As a result, he misunderstands the Chinese custom that prohibits public display of emotion and declares that Chinese mothers have no affection for their children.

A final topic Knollys considers in relation to the Chinese character is death. This topic would, like that of maternal feelings, seem to be one with congruences in Victorian and Chinese practice that could create cross-cultural understanding. Victorian mourning customs that included making jewelry from the hair of the deceased would seem to be able to accommodate Chinese burial customs. Knollys, however, finds them repugnant:

the Chinese funeral ritual is a "repulsive, unfeeling ceremonial" (ELC 15). Cemeteries that Fortune had found so dignified decades earlier Knollys ridicules as holding "gaunt graves," and he is disagreeably overwhelmed near Hankow by a necropolis with a "perimeter of nearly nineteen miles" (ELC 126). Unsurprisingly, then, he also dismisses the tenets of ancestor worship, "which at first appear to pivot on some of the better and softer feelings of our nature," as "fetish superstition" that stands in the way of reason (107). An example of "sepulture" that prevented the construction of a modern road also elicits his characteristic contempt of Chinese culture (ELC 106). Ancestor worship and attendant burial practices such as Knollys notes were a serious obstacle to modernizing the infrastructure—building railroads, establishing a telegraph system—but Knollys's sarcasm undercuts his authority to say so.

As mentioned earlier, Knollys went to China with a substantial knowledge of its recent history and firm views on Britain's policy toward it. During his travel, his impression of China is partly filtered through English officers, merchants, missionaries, and other Europeans in China, but it is also gained from sightseeing in the company of his Chinese interpreter and from direct experience. It is the latter I now wish to pursue, for Knollys uses it to bolster his support of British political and economic endeavors in China.

Following the lead of his contemporaries in London, Knollys employs the methods of social exploration to help develop his argument.[32] The purpose of social exploration in England was "to draw attention to inequalities in English society and to force upon the reader an awareness of his social blindness."[33] The investigation of manners and customs by Victorian travelers in China shares such an informational purpose, and in drawing attention to cultural chasms it influenced both humanitarian work and British policy toward China. For Knollys, exploration of Chinese culture has a predictable result.[34] He sees men in the torturous cangue and other cruel punishments administered by the Chinese justice system that make him declare that the Western assessor system, in place in the concession areas, seems kindly in contrast. However, opium presents the usual difficulty in arguing the benefits of imperialism. Knollys's tactic is to marshal personal experience in defense of the opium trade.

Knollys's personal exploration of opium dens is in the tradition of Dickens and Wilkie Collins, who were drawn to the low life and fascinated by the sordid: "On many occasions I repeated my visits to the opium shops and always with the same result" (ELC 257). Although the atmosphere is decadent, his descriptive imagery makes it vaguely domestic: the room contains "numerous divans"; the opium apparatus is compared to an "ink-jar"; the drug is "treacly-looking"; the smokers appear emaciated but "perfectly quiet, sluggish drunkards."[35] Such empirical evidence yields an argument in homespun language that makes opium more a social than a moral matter:

> I found that these so-called dens by no means reveal any patent amount of evil, except the wasting of money, and as I investigated more and more the whole question of opium, I became more and more persuaded that the wholesale denunciation of our national wickedness, apparently ignoring the fact that an enormous amount of opium is grown in China itself, contains a good deal of catchpenny claptrap. It would not be listened to by any reasonably wise man for five minutes consecutively if the matter were argumentatively presented and fairly weighed, and if instead of the begging-the-question title-page, "our iniquitous traffic in opium," were substituted "British commerce and the exportation of papaver juice." (ELC 257)

This discourse de-exoticizes opium, but Knollys's exploration goes further. He inspects consignments of opium at "those merchant princes, Jardine and Matheson" (ELC 142), a company that, as previously noted, had made its fortune in smuggling opium before the Opium War and now was engaged in the legal opium trade. Next Knollys is eager to see if he "might experience to some small extent the sensations of an opium smoker's gratification" (ELC 261). He signals the hypocrisy of his claims for the harmlessness of opium in that he lacks the courage to lie down among addicts in opium dens. Instead, he "induced a wealthy Compradore—Chinese agent of an English mercantile establishment" to invite him to his home to make the experiment.

Even under such controlled circumstances, it is a dramatic scene, and Knollys seems a bit disappointed that not "the slightest gratification" resulted, although the reasoning of the "papaver juice" passage quoted above suggests that the drug had some effect. His experience is different from that of Archibald Little, who tried opium as a cold remedy and misjudged the dosage; it made him so ill that he decided the cure was far worse than the disease. In contrast, Knollys, outfitted in his opium-eater's clothes, presents himself as imperial Everyman to whom opium does no violence.

Knollys's experimentation is but an echo of that East End exploration that, Leask notes, had led De Quincey to an addiction that he twisted into an "apologia for imperialism as the means of stimulating [China's] torpid and internally fissured national culture."[36] Several years after the opium trade was officially ended in mainland China, Somerset Maugham indicates the extent to which these arguments about the politics of opium ceased to matter. He describes a Hong Kong opium den in *On a Chinese Screen,* based on his 1921 visit to China, as a "neat enough room" where there are men in various stages of addiction. At the end of the room, the proprietor's family is gathered in "a cheerful spot, comfortable, home-like, and cosy." Maugham's passage shows opium entirely naturalized, being merely the means of working-class livelihood. He concludes: "Fiction is stranger than fact."[37] With this turn of phrase, Maugham detoxifies the arguments of those like De Quincey and Knollys so that opium does indeed seem no more sensational than "papaver juice," and the trade disputes and wars behind it become unnecessary.

Knollys's experimentation with opium appears to have emboldened him to explore China accompanied only by several Chinese servants. A houseboat journey up the River Min near Foochow (an excursion also taken by Cumming, Bird, and numerous others) makes him feel more positive about China than did any of the other experiences he had there. Abandoning his military bearing and satirical eye, he becomes, simply, traveler. On a six-mile trek inland, he meets village people, who serve him a cup of tea that thaws him enough to make him remember the name of their village, Yuenki—no small feat since he never bothers to give the name of the interpreter who accompanies him. He clambers by moonlight through banyans and bamboos, wades through shallow streams, admires waterfalls, is chased by dogs, gets lost and found. Finally, drenched in a violent thunderstorm, he is "compelled to sit on deck in what I may describe as coolie costume" (ELC 317). Moonlight and a bit of opium taken for fever evoke a rapturous paean to "jagged mountain crests" and "a startled night bird" that he compares to a nightingale. Unity with nature, Englishy metaphors —it is a moment that catapults China into the realm of high romanticism.

Social exploration allows Knollys to exchange his officer's uniform and satirist's pen for oriental dress and an opium pipe, a world of dreamy sensualism for one of discipline and contention. It is a pleasant contrast to his investigation of missionary life and a world where rank and class divide and separate people. "The Missionary Question" is a long chapter that, as Pat Barr mentions, "aroused the fury of the mission press" in England.[38] It is easy to understand why. The dispute between missionaries and the merchant community that upset Cumming is inflamed by Knollys. Cumming focuses on opium as the cause of the dispute and obstacle to Christianizing China. Knollys, who applauds the opium trade as good for Britain and harmless to China vehemently blames the missionaries for their own failure.

In particular, he heaps opprobrium on Protestant missionaries for craving social status and lacking commitment to their work: "The missionary business in China" is "run by that class . . . one grade below gentlemanship, and from which the majority of the Chinese Protestant missions are recruited. Poverty stricken and without prospects at home, out here they are provided by the various missionary societies with an assured and liberal income . . . " (ELC 205). Knollys waxes eloquent on "missionary luxury," the supposed extracting of funds from supporters at home to live an affluent life in China. A decade later, Bird raised this raw issue with one of her missionary hosts, provoking a defensive response: "She very kindly offered to enlighten me as to the cost of furnishing in Western China" (YVB 291). The use of missionaries as ammunition in Victorian accounts of China is a constant reminder of the conflicted morality of the British role there.

Knollys says his criticism is not directed toward the China Inland Mission (CIM); however, his mockery of missionaries "with a deficiency of clean linen and h's [aitches]" is rather plainly directed to the CIM, many of whose missionaries had little formal education. Founded by the charismatic leader Hudson Taylor in 1866, the CIM recruited missionaries from all classes and religious persuasions. The number of Protestant missionaries rose dramatically from fewer than two hundred before 1864 to more than twelve hundred by 1881; the number of communicants was perhaps only fifty thousand (of China's four hundred million).[39] Controversy raged in Britain over the expense of supporting so many missionaries with so few converts.

Knollys's criticism of missionaries again alludes to Swift's *Gulliver's Travels*—in this case to Gulliver's journey to Laputa—to convey the image of mission work as misguided. His acerbic remarks about a Roman Catholic orphanage where footbinding is practiced so as to make the girls marriageable serves as a prime example of this.[40] Knollys's general conclusion about the expectations of Christianity in China may also be glossed as Laputan, rather like turning cucumbers into sunshine: "Those who assert that thus far missionaries have made numerous sincere Christians are governed by delusion or are guilty of fraud" (ELC 209). Missionary failure, whether resulting from bad science, morality, education, or social rank, to Knollys besmirches British competence and prestige. Apparently offering a self-portrait as an alternative, he thinks that religion would be best served by "highly educated" gentlemen "who wear well-cut, well-brushed clothes; who are men of the world, of tact and discrimination . . . whose experience is varied and conversation interesting" (ELC 211). In the end, Knollys makes missionary failure turn squarely on class.

Knollys's account of China fits what an ethnologist has called an "author-saturated" text, one "in which the self the text creates and the self that creates the text are represented as being very nearly identical."[41] The military officer-globetrotter and the narrator of *English Life in China* appear alike in their feelings about English superiority and "the instinctive submission" of the Oriental. Knollys adduces his own military bearing and ability to command in such a way as to support this idea.[42] Once when more than a hundred luggage carriers race on board ship to vie for employment, he deftly establishes order. The men, "keen for hire and shrouded in darkness, who could have brushed me aside like a fly, never dream of disputing the self-assumed authority of the single Englishman" (ELC 67). Later he says that the "demeanour" of the Englishman exercising this kind of authority must be a "more masterful one than would be wise or indeed would be tolerated in a civilised city," which to him adds proof of an inequality between the races (ELC 230). Perhaps misunderstanding the traditional

Chinese respect for authority, not to mention that the behavior of the men might suggest a desperate desire for work, the luggage-carrier incident assures Knollys of his own racial superiority.

Ironically, Knollys's heroic stance leads him to a sense of foreboding about the British presence in China. His consciousness of the relatively small number of Europeans in China in contrast to the huge Chinese population and the combination of threat and firepower by which Europeans maintained their authority there seems a prologue to the fear of what, a little later in the century, would be termed "the Yellow Peril."[43] As mentioned, at the end of her travel book, Cumming worries that thousands of emigrating Chinese portend a threat to future racial balance. Some years later, Bird opines that the real "peril" is a Chinese threat to British mercantile dominance. A combination of these racial and political tensions inspire Shiel's *The Yellow Danger* (1899), one of the invasion novels that appeared toward the end of the century. In Shiel's work, starving millions of Chinese and Japanese invading Europe are conquered by means of germ warfare and a coalition of the allied armies of Europe, America, Canada, and Australia. It is a fable Knollys almost predicts: "The slight moral force which keeps the rabble in order is most remarkable, and usually perfectly efficacious, but it may snap—occasions have arisen when it has snapped" (268). This threat and counterthreat makes him restive about his version of China and the imperialist mission he supports.

Isabella Bird Bishop in Chinese Dress.
Photo; Isabella Bird, *Yangtze Valley and Beyond.*

five

In Search of Elysium

Isabella Bird (Mrs. Bishop)

ISABELLA BIRD DIED a week short of her seventy-third birthday with her boxes packed for a new journey to China. Her desire to return to it, of all the countries she had visited, indicates something unresolved in her feelings about the country. Her style had always been to plunge forward to overcome all obstacles to her goals. At the end of it would be a book that crowned her sense of conquest of a little-known land. China was a climactic journey for Bird, representing the best and worst of her long years of travel, but despite her lengthy sojourn and her big, "definitive" book on it, something about the country eluded her. Complicating her feelings was her sense of rejection due to the lackluster sales of *The Yangtze Valley and*

Beyond (YVB), attributable to the unfortunate timing of its release just at the outset of the Boer War.[1] As her health was failing, the ecstatic, other-worldly moments she had experienced in far-western Szechuan were drawing her back.

It had not been an easy journey. When Bird set sail in January 1894, her main travel goal was Korea, but she soon had to flee because of the Chinese-Japanese war. She then spent fifteen months (1895–96) in China, restlessly journeying to Shanghai, then to Cheefoo, Tientsin, and Mukden, where she stayed with missionaries at the China Inland Mission, returning to Shanghai in the summer of 1895 to plan a trip through the Yangtze valley. There were difficulties obtaining the authorities' permission. Exasperated with the delay, she traveled to Peking to secure the necessary papers. The desire to escape the social constraints that motivated her travel developed new depth and urgency in China. She needed to flee the very places in which she sought refuge. The forces of gender, class, and patriarchy Bird found so restrictive in European society pursued her in new, threatening ways that riddle her portrait of China with conflict and contradiction. *The Yangtze Valley and Beyond* is based on a notion of three Chinas described separately but also overlapping, jostling one another as pedestrians on a narrow, crowded thoroughfare. European residents of China, the Chinese, and the aboriginal Man-tze (akin to Tibetans) are alternately romanticized, excoriated, and praised.

Bird's numerous biographical accounts stress her fearlessness as a traveler, paradoxically combined with chronic illness, pain, and exhaustion.[2] As a child her attachment to her father, as an adult her intense relationship with her sister, and at age fifty her marriage to Dr. John Bishop are indices of Bird's sense of duty to home values that called to her from abroad. When abroad, however, she evaded that sense of duty by plumbing the ever farther depths of the unknown that her books of travel celebrate.[3] Bird represents a middle-aged version of that fictional traveling forbear Corinne, who lives alone in her own home, works for a living, chooses her own friends, travels freely, and in Ellen Moers's words "turned the heads of young women from Yorkshire to New England."[4] Expressing a similar freedom in her books, Bird is neither daughter, sister, nor wife, but traveler, commentator, journalist, and ethnologist.

Bird begins her book with a subtext, a woman's claim to excellence in male-dominated fields, in an informational introduction packed with geographical data on China and an attack on the "spheres of influence" policy by which China was being carved up by England, France, Germany, and Russia. The chapter thus self-consciously establishes her as an authority with a wide knowledge of the country, an explorer whose experience adds weight to her role as pundit. Bird had been the first of fifteen women made fellows of the Royal Geographic Society in 1893, an honor that came after a good deal of soul-searching by the all-male society and that was soon after undermined by a vote to forbid any further election of women fellows.[5] Several years later, Bird seems determined to debunk such male bias toward women's achievements with a persuasive display of expertise. Her letters to her publisher, John Murray, during the time of composition of the China book indicate her anxiety over factual details and her research being hampered by the difficulty of borrowing books by Colborne Baber and Capt. Gill, two sources she relied on for geographical information.[6] China, a subject so vast and with so many published precedents, would not yield just another book of travels for Bird. She would end her publishing career with a carefully documented tome.[7]

While the introduction of *The Yangtze Valley and Beyond* implicitly confronts the patriarchal order outside of China, chapter 1 attacks the nexus within. This chapter is on Shanghai, that city, like Hong Kong, virtually invented by the British after the Opium War. There were scarcely fifty foreigners in Shanghai in 1844; in 1860, only 569; but the number leaped to more than five thousand only five years later.[8] The once swampy, agricultural village had been transformed into a modern European city by the time Bird saw it—a transformation that she concludes, after extensive fault-finding, is politically laudable. Donning the helmet of Britannia, she declares: "Shanghai in every way makes good her claim to be metropolitan as well as cosmopolitan, and, in spite of dark shadows, is a splendid example of what British energy, wealth, and organizing power can accomplish" (YVB 24). The seasoned traveler and colonial observer could reach that patriotic conclusion only after underlining how personally unappealing she finds it: "Those of my readers who have followed me through all or any of my eleven [*sic*] volumes of travels must be aware that my chief wish on arriving at a foreign settlement or treaty port in the East is to get out of it as soon as possible, and that I have not the remotest hankering after Anglo-Asiatic attractions" (YVB 15). In addition to the antisocial element in Bird's attitude toward Shanghai is her tone of distress. To a visitor, a globetrotter, it looked too much like home.

In Shanghai, Westerners resided in the concessions, the areas secured for them by treaty and in which they lived subject to their own rather than Chinese law. Housing, clothing, food, places of business, clubs, parks, and the famous Bund emulated European models. There were newspapers and magazines suited to various interests, including Shanghai's *North China Herald,* the *Rattle,* a humor magazine, and the scholarly *China Review,* published in Hong Kong. For much of the year there was a frenetic round of dinner parties and sports, and, pervading all, an aura of luxury and license. There were, too, wealthy Chinese who adopted Western styles and lived in the concessions. Just as, later in her book, Bird would enthuse over the comfort of her corset-free Chinese dress, it was freedom from confining Western roles she sought abroad. For the political commentator that Bird sometimes styled herself, there was a more pertinent story to be told.

Bird's first brief visit to Hong Kong and Canton at Christmas 1878 (already mentioned, in chapter 3) shows her insistence on firsthand experience. The visit also kept her in the company of the missionaries and diplomats with whom she stayed, well insulated from any real contact with the Chinese. Eighteen years later, she wanted a broader experience of China. This included a visit to Chinese Shanghai that lay beyond the European city; however, "to mention native Shanghai . . . brands the speaker as an outside barbarian, a person of 'odd tendencies.' It is bad form to show any interest in it, and worse to visit it. Few of the lady residents in the settlement have seen it" (YVB 25). She critiques the city and the project it represents by positioning herself outside the European community, yet maintains an insider's vantage point.

Bird shares the traveler's claim of impartiality in observing the colonial world, a claim invariably used to criticize the colonizers, as when Cumming, the "unbiased stranger," comments on the water and sanitation system in Hong Kong and when Knollys, arguing that "the casual amateur has greater facilities for hitting blots than the bigoted professional," ridicules missionaries (ELC 204). The aim of the criticism is to exculpate the traveler from any responsibility for the crimes of the colonial world. In the passage cited above, Bird's criticism of European Shanghaiese absolves her from complicity in the embarrassing disparity between the living standards of Westerners and Chinese. Moreover, the sarcastic tone of her comments shows the enormous gulf that existed not only between her and the permanent European residents, but also between them and the Chinese. Bird's touristic interest in the Chinese city makes her attack on Europeans less innocent, however, for squalor as object of sightseeing is exploitative in its own way. Finally, by dissociating herself from "lady residents" and allying herself with male residents—traders, clerks, explorers—she unwittingly joins with the very hegemonic forces she sought to undermine. Negotiating touristic impulse, patriotism, humanitarian instincts, and her need to escape conventionality results in conflicting views of both Chinese and English residents.

The layered conflicts in Bird's response to Shanghai are mirrored by the hostility of the Anglo-Chinese toward travelers. It is unclear exactly when Bird's visit to the Chinese city took place, since she notes that she stopped in Shanghai ten times, but one of her last stays was in June and July 1896, shortly before a satiric vignette bearing a resemblance to Bird's account appeared in the Shanghai *Rattle*.[9] A "James Porson, Globetrotter" is guided to the Chinese city by an agent who finds foreign visitors tedious at best. In her book, Bird, four feet eleven inches in height, and portly (Porson = "porcine"?), tells about the difficulty of finding an escort, finally persuading Mr. Fox from the British consular office to act in that capacity. The fictional Porson, who is collecting material for a book, strongly objects to European exploitation of the Chinese, and after his tour pays his ricksha driver ten shillings, while his consular guide pays *his* driver fifty cents. The disparity in payment causes a brawl between the two drivers, and both are arrested. The guide gleefully takes the opportunity to teach Porson a lesson: Don't interfere with "the equilibrium of local conditions."

A chastened-sounding Bird also appears to have learned a lesson. She ends her description of the startling, multifarious visit to Chinese Shanghai with an admission: "I was less surprised than before that so many of its [foreign] residents are unacquainted with the dark, crowded, narrow, foul, and reeking streets of the neighboring city" (YVB 26). Bird's abashment over the gulf between the East and West within this corner of China demonstrates the problem of interfacing practice and criticism, of exteriorizing objection and internalizing acquiescence to imperialist practice. The process of "naturalizing" the Chinese, fitting them into their landscape, presents for Bird the conflict between the idealization of Rousseau and the pessimism of Nietzsche. She would be further aggrieved by this conflict as she traveled west in China and found poignant reminders of it in Ichang, where a cultured Belgian priest, all his sensibilities rebelling against Chinese life, felt anguished by his "failure to love" the people (YVB 97). Bird's confrontations with race as a moral issue diminished the sense of freedom she sought in her travel.

The relationship between gender and power, in contrast, Bird approaches with zest. Her criticism of Shanghai business and social activities falls upon many decades of debate in Britain over the conduct of affairs in China, most notably over the opium trade and missionaries, as mentioned in earlier chapters. Bird participates in this debate not by questioning politics or ethics but efficiency. Her aggressive presentation of the trade topic, like that of Mary Kingsley in her *Travels in West Africa,* exhibits a new tension between gender and patriarchy.[10] These women travelers did collaborate in the ideology of their homeland in relation to trade, but rebellion from conventionality was their inspiration for it.

By commenting on a frankly gendered topic such as trade, Bird distances herself from the more traditional manners-and-customs descriptions of lady travelers. At times she goes so far as to echo the point of view of a grumbling oldtimer, rather like that of Archibald Little, to whom she refers ten times in her book. In deference to his advocacy of modern mining in China, Bird conscientiously notes every coal seam she sees in her travel, once even taking the time to inspect one, while she relegates Alicia Little's more conventionally feminine humanitarian work to a footnote (YVB 237). This is not to say that Bird simply adopts a male point of view. Her attention to the perspective of men in *The Yangtze Valley and Beyond* may be better understood by looking at its ironic consistency with *The Golden Chersonese and the Way Thither,* her account of a five weeks' tour of the Malay states in 1879. In this book, according to Susan Morgan, Bird's "feminine imperial discourse" mirrors the "feminine cast" of the colonial administrator Frank Swettenham, who advocated the "importance of sympathy and gentleness in ruling British Malaya."[11] For Bird, the masculine and feminine intersect in the work of empire.

Bird's remarks on British commercial interests in China associate her with the male world of business and politics. Taking advantage of a mature woman's prerogative—she was sixty-four in 1895—she takes a bold stand by casting aspersions on the young Western clerks in Shanghai: "Of the men I write tremblingly! . . . May it be permitted to a traveller to remark that if men were to give to the learning of Chinese and of Chinese requirements and methods a little of the time which is lavished on sport and other amusements, there might possibly be less occasion for the complaint that large fortunes are no longer to be made in Chinese business" (YVB 20). By framing men's work and business issues as matters of character and morality, Bird adopts a conventional feminine role and demonstrates a blending of masculine and feminine in the work of empire.[12]

Bird performs a similar blending of masculine and feminine by allying trade issues with her own professional interest as a lady traveler and travel writer. She makes trade a dimension of her travel and herself a chamber-of-commerce representative: "My interest in the subject led me to make continual inquiries into the local trade" (YVB 304). She provides lists of items for sale in shops and offers advice on the kind of products, from cloth to canned goods, that British merchants might sell in Chinese villages. Like Lysistrata declaring "War is the business of women," Bird challenges the affiliation of trade solely with the male gender by coupling masculine and feminine in the context of diplomacy and consumerism. The Hangchow hospital, for example, produces "remarkable goodwill toward foreigners." She writes that "it has been remarked by Consuls Carles and Clement Allen in their official reports that missionaries unconsciously help British trade"; articles that the missionaries introduced for their own use "commend themselves to the Chinese"; the hospital drugstore had "created a demand for such British manufactures as condensed milk, meat extracts, rubber tubing, soap, and the like, condensed milk having 'caught on' so firmly that several of the Chinese shops are now keeping it on sale" (YVB 45). By taking aim at two warring factions within the foreign enclaves in China, she links traders, missionaries, and the humanitarian efforts of Western hospitals. In other words, business and humanitarianism, diplomacy and morality, consumerism and religion, masculine and feminine are all intertwined in her account of China.

On 10 January 1896 Bird began her journey to the interior of China, first taking excursions by houseboat to Soochow and Hangchow, then traveling nearly a thousand miles by steamer up the Yangtze River, reaching Ichang. From Ichang she emulated Archibald Little and hired a wupan, a small houseboat, to carry her through the river gorges as far as Wan Hsien. At that point she left the river and traveled three hundred miles over the Chengtu plain to Paoning Fu, then another three hundred miles west to the mountains on the border of Tibet. On her return, she traveled on a Yangtze tributary from Chengtu to Suifu, where she rejoined the Yangtze, sailed to Chungking, finally returning to Shanghai on 27 June 1896. This journey would not be an easy one even today, and at its extremities is to places still difficult to reach. Few Europeans had traveled so far west in China in Bird's time, though two years later the Littles, inspired by her, made a similar journey to the borders of Tibet. Bird and Mrs. Little lay claim to being the first European women to travel to, respectively, Matang and Tachienlu.

The preparation Bird made for her arduous journey almost suggests that she did not expect to return from it: it consisted of divesting herself of most of her luggage, equipping herself with a camp bed and mosquito net, and hiring an interpreter. When her role model for this trek, Capt. Gill, had taken the trail she meant to follow, he had had a large number of tin boxes constructed to hold his considerable gear. He specially notes that each box contained a quantity of English candles (though dripless Chinese candles made of a natural wax were available), curry powder, and dehydrated English vegetables.[13] Bird follows his lead regarding curry powder and adds a luxury of her own to her travel kit: chocolate. Archibald Little, too, mentions "cooking his Cadbury" as an indispensable solace during his Yangtze journey. Bird's minimalist approach to travel in Szechuan does not reflect an attachment to Chinese food and amenities, but rather stoicism. And though there is the seasoned traveler behind her preparations, there is a will in them to leave English life, and perhaps life itself, behind.

Escape from English life does not, however, mean Bird wants to abandon all the forms, as indicated by the importance she attaches to hiring an interpreter. This person was responsible for arranging her travel needs and negotiating with the retinue she would have to hire. He was a buffer between her and the Chinese system, smoothing the cultural differences she needed to hurdle en route. An important criterion when she hires her majordomo, Be-dien, was that he "had not previously served Europeans" (YVB 53). Her reason for this becomes clear in her description of him a few lines down: "He was proud and had a bad temper, but served me faithfully, was never out of hearing *of my whistle* except by permission, . . . and never deserted me in difficulties or even in perils" [emphasis added]. Be-dien is described with the language one might use about a good dog, apparently well-trained by Bird, his first master. The whistle convention, also employed by Lucy Duff-Gordon for her beloved dragoman Oman in Egypt, does nothing to mitigate that image. Bird's requiring a *lack* of experience as a job qualification seems aimed at securing docility and loyalty in her servant; moreover, it obviates having to compete with a previous model of authority. She means to be in charge, though Chinese culture proves a rather solid impediment to that aim.

Gender and patriarchal forms enter her employer-employee relationship despite Bird's attempt to neutralize them by her hiring policy. That she becomes less a leader and more a "barbarian" allowed to give commands is indicated in material very similar to the journal she wrote en route. Be-dien grows less "faithful" and more complex as the journey progresses. During the river journey he is but a phantom presence, but he materializes for balking at accompanying Bird overland. Be-dien, who is from the east coast of China and unfamiliar with rural Szechuan and its language, handsome and "fairly educated," now becomes "helpless, useless, lazy, unwilling, and objectionable all round" (YVB 191). Bird's exasperation indicates a shift in the balance of power, for she must persuade him to continue in her employment —and just how grudgingly soon becomes clear. At the next overnight stop, Be-dien appears to have secured for her the worst inn room in all of China:

> It was long and narrow, and boarded off from others by partitions
> with remarkably open chinks, to which many pairs of sloping eyes were
> diligently applied. . . . The floor was a damp and irregular one of mud,

> partly over a cesspool, and with a strong tendency to puddles. On the other side of the outer boarding was the pig-sty, which was well-occupied, judging from the many voices, bass and treble. . . .
>
> The walls were black and slimy with the dirt and damp of many years; the paper with which the rafters had once been covered was hanging from them in tatters, and when the candle was lit beetles, "slaters," cockroaches, and other abominable things crawled on the walls and dropped from the rafters, one pink, fleshy thing dropping upon, and putting out, the candle! (YVB 201–2)

A grim scene, that, and the complicity of Be-dien in making her suffer it is evident, for instead of helping her set up her camp bed and arrangements to secure herself from vermin, he "left me very much to carry it out myself."

The reason Be-dien asserts himself is more than a fit of pique. The next day, Bird makes passing reference to the departure of a Mr. Thompson who had accompanied her from the China Inland Mission at Wan Hsien. A radical change in Be-dien immediately after this man departs makes it impossible to miss the connection. The European man proved an oppressive presence, a symbol of China's conquerors to whom those such as Be-dien resentfully submitted, a submission ironically indebted to the powerful hierarchical and patriarchal order embedded in Chinese culture. But Thompson represented unwonted patriarchal authority to Bird also. When he leaves, she relaxes and Be-dien takes charge. The chairbearers, who previously made her feel that their labor was a source of "unbearable pain" (YVB 198) now protest when she walks to save them from having to carry her uphill, and "I found my cloak put over my shoulders for me, a wooden stool brought for my feet, sundry little comforts attended to" (YVB 203). Perhaps more meaningful to her, the men point out objects of possible photographic interest. The heretofore faceless laborers are suddenly humanized due to their filial attentions to Bird and an intelligent response to her photography. Bird achieves this respectful relationship with her employees by balancing female subordination with her employer's right to command, a balance achieved less by choice than by the conditions of her travel.

Traveling alone (in the sense of organizing her own travel plans), a woman obviously needed to be able to command the respect of her often numerous entourage of servants (Bird hired 134 men over the course of fifteen months in China).[14] Birkett has discussed strategies based on race and gender that women travelers employed in this effort, including that masculine symbol of authority, carrying a loaded revolver. Real danger compelled Bird to adopt this measure in China, but she never brandished it as May French-Sheldon did in Africa. On one occasion when a mob pursued Bird she planned to shoot for their legs if they broke through the door of her inn room; however, she preferred a more conventional means of securing employee loyalty: she could get bearers to shoulder seventy-pound burdens for thirty miles a day because she paid them well. "I decided . . . to buy my own experience," she announces (YVB 190). On the other hand, it is clear that her chairbearers would not tolerate being infantilized; they choose the pace and schedule for food and rest, placing Bird virtually at their mercy. The forms of Western society she found so stifling and from which she sought escape in travel, the exhilaration of exercising authority, is challenged in Szechuan by those near the bottom of the social scale, laborers of the "coolie" class who will not gladly be governed by a woman.

Despite their conflicting ideas about gender and authority, both Bird and her retinue have moments of high-spirited fun. As Archibald Little observes, the roads in Szechuan were often nothing more than a narrow bank separating irrigation ditches and fields: "Drop the willow-plate" landscape stereotype, Bird advises (YVB 220). On such a path, Bird meets a corpulent mandarin in an ornate sedan chair that her chairmen manage to tip into a ditch, then speed off in great mirth, much to the approval of Bird herself. The spirit and self-image of these chairbearers is more tellingly revealed when steep mountain trails make chair travel too perilous. Bird walks, and her bearers then hire servants of their own to carry the empty chair so they can enjoy the adventurous trek into the unknown with their arms swinging freely.

If Bird's chairbearers enforce a gendered rule over her, it is nothing compared with the way strangers "occidentalize" her. I use "occidentalism" as a companion term to "orientalism" in the sense Said uses it, as a method for the West to define and express authority over the Orient. Occidentalism, then, means the methods the Chinese use to define and express authority over Westerners, for racism and ethnocentrism are not limited to Westerners. Fear and wariness of strangers, of those outside the neighborhood, or of those who look and dress differently than the "insiders" is a common phenomenon that has onerous possibilities when power is involved. Power gives this fear grave consequences. Like the power of numbers and of guns and might, the power to ostracize and show hostility turns fear into a method to hurt the stranger. East and West are both perpetrators and recipients of this method, though travelers do not usually think of themselves in these terms. Bird does not, and is taken by surprise at expressions of "occidentalism" numerous times.

Early in her account, Bird encounters a fairly benign example of this phenomenon in the "overweening self-conceit" of the Chinese. Victorian travelers were stunned by what they viewed as an unwarranted feeling of superiority the Chinese held toward them. Bird is particularly inflamed at expressions of ignorance on which this claim is based. These include beliefs that "the Queen of England is tributary to China," that outside of China there are five kingdoms, one inhabited by dog-faced people, and that "the missionaries come and live in distant places like Wan and Paoning in order to find out the secret of China's greatness" (YVB 173–74). Western might, technology, learning, religion, and culture could not quench Chinese disdain for foreigners. The division of the world into "Chinese" and "barbarians" had the power of a genetic trait in Chinese thinking. As the wisdom of Lao-Tzu puts it: "What is firmly rooted cannot be pulled out" (*Tao-te Ching* LIV). According to the reasonable explanation of the missionary Arthur Smith, foreigners' ignorance of the Chinese language, customs, and culture makes "many Chinese unconsciously adopt towards foreigners an air of amused interest, combined with depreciation."[15] Used to overcoming all manner of daunting obstacles in her travels, Bird was unprepared for the racial pride of the Chinese or their more serious challenges to her sense of superiority to them.

The forms of occidentalism Bird encounters are many: Be-dien and the chairbearers presented a challenge based primarily on gender; the mandarins based their views on race. The crew and sixteen trackers she hires to man her wupan, her small houseboat, may be said to add social class to that list. At the outset, Bird says these men "looked too low to be human" (YVB 131). They sense her contempt and repay it with a chilly gesture. In windy weather, with the temperature at thirty-eight degrees Fahrenheit,

Bird's Trackers at Rest on Her Wupan. Photo by Isabella Bird, *Yangtze Valley and Beyond.*

they refuse to put out a plank to ease disembarking and she falls into the river. After sitting on shore in wet clothes for many hours, she changes her view of these men and on occasion apologizes for her failure to observe Chinese etiquette regarding entering and leaving boats and sedan chairs. The "low" laborers keep her on the defensive with her firsthand experience of "democratic China," that nineteenth-century term reflecting Westerners' observation of China's mingling of the classes. It takes some effort for her to admit that the men eventually win her sympathy and "in some sort my admiration" for their "honest work, pluck, endurance, hardihood, sobriety, and good nature" (YVB 155). That approval is weighed against the constant resistance to her authority shown by the trackers and the *lao-pan,* the "captain" of the wupan.

The Sino-patriarchal system represented by Bird's bearers and trackers is so entrenched that Western patriarchy seems pliable in contrast. For all the constraints of home society, Bird and many other Victorian women managed their own affairs and traveled freely whereas in China women were virtually unseen and literally hobbled by footbinding. From another point of view, Victorian society protected women and offered them status as "the angel in the house," as Patmore's famous poem puts it. In China, Bird discovers that neither the unconventional New Woman nor the traditional keeper of hearth and home was an image from which she could derive any sustenance. The evidence of this comes to her as a violation she experiences in yet another form of occidentalism when she becomes the object of surveillance and trespass. At nearly every inn in which Bird stays, other guests, usually male, peer at her through chinks in the walls, sometimes deliberately drilled for the purpose. Robert Fortune could resign himself to being an object of touristic interest, but Bird is unnerved by it. She makes lame jokes about being watched writing, but the intrusion deprives her of the psychological freedom she sought in travel.

The uninhibited expression of curiosity extended to Bird is so irritating to her that she forfeits an unparalleled opportunity to view Chinese home life. The owner of an exquisite country mansion sees her photographing his home and is so pleased that he invites her to stay for a few days so she can photograph his family.[16] Echoing Cumming's fear of contamination by entering a Chinese home, Bird refuses this offer because of both her "grave doubts" about the reception she would get in the women's quarters and the "stifling curiosity" of the women on intimate details of her life and appearance (YVB 227).[17] Once again, Bird's claim of privilege as a tourist, her desire to observe freely, is fettered by a reciprocal Chinese desire to observe her. In a more general way, she recognizes that the act of observation or sightseeing is reconnaissance, an expression of power evidenced more particularly in her writing. She might not have initially intended to write a book on China, but her copious journal-letters were meant for wide circulation. Observation means taking something away—revealing, exposing through verbal or pictorial images (she also took hundreds of photos). Claiming this right for herself, she resents it when others make her the object of a similar claim.

The reciprocity of the "gaze" has still more ominous implications for Bird. In the Cultural Revolution phase of China's history, Chairman Mao forbad his countrymen to allow themselves to be photographed by foreigners. In addition to the various political motivations for this stricture, it contains the essential fact of the exploitative gaze. While Bird never equates her own sightseeing trek with Chinese curiosity about her as a mutual form of objectification, the Chinese instinctively react to her gaze as a form of power.

Bird does what she can to minimize the power of the gaze by keeping as much as possible to less-traveled routes and inns in hamlets where "at very small expense" she can become friendly with the village headman and a few other people by sharing tea and tobacco and showing some of her photographs (YVB 258).[18] On such occasions, she gathered some insights into contemporary Chinese life, local views on taxes, prices, and so on, but her interest is not particularly piqued by local issues. Cumming, for example, would have included every detail of such conversations. For Bird, the conversations are mainly a means of easing her passage to more distant parts.

In order to gain a peaceful evening, though, Bird first had to reach a safe haven. The day's journey often entailed physical threat. Bird is several times verbally assaulted, pushed, and pelted with mud. Her travel in Szechuan during a period when strong antiforeign feeling was building toward an eruption contributes to the level of violence hurled at her. These attacks provoke perhaps the only instances in her travel books in which she appeals to conventional feminine forms to reprove native culture. She complains that the Chinese insult her feminine modesty, and that if she had a European man with her, she would not be subject to mistreatment.

Ironically for her, her clothes are partly to blame for provoking these mob attacks. Years earlier, she was outraged when readers described her Hawaiian riding costume—a wide skirt over trousers—as masculine.[19] For Bird, the issue was not what represents a more female or male form of attire but that the riding costume demonstrated common sense. Apparently still smarting from the description of her "masculine" attire, she says she could never be "reconciled" to the trousers Chinese women wear (YVB 238). Instead, she dons an eclectic combination of Chinese gown, Japanese sun hat, and English shoes and gloves that she deems sensible, and the Chinese think "a confession of foreign inferiority" (YVB 206). Bird's readers, from Queen Victoria on down, might admire her individualism, but the Szechuanese did not.[20] To the tradition-minded Chinese, Bird was one more instance of foreign trampling on custom.

The costume could have cost her her life at Lo-kia-chan, a small town she visited on a sightseeing expedition. There her dress seemed bizarre, while her "open chair" (a simple bamboo armchair attached to carrying poles) was thought masculine. A mob of two thousand men, gathered for a theatrical performance, set upon her and a missionary's wife, Mrs. Horsburgh, with both epithets and stones. Bird was knocked unconscious by a rock hitting her behind the ear, a blow she says it took a year from which to recover. If we are to believe Bird about the composition of this and other mobs she encountered, both as to size and gender, it is hard to see whether it was her infraction of custom or because she represented the hated foreigner that was more to blame for arousing the violence. For her part, Bird echoes the language of the social explorers at home in summoning images of the demonic to describe her encounters with these angry crowds: "No one who has heard the howling of a Chinese mob can forget it—it seems to come up direct from the bottomless pit!" (YVB 342)

But to the Chinese, she, too, symbolizes the demonic Other. In calling Westerners "foreign devil" and "child-eater," they joined their well-documented distrust of foreigners to folkloristic explanations of diabolical behavior they attributed to the "barbarians." As Bird notes: "Slanders against the missionaries were circulated and believed, and the special one that they stole and ate infants, or used their eyes and hearts for medicines, was disagreeably current in Kuan Hsien" (YVB 341). Levi-Strauss argues that superstitions denote "a kind of wisdom" that it is madness on the part of the modern world to reject since it enables the believers to achieve a certain cosmic harmony.[21] Seen in this light, the extravagant accusations the Chinese made against foreigners may be read as tropes; infants are "stolen" by being Westernized. Bird recognizes this, too. Despite the fact that she thinks Chinese culture ought to be anglicized, she sympathizes with those who fear that missionaries aim "to subvert Chinese nationality, to wreck the venerated social order" (YVB 254). Western imperialism in China, whether represented by soldiers, merchants, missionaries, or travelers, was intent on a combination of displacing, preserving, and reconstructing Chinese society.

"Beating the Foreigners and Burning Their Books." Cartoon in *Illus. London News,* 24 Aug. 1895: 246.

Bird titles her book after a significant geographical feature of China, but the "valley" may also be seen as a metaphor describing the central part of her story. Her sojourn on the great river and into Szechuan, though off-set with satisfying experiences and claims for personal heroism, is marked by images of danger, affliction, and pain. She has a few serene moments developing photos, using night as her darkroom and the river as her wash, but there are miserable, cold days in wet clothes and even more miserable nights in inns shared by hogs and coffins, physical threat, and duty-visits to missions. The "valley" is inhabited by a Scylla and Charybdis of rioting Chinese and benighted missionaries, neither of whom is depicted as an en-tirely worthy candidate for redemption.

Acting on her late husband's belief in medical missions, Bird offered financial support to these institutions and established a hospital in her sister's name in Paoning, as she had earlier done in Mukden.[22] Victorian human-

"The Conversion of Chou Han." Cartoon in *The Rattle,* May 1896: 9.

itarianism found ample opportunities in medical missions, all the more because of the low opinion the West held of traditional Chinese medicine throughout the nineteenth century.[23] Bird views the Hangchow hospital, for example, as a "good investment" because its exhibition of Western methods of healing will counter superstition in Chinese medical practices and belief in demonism (YVB 42). Such formal claims for the benefits of medical missions, however, must be seen in the light of the penitential nature of Bird's tour. Grief and guilt over the death of her sister and husband had earlier led her to take a nursing course, and later to get rebaptized in preparation for missionary work, both fields for which she found herself unsuited and quickly abandoned.[24] Now she was endowing infirmaries and visiting lonely, threatened missionaries to buy solace.

The antiforeign, fiercely antimissionary sentiment in Chinese society in the 1890s would reach full boil in the Boxer Rebellion.[25] Knollys had acknowledged the sentiment by passing along a joke: When asked about possible danger from rioting Chinese, the boat captain shrugged, saying "'there is nothing to fear from outrage. There is not a Christian within 100 miles of us'" (ELC 118). The demonization of missionaries as child killers and practitioners of various sordid behaviors was fueled by pamphlets traced to a bookstore owner by the name of Chou Han in Hunan. A cartoon in the *Rattle,* the humor magazine, in 1896, shows Chou drafting "sermons" on the "FOREIGN DEVILS." Such cartoons and propaganda, discussed more fully in Cohen's *China and Christianity,* depict physical attack of Christians and a vicious version of their doctrines. But in addition to the animosity incited by the pamphleteer, there was a more general hostility to foreigners, from the court under the empress dowager to scholars, officials, and the people at large. Missionaries were a direct challenge to traditional religion and ethics, and the aggressive and arrogant foreign traders and diplomats, with the economic hardships and political humiliation they represented, threatened the very fiber of Chinese national life. Added to these problems brought by outsiders were those caused by internal change, such as the development of a north-south railway and changes in the taxation system that rendered the Grand Canal, and a wide range of services and occupations dependent on it, obsolete.[26] Missionaries were accessible targets for expression of these hostilities and resentments.

Despite her formal support for missions, Bird was unenthusiastic about them. In travel, she sought freedom from form; missionaries represented the hard hand of convention denying that freedom.[27] In her early travels, she boasted of giving missions a wide berth, though at home she was conventional enough in her religious practice. After her tour of China, her lectures about the missions always insisted on two points: their need of reform and their value as a means of bringing Western civilization to the

Chinese: "Christianity does produce an external refinement among those who receive it" (YVB 246; cf. 325). This point of view echoes the *London Times* series of articles in 1863 arguing that missionary work should consist, first, in introducing Western civilization, and religion only secondarily. At the end of *Yangtze Valley and Beyond,* Bird extends her argument by describing missionaries as agents "in the awakening of empire" (YVB 513). Bird was one who believed missionaries could and should effect cultural hegemony over China, rather than solely press Christianity on it.

Years earlier, Cumming offered a saccharine discourse that sharply contrasts with Bird's censure. To Cumming, "all the regiments of the Grand Army . . . one and all are surely undermining the old idolatries" (WiC 151). In contrast, Bird offers pitiless images of misplaced religious idealism among missionaries; for example, the women missionaries in Mien-chow who labor for two years while living in a mud-floored house without privacy: "Under these circumstances their love and patience had won twelve women to be Christians" (YVB 319). Bird makes these missionaries seem merely pathetic, but her description of the Rev. Horsburgh preaching is scathing in its indictment of his ineffectiveness, as indicated by the manner with which it is received: "A distracting babel—men playing cards outside among the throng, men and women sitting for a few minutes, some laughing scornfully, others talking in loud tones, some lighting their pipes, and a very few really interested" (YVB 319). This is not a passage likely to inspire much openhandedness among mission supporters at home, nor does it sympathize with the Chinese. Rather, it conveys the sense of Western obtuseness and Chinese obstructionism, both of which irritated Bird.

She remains respectful but noncommittal toward Bishop Cassels, one of the Cambridge Seven, a group endowed with money, social standing, and athletic prowess that had been recruited by Hudson Taylor for the China Inland Mission, and whose zeal had popularized missionary work. Unlike the Rev. Horsburgh, Cassels maintains order during his service, but Bird suggests the fruitlessness of the effort by maintaining that the English *Book of Common Prayer* is unintelligible and untranslatable to a Chinese context. As if validating Bird's misgivings about Cassels's work, in the Boxer era his little cathedral was destroyed and his congregation dispersed.

Despite her tepid enthusiasm for missionary work, Bird does not hesitate to weigh in with suggestions for improving it.[28] She is well aware of the result of nearly sixty years of missionary work in China, which according to missionary Arthur Moule's accounting in 1891 constituted forty thousand Chinese Christians in a population of four hundred million.[29] Looking for a scapegoat whom no one else has mentioned, she surprisingly finds one in women—or mothers, to be more precise. Although she praises women's work in China, she questions the usefulness of married women with "the inevitable baby" (YVB 79). Privately, she reveals a prudish embarrassment over the connection between sexuality and motherhood that she imagines is shared by the Chinese. She faulted married women for being a source of "scandal among natives caused by the ceaseless . . . maternities." These, she says, created "a waste of working power" as mothers devoted themselves to their children and husbands, and other women missionaries often had to help nurse the mothers and children.[30] The idea that motherhood was somehow culpable for the singular lack of success in converting the Chinese to Christianity reveals Bird's own emotional makeup, "absolutely no maternal instinct whatsoever," according to Barr.[31] This daughter of an Anglican clergyman also thought that the Chinese "appreciate the celibacy, poverty, and asceticism of the Roman clergy" (YVB 98), values that did not exactly match the Chinese perception of the Catholic clergy nor their own culture (Bird seems unaware of the contemporary Chinese hostility to Catholics due to their excessive demands for restitution after the destruction of their missions in riots and the demand that Catholic bishops be given the civil rank of mandarins). In projecting her personal views on both missionaries and the Chinese, Bird shows a shortage of empathy for both.

It should be added that Bird's attitude was not shared by other childless travelers. Cumming, for example, takes a special interest in the plight of orphans, and she praises the compassionate maternalism of missionaries operating orphanages. In her critique of women missionaries Bird may have seen her own unencumbered state as a model for women's professionalism, just as Knollys had seen his gentility as a model for male missionaries. Bird's contribution to the contemporary debate on missionary work draws attention to her own tenuous connection to women's participation in the work of empire. Priding herself on her independence, intellectual capacity, and daring; identifying with the "male" field of exploration; rejecting stereotypical female work and roles—she plots a course for herself that alienates her from society both at home and abroad. As with other women who achieve success in male-dominated fields, from George Eliot to Margaret Thatcher, Bird felt it politic to dissociate herself from feminism and sisterhood.

Although Bird has a good deal to say about missionaries individually and in general, she temporizes on that cause célèbre of Victorian travelers in China, opium. Her presentation of "The Opium Poppy and Its Uses" reflects a sense of duty to comprehensiveness, rather than moral indignation. She slips criticism of opium into a subordinate clause to imply that it may not really be so bad: "If one could disabuse oneself of the belief that opium is the curse of China . . . "; then she adds a long passage painting a vibrant picture of "these millions of corollas, in all the glory of their brief and passionate existence" (YVB 342). Her being in the midst of a field of poppies in deepest Szechuan naturalizes the opium; exoticism gives way to normalcy. As proof, opium prompts a rare willingness on Bird's part to try Chinese food: she ate a dish made from the lower leaves of the opium plant. She says it tasted like spinach (YVB 232). All sides of the opium issue had been debated repeatedly by the time Bird saw fields of poppies in Szechuan. Instead of arguments, she presents anecdotes.

The central part of Bird's story, the journey on the river and visiting missions, portrays a very divided view of China. There are fine, romantic sights such as the forested "Chinese Switzerland" (YVB 109) and the "Chinese Chatsworth" (YVB 221), and village houses with their upturned roofs give China a photogenic quality. Junks being warped through a Yangtze gorge are an example of the sublime: "A glorious sight the Hsin-tan is as seen from our point of vantage, half-way up the last cataract, a hill of raging water with a white waterfall at the top, sharp, black rocks pushing their vicious heads through the foam, and above, absolute calm. I never saw such exciting water scenes—the wild rush of the cataract; the great junks hauled up the channel on the north side by 400 men each, hanging trembling in the surges" (YVB 119). Bird's description of the river gorges bears some similarity to the language used in arrival scenes.[32] However, the effect in this case is not conquest but threat of annihilation: "The tremendous crash and roar of the cataract, above which the yells and shouts of hundreds of straining trackers are heard, mingled with the ceaseless beating of drums and gongs" create "a pandemonium which can never be forgotten" (YVB 123). For Bird, the beauties of China are inextricable from its dangers.

At other times, the danger is evoked by visible signs of decay. Using imagery reminiscent of Knollys, Bird describes towns as "an inconceivable beastliness of dirt" (YVB 246) and food that requires "very-old fashioned Anglo-Saxon words" (she does not list them) to do it justice (YVB 152). Waiting three days for her boat, which is twenty-fifth in line, to take its turn to traverse the rapids, she is so terrorized by a crowd of men and boys that she questions their humanity. Later, in the face of threatening mobs she stoically tries to sit up straight in her chair rather than "appear hurt, frightened, or annoyed" (YVB 216). The dangers of the river journey, the threatening mobs met on the overland journey, the fruitless labor of the missionaries—all these cloud her journey through Szechuan. It is not only "foreign settlements" that prompt Bird to escape as soon as possible, but any well-traveled route in populous places. It is the "beyond," the unknown, that draws her.

At the last mission station, after being knocked cold by a rock, Bird surveys the scene with a mystic sensibility: "Perfect quiet" prevails in a crowded street; snowy peaks beckon from across the Chengtu plain; and "everywhere living waters in their musical rush echoed the name of the great man [Li Ping, engineer of the ancient irrigation works in the Chengtu plain] who before the Christian era turned the vast plain into a paradise" (YVB 328). This illumination has a surprising result: "Why should I not go on, I asked myself, and see Tibetans, yaks, aboriginal tribes, rope bridges, and colossal mountains, and break away from the narrow highways and the crowds, and curiosity . . . of China proper?" (YVB 331). All the informative material poured into her book—the detailed examination of Chinese customs, the dutiful inspection tour of missions—are for Bird a form of *pao,* the Chinese system of anticipatory payment for a favor to be asked. Having paid in advance for the chance to experience the "beyond," she demands escape from the beaten paths of China proper.

The tone of *The Yangtze Valley and Beyond* changes dramatically after

Man-tze Village. Photo by Isabella Bird, *Yangtze Valley and Beyond.*

that. In ordering gear and hiring bearers Bird assumes a sense of command that had recently been relinquished to Be-dien and others. Now she compares herself to General "Chinese" Gordon, the British commander of the Ever Victorious Army: "'I am my own best servant'" (YVB 355). The steamy heat of the Chengtu plain gives way to an "invigorating and delicious" forty degrees in the mountains (YVB 365). Page after page of euphoric, superlative-laden images of forests, icy rivers, and snow-capped mountains contrast to the morose march across the plain. Now nine-thousand-foot mountains—"broken up by stupendous chasms and precipices . . . the higher like needles, the lower crested by villages, to all appearances inaccessible"—invite her to "penetrate" them (YVB 372). She finds the explorer's thrill of discovery and conquest once she crosses the Chinese border.

What these glorious scenes represent for Bird is freedom, but, like the heart-stopping rope bridge, not unlike a bungee jump, that she admires but will not use, it is not within her grasp. This sense of the unattainable—

of something lost before even gained—is strangely presaged by a group of Tibetans going down the mountains while Bird is on her way up: "I envied them the altitude and freedom to which they would return from the cramping grooviness [conformism] of China" (YVB 361). Altitude, mountains, freedom, solitude are the stars in her geographical/metaphysical pantheon, and she will take almost any risk to experience them, be it riding to the edge of an erupting volcano in Hawaii, defying ice and snow in the Rocky Mountains and Kurdistan, or now, faltering through an April blizzard in the dark with her bearers near collapse from altitude sickness.

Bird has nothing but praise for the Man-tze, to her all jovial, agreeable-looking, and colorful in red woolen clothes and unusual headgear. In contrast to the rowdy mobs she encountered earlier in her journey, she finds the curiosity of the Man-tze "tempered by politeness" (YVB 394). The item most frequently mentioned in her account of the Man-tze is the beauty, "even in middle life," of the women who are "loaded with silver and coral ornaments, plied the distaff as they joked, and were free, not to say bold, in their manners" (YVB 410–11). So unlike the hobbled Chinese women, the freedom of the Man-tze girls is symbolized by their unbound feet, and when Bird needs an escort to the next village, a pair of "handsome laughing girls" provides it (YVB 409). She compares the tiered, flat-roofed, nearly windowless Tibetan-style houses to those of the Ainu in Japan. In a short chapter, she summarizes information she was able to glean about Man-tze marriage and the position of women, religion, burial customs, health, and agriculture. In view of her complaints about dirt in China, it is an indication of her idealization of the Man-tze and their scenic, mountainous country that she notes without comment the Man-tze "have no soap, and never wash" (YVB 446). The thundering rivers, the whir of perpetually moving prayer wheels, even the bear-like Tibetan dogs seem tokens of freshness and freedom to Bird. Ultimately, the mountains of western Szechuan represent for her the possibility of otherworldly ecstasy and untrammeled freedom, so difficult to find in life's earthly journey as represented by China proper.

The inns in which Bird stayed in Szechuan were a particular misery, but among the Man-tze, where food is scarce and inn rooms are roofless, her description becomes romantic. The language of scientific exploration and ethnography are replaced by the imagery of Coleridge's "Kubla Khan." She "crossed the bridge and shortly entered paradise," an incongruous mix of aromatic plants, lamaseries, and "peaks of unsullied snow" (YVB 402–3). Eating by the light of a full moon in the chill, rarefied air at eight thousand feet, "away from crowds, rowdyism, unmannerly curiosity . . . and from many a hateful thing," even her rheumatism disappears: "Anything might happen afterwards, but for that one day I had breathed the air of freedom, and had obtained memories of beauty such as would be a lifelong possession" (YVB 408). The experience is akin to the shriving of a religious pilgrimage, the restoration of grace to sustain the pilgrim through the perils of life.

Bird internalizes the Victorian view of China as a static, changeless place so that her encounters with an ingrained cultural system present unbreachable barriers to understanding. At the last government outpost, Chinese officials try to prevent Bird from venturing further west. They make trouble over her passport and warn her of warring barbarians beyond the border. She insists they were "quite quenched" with her arguments (YVB 393), and she marches out the gates and improbably baffles an equestrian guard sent to obstruct her passage. Bird sees the Chinese as obstinate recalcitrants, though they no doubt felt both protective of her and self-conscious about the perilous paths, uncertain weather, scarce food, and poor lodging in the region. For Bird, English superiority suddenly supersedes all other concerns. She never questions her right to travel or to extend her gaze in sovereign territory. When the Chinese official arrives in a Man-tze village soon after her, "the delicious sense of freedom in which I had been reveling vanished" (YVB 417). The personal freedom, from claims of form, gender, and patriarchy that "China proper" denied her leave her feeling she has a score to settle.

part three

Women of Empire

Family of Literati Active in the Anti-footbinding Movement in Western
China. Photo by Alicia Little, *Intimate China*.

six

Orientalizing Feminism

Mrs. Archibald Little (A. E. N. Bewicke)

"IT'S A WELL-KNOWN SAYING that the women lost us the Empire." Helen
Callaway quotes this trenchancy of Sir David Lean in her *Gender, Culture
and Empire* to introduce her argument that women are either ignored or
represented negatively in reconstructions of the colonial record.[1] Women
of the Empire were accused of "refusing to adapt" and drawing men away
from their work.[2] They are often represented in men's memoirs and novels, Callaway adds, as racist, self-centered, and with a snobbish attachment
to social distinction, though individually and as a group their response to
colonial life and the native population was far more complex. Mrs. Little
exemplifies such complexity. Being both the wife of a merchant and a

writer, she plays a dual role in the story of Victorians in China. In her personal life and in her books, she depicts Women of the Empire as a diverse group whose allegiance to English life and interactions with local culture cover a broad range of possibilities.

Before Mrs. Little married, she had published at least nine romances under her maiden name, A. E. N. Bewicke.[3] She was also a feminist who put her writing skills to work in *Mother Darling* (1885), a novel advocating the reform of laws "'to establish the rights of mothers to their own children.'"[4] The novel had a considerable impact on this cause. When the author married in 1886 and went out to China with her husband, she changed her identity and immersed herself in her new life in Shanghai, Hankow, Peking, and western Szechuan. After she resurfaced as Mrs. Archibald Little in 1896, she published a dozen books with China as text and setting.[5] This prolific output demonstrates the author's investment in China, not only as a writer but as part of the British establishment there. She found in China and the colonial experience new subjects for the social activism that she had expressed in her earlier work in England.

Little's voice adds considerably to that of the other travelers discussed in this book, in both subject matter and tone. Her novels set in China focus on British life there. *A Marriage in China,* her first and boldest China book (finished in 1893, it did not appear in England until 1896), examines the effect of colonial administration policies on people. Little's nonfiction shifts attention to herself and life in China. *My Diary in a Chinese Farm* is a highly personal record of events in the summer and autumn of 1893, when the Littles fled steamy Chungking for a rural cottage.[6] In *Intimate China* (1899), the author compiles manners-and-customs descriptions collected over an eleven-year period. These texts in different genre provide a comprehensive picture of Little's involvement in China that culminates in her humanitarian work against footbinding, starting in 1895 and described in *Intimate China* and *In the Land of the Blue Gown*.[7] Little's writing and humanitarian work have overlapping discourses on colonial life and the Chinese that feminize orientalism.

By "feminizing orientalism" I mean that Little uses gendered strategies in representing China that are both feminine and feminist. The effect of these strategies is the creation of an orientalism that differs from the meaning made current by Said. In Said's interpretation, orientalism is a masculinist method based on the imaginative expressions and political structures developed by men to exert power and authority over the Orient. Following this argument, oriental women exist solely as sensual objects, while Western women are extraneous to the production of orientalism. Obviously, Western women's orientalisms do not neatly fit Said's ideological framework. Deprived of the historical agency that European men possessed, European women developed an orientalist point of view from a position of inferiority within the ruling hierarchy. They may, in some respects, reflect the ideological bent of their era, but others who like Little question Western male superiority, also subvert it. In the account of her own life and travel in China and in the fictional characters she creates, male orientalism is often as flawed and tyrannical as the infamous Shanghai garden that Chinese were prohibited from entering. Her statement about this prohibition—"This never can seem quite right"—is an indication of her willingness to speak out against injustices (IC 21).[8] As a result, her writings both criticize Western male orientalism and offer a female alternative to it.

In *A Marriage in China,* Little plunges into the emotional vortex of colonial life, dealing candidly with issues of morality, gender, and race. The protagonist, Claude Fortescue, is a consul posted to Chungking, where he and a few missionaries are the only foreigners. He becomes a sinologue, deeply attracted to Taoist philosophy, and a fluent linguist who waxes "enthusiastic over everything Chinese" (MiC 101). Thus seduced by China, in his loneliness he is also attracted to a kittenish slave girl (never named in the novel). He buys her freedom and they soon have a son, and later a blue-eyed daughter.[9] While on home leave, Claude falls in love with Lilian Grey, a youthful, idealistic heiress, then mysteriously decamps. The larger story of the involvement of these characters is played out in China, where, the novel implies, the complications in Claude's life are essentially scripted by colonial administration: *A Marriage in China* is premised on administrative policies that discouraged marriage and encouraged concubinage among junior officers. The authenticity of Little's tale may be inferred from the uproar it caused among the Western establishment in China at the time of publication; despite Little's protestations, readers identified the original of several of her characters.[10]

It is important to understand the historical background Little draws on to appreciate how central it is to her novel. Junior officers were not allowed to marry in the first five years of colonial service.[11] A lewd cartoon in the *China Punch* of a soldier, with its caption "'On Horror's Head Horrors Accumulate,'" alludes to the preoccupations these regulations promoted.[12] As late as 1929, employees in the colonial service in India were recruited at age twenty-six and forbidden marriage for three years.[13] Little's novel draws attention to the toll such regulations take on consuls, the representatives of the British government in each city opened to foreign residence by treaty, who spent six years in their outposts before getting a home leave. Several of these characters break down from either physical or mental illness.

The reasons for prohibiting junior officers in the colonial service from marrying were first of all economic. Transportation costs for wives and children and higher salaries and living expenses for family men were avoided by the marriage restrictions. Secondly, single men could be posted to areas deemed unsuitable for European women and children. Little's novel openly criticizes these policies and their rationale in a number of ways. For example, missionary families with young children thrive in the very place supposedly too inhospitable for a consul's wife. The novel also includes discussions among the characters in which they criticize the policies that give rise to Claude's union with the Chinese girl. An outspoken missionary, Mrs. Betterton, disputes the idea that unmarried officers lowered the attrition rate caused by family pressures to return home: "'I have no patience with that idea, that wives are a sort of lap dogs . . . if a wife would find it dull with her husband beside her, what must a man find it all by himself'" (MiC 26–27).[14] *A Marriage in China* thus proposes that the hearth-and-home values idealized in Victorian life are deliberately sabotaged by colonial policy that forbids junior officers to marry.

Perhaps the greatest irony of the policy is that it in effect institutionalized concubinage as an agency of colonial administration. Concubinage was deemed useful to insure virility, and according to Stoler "in Asia and Africa, corporate and government decision-makers invoked the social services that local women supplied as 'useful guides to the language and other mysteries of the local societies.'"[15] *A Marriage in China* expressly notes this when Claude defends his relationship with his Chinese mistress by saying he is presently studying the works of Confucius and finds the Chinese girl "of inestimable service" in this task (MiC 50). However economically and politically beneficial were the policies that accommodated concubinage, in the novel they lead to the main conflict for the protagonist. Claude is so tormented by the tension between his emotional needs and the pressure of conventional morality that he suffers a mental breakdown. To complete the picture of institutional sources of private woes, the novel adds the detail that, in the name of righteousness, Claude is ostracized by the several missionaries at his outpost.

It should be noted that as the number of European women in a colony increased, concubinage was discouraged, as early as the 1860s in India.[16] Little's novel on the evils of concubinage in the 1890s points to a somewhat later but parallel development in China. The British empire officially banned concubinage in 1910, though the ban had little effect. In Africa, the directive was mocked for its "impracticality."[17] Ironically, the French were encouraging concubinage at the same time the British banned it.

The focus of Little's novel on the English rather than the Chinese characters results in a feminine orientalism that foregrounds the effect of colonial policy on Englishwomen. In Lilian Grey, the Women of the Empire are represented by an icon of purity—a model wife and benefactor of the unfortunate. Her role is played out through the somewhat exotic circumstances in which this etherealized lily meets Claude, then goes to China, chaperoned as it were, by a group of missionaries, and accidentally bumps into him, now mad and broken, while waiting for her junk to negotiate the Yangtze River gorges. She is shown interacting with the Chinese only once. She briefly becomes a governess to a missionary's children and an assistant to a medical missionary in Chungking. Were it not for the vivid local color Little provides, Lilian could be in her home at Northampton. Nor is she contaminated by colonial life; it is left to the minor characters to relieve their boredom with marital infidelities and various self-indulgences. In her first China novel, Little's heroine does not stray from the role of domestic angel.

Marriage, however, turns Lilian into a martyr to her husband's impurity, a martyrdom heightened by many plot devices that seem deliberately the reverse of those found in *Jane Eyre*. Unlike Bertha Mason hidden in the attic, Claude's concubine and children are a secret to no one but the bride. No one stands in the church door to claim an impediment to the marriage of Claude and Lilian; instead, Mortimer, Claude's friend, flees Shanghai when he hears of the wedding plans rather than forestall it. No mad Bertha rends the bride's wedding veil; instead, the Chinese girl sends Lilian a beautiful piece of embroidery as a wedding gift. Finally, no deus ex machina resolves the marital dilemma. Instead, secrecy and guilt wear Claude down, and discovery causes Lilian to suffer a miscarriage. In *Jane Eyre,* the plot devices are part of a feminist theme to reduce inequalities between Jane and Rochester and promote conventional morality by averting a bigamous union. In *A Marriage in China,* they subvert conventional morality and turn the independent heiress into a victim.[18] The conspiracy of silence that gives tacit approval to Claude's double life also criticizes a policy that undermines the values of home society and leads to deception and betrayal.

While Lilian serves as a symbol of ideal womanhood, the Chinese girl's representation is more complex and inconsistent in that it layers the discourses of feminism, conventional morality, and racism. The Chinese girl first of all documents the historical consequences of colonialism, as indicated in the discussion above. Sexually exploited, she then becomes symbolic of the Englishman's moral failure: "What need to describe the various stages—various gradations of feeling by which men brought up with Christian principles, amongst beautiful, high-minded English girls, at last sink to allying themselves with a Chinese girl of unknown parentage, too well-known character! So many of his set have done it before him! So many of his set will continue to do it" (MiC 101). The narrator connects moral failure and racism, the girl corespondent of the Englishman's "sinking" into an irregular union.

The comment on the frequency of situations like Claude's notwithstanding, Little takes care not to charge her character with irresponsibility, perhaps out of a sense of national pride. Injustice to the girl is rationalized by crediting Claude's interest in her with saving her from early death. He treats the girl considerately and always makes arrangements for her and the children, even when he casts them aside.[19] The story line reflects Little's attention to authentic detail in that the economic advantage of concubinage, so far as colonial administration was concerned, was that any expenses it incurred were borne by the individual. But Little frames this cold reality in moral terms that emphasize the human dimension that colonial policy ignores. A Shanghai clergyman reminds Claude, "a deed once done always remains" (MiC 181). This insistence on the Englishman's moral and economic responsibility for the concubine and her children shows a progressiveness in the fictional world that did not necessarily match contemporary reality.

While the male protagonist of Little's novel incorporates orientalist attitudes, the narrator often takes an opposing view, for example in crediting the Chinese girl with conventional (English) feminine virtues. She may be nameless, but she is nonetheless accorded engaging wifeliness and maternal feelings. She surprises Claude with his favorite Chinese dishes, learns "to read his moods, forestall his wishes," and yet makes no demands on him (MiC 105). She keeps the children "clean and comfortable and apparently loved" (MiC 179). And Little cannot help but connect her with the issue she championed in England but that remained unreformed in the East—a mother's rights. When Claude marries Lilian, he thinks of taking the children from their mother and placing then in a school for Eurasian children, but "he wondered what right he himself had to do this. What gave him the authority to dispose any further their lives, or hers? He believed not even law" (MiC 180). By suggesting that even a "soulless" mother had a right to care for her own children, *A Marriage in China* breaks away from male orientalism and affirms support for Chinese women.

The children, Eurasian children, serve further purposes in this novel— one as realistic social cause, the other as trope. In tackling the subject of Eurasian children, Little combines feminine discourse and social activism. Schools for Eurasian children were a cause célèbre for missionaries and European women, as Little mirrors in her novel when Lilian, who wants to be useful, thinks of teaching at the Eurasian school that her missionary cousin supports. Evidence of public concern for the care of Eurasian children in China appeared as early as 1867, when the *China Punch* carried a cartoon about a man who doesn't want to be mistaken as the father of a Chinese child. The retort of the *amah* (nurse or nanny) places the subject

THE RETORT COURTEOUS.

Mr. Hurrycombe (*with the umbrella*): I wish you'd take your ugly old face to the other side of the road, Amah, when you want to talk to your coolie friends. Ah—people—ah—will think its my child.

Amah (*who understands perfectly—with emphasis*): Who you talkee so fashion? Allo man savy this chilo b'long *gentleman* baby.

Amah and Eurasian Child. Cartoon in *China Punch,* 8 Nov. 1867: 96.

in perspective. She says that everyone understands that the child is a *gentleman's* baby.[20] In 1871, the *Cycle,* another Anglo-Chinese journal, published an impassioned plea for the establishment of an Eurasian orphanage in Hong Kong. The writer argues that both race and morality demand it: half-European children "have a blood or race claim upon every foreigner" and thus deserve to be saved from the "constant contact with the degrading vices of the Chinese." The latter claim alludes to the idea that the mothers of Eurasian children may have been prostitutes and therefore would corrupt their children.[21]

The anomalous situation of Eurasian children is, above all, racial. Claude's paternal responsibility is clouded by race, which is also the cause of his inability to love his children. His self-recriminations introduce the ideas about eugenics that began circulating at the end of the Victorian era: "he, who so believed in purity of race, with whom the doctrine of heredity was not a creed but a thing proved saw himself responsible for having brought [these children] into the world" (MiC 103). His feelings reflect the climate of opinion indicated by Knollys's brutal words: In Hong Kong "the muddy-complexioned children, many of whom are the hybrid off-spring of effete Portuguese fathers and half caste native mothers, arouse a disgust not entertained toward the pure-blooded Chinese children" (ELC 49).[22] Eurasian children, though, are not only inheritors of the genes of their parents, they are the visible reminders of collective guilt for Western encroachment on Eastern society. In practical terms, this meant they were isolated as if they would contaminate their racially pure brethren.

Little's novel goes quite far in challenging prevailing views on the care of Eurasian children. One character, Mrs. Robinson, sympathizes with them, criticizing their treatment, "as if they were to blame in any way" (MiC 163). The novel also attacks the cruelty of the regulation that schools for Eurasian children required severing all ties between the children and their mothers. Ashamed of his lack of paternal love, Claude balks at sepa-rating the children and their mother, but it is left to his wife, the guardian of morality, to resolve the complications in his life. After Lilian's miscar-riage, she is told she can never bear children and that she must keep busy as a way of insuring psychological health. The doctor advises: "'Let her work! Let her be useful!'" (MiC 292). Lilian then shifts into Jane Eyre–Dorothea Brooke mode, insisting on rehabilitating the stigmatized Claude and supporting him with her inherited money.

Little resolves the issues of Eurasian schools and racial divisiveness by ending the novel with an idealized portrait of acceptance and success for all her characters. Lilian and Claude take charge of his children and re-turn to England, which is shown to be more tolerant of racial diversity and unconventional families than the colonial world. The boldness of this end-ing may be judged by a review of *A Marriage in China* that takes the opportunity to repeat "the warning recently given by Olive Schreiner to dwellers in South Africa, '*Keep the breed pure.*'"[23] Little's novel, however, rises above such blatant racisms. In England, the Fortescues achieve a re-spectability they could not have in China, where a Shanghai matron huffs: "One could never call there with those illegitimate children hanging about" (MiC 304). Restored to the balm of English life, Claude becomes a profes-sor at Cambridge and grows to love his children: "The first agonizing sense of shame began to give place to a gradually growing pride in their acquirements" (MiC 309). Finally, the novel may also be said to encourage inter-racial marriage. Bright futures are predicted for the children, the boy as a scholar who will help revolutionize China, and the girl, whose eyes are "found piquant in England," as the wife of a "Cambridge professor with a lively interest in race distinctions" (MiC 309). It seems, in the end, that colonial life is the villain, Britain the panacea.

Courageous as *A Marriage in China* is in dealing with mixed-race children, its "Angel in the House" iconography preserves the status quo and endorses a double standard for both racial and moral matters: men who stray from the path may be redeemed by a virtuous woman, but the woman who strays is left without an anchor. The complementary half of this standard is the thesis of a novel that appeared at the same time as Little's, *Chun Ti-kung, His Life and Adventures,* by Claude Rees. *Chun Ti-kung* takes a hostile view of a British woman who steps out of the "angel" role by crossing racial barriers. She unknowingly enters into a bigamous marriage with a Chinese man and then drowns herself and her baby when she learns about his Chinese wife. Little supports the premise of her Shanghai friend's novel when she writes in her travel book *Intimate China* that Englishwomen who marry a Chinese man risk bigamy and abandonment, and she cites recent cases in Shanghai as proof. Little's and Rees's books share in the policing of women's behavior. European women's generosity to colonial subjects is approved only insofar as humanitarian efforts are concerned, or when a power relationship is maintained. For Little, feminine discourse, conventional morality, and racism complicate her representation of China.

The voice missing in this discussion is that of Chinese women. Little seems self-conscious about this silence and makes an effort to address it in her wrap-up of *A Marriage in China.* Claude's concubine has to be disposed of when he and Lilian take custody of the children and return to England, so she is married off to a Macao Portuguese with whom she has many children—Spivak's claim that "the subaltern cannot speak" when the discourse is not their own is painfully current in Little's novel.[24] However, Little ironizes her own plot device. Since the exploitation and chauvinism embodied in the character of the British consul is unambiguous, he needs to be forgiven by the Chinese girl to make the ending palatable. This is achieved by having the girl raise her offspring in the Church of England in memory of Claude, but then Little sabotages her character's rehabilitation with a narrative aside: the girl "had had a soul all the time, if Claude Fortescue had but known where to find it" (MiC 311).

If on the whole the Chinese girl approximates the sensibilities of ideal English womanhood, Lilian's experience corresponds with the exploited and abandoned concubine. The feckless Claude, meanwhile, represents male power and authority as a force that links the Chinese girl and the Englishwoman as Women of the Empire. Deprived of agency, they exist as pawns to colonial regulations and individual European men, both sacrificed to the imperial mission. The "women who lost us the Empire" are those who surrendered themselves to it.

As a novelist, Little mixes feminine, feminist, racist, imperialist, and humanitarian perspectives that alternately indict and support institutionalized orientalism. These sometimes contradictory perspectives also appear in her nonfictional writing about China, both in autobiographical material and descriptions of Chinese culture.[25] As a Woman of the Empire, Little enjoys the privilege Western authority lends her, yet she is also aware of the tenuousness of her position—the illusoriness of her own authority both within the circle of British colonial life and in relation to the Chinese people. The result in her books of travel and description is a blending of arrogance toward and sympathy for the Chinese.

Images of Little's own domestic life, especially scenes from her summer in rural Szechuan described in *My Diary in a Chinese Farm,* illustrate this blending. Once when her husband was away on business, the steamy heat prompts her servants to hang her mosquito net from a tree and move her bed outdoors; she admits, "I was ashamed to say I was afraid" (DCF 18). The complication arises when her "soldier coolie" finds the mosquito net an attractive contribution to a night's rest and places his bed next to hers. Little has no revolver to back her up as Bird does, only her womanly honor. She has slender control of her situation and command of a very small space, and yet she forces the man to remove his bed. The man acknowledges Little's power over him and he respects her integrity. Whether sex or a mosquito-free night was his main interest, the mosquito net remains an emblem of the flimsiness of female power.

Little's depiction of female power tends to follow the lines of literary naturalism in her description of life on the Chinese farm, where the cruelties and tyrannies of everyday life, some accidental, others the product of ignorance, pettiness, and private demons, are evident. There are recurring scenes of domestic violence in the mistreatment of the daughter-in-law as household drudge and of the sick child, who is beaten and denied available (Western) medical treatment. Little takes no initiative against these injustices. Elsewhere she offers an interpretation that mitigates the violence when she compares Chinese and British culture: "In a Chinese city one does not at night hear the cries of women as one too often does in London" (IC 180). This defense of cruelty on the Chinese farm screens the racialism and feminine passivity that condones it.

When her own actions are the cause of suffering, however, this passivity reduces the distance between Little and the Chinese. During the Littles' stay on the farm, thieves make off with a large portion of their personal possessions. To find the culprits, the Chinese authorities torture the farmer's son for collaborating with the thieves. Then the farmer's daughter, whom Alicia has hired to do some needlework, develops ophthalmia, supposedly because of the needlework. The Littles abandon all claims to their possessions, "unable any longer to bear the thought of the misery, we have any how been the means of bringing upon these poor people" (DCF 60). The episode shows that, even when foreigners have benign intentions and seem rather the victim than the agent of misdeeds, their presence brings grief to local people. The only solace Little finds in the situation is an understanding of the common humanity of the East and West: "that great Division of the Human Race, called Chinese, consists not only of China-men but of real men and women, with simple wants and wishes not after all so unlike our own" (DCF 74). "Unity out of adversity" is part of Little's feminization of orientalism.

Countering the threat in the mosquito-net episode and the disturbing life on the Chinese farm, Little offers sentimental domestic images that soften the image of China. Especially notable in this regard is a chapter in *Intimate China* devoted to the family dogs, an essay arising from the loss of a cherished Peking pug: "I have sought to take the edge off my grief by writing some account of Shing-erh" (IC 455). The uniqueness of the subject in China travel books gives it value. The pet breaks down cultural

Alicia Little with Her Lion Dog and Szechuan Pony.
Photo; Alicia Little, *My Diary in a Chinese Farm*.

barriers: children want to play with it; adults compare dog lore. Through the international language of pets, Little's pug also leads her to appreciate their human owners: "There must be some subtle unnoticed quality in the Chinaman to breed such dogs" (IC 456). The significance of Little's handling of this domestic subject may be seen when comparing it with male comments on a similar topic. Robert Fortune, who was more disposed to speak kindly of the Chinese than many of his compatriots, had his pride ruffled by Chinese hunting dogs, as did Knollys and Ready. These dogs "are clever," says Fortune; "They are not, however, to be compared for a moment with our English dogs" (JTC 153). The gendered response aroused by dogs, though perhaps unsurprising, has its own interest. For the Englishmen, hunting dogs arouse chauvinism, but for Mrs. Little the lapdog summons cross-cultural understanding.

Moving out of the domestic sphere into the public, Little takes on one of the more politically and emotionally charged phenomenons of the time —mobs of hostile men attacking foreigners. The motives for these attacks have been mentioned in previous chapters. Here I want to focus on the strategies Little uses that, first, distinguish her from Bird, and, second, characterize her feminized orientalism. The different approaches of the two women demonstrate the fact that women's orientalisms are not monolithic.

As mentioned previously, Bird was stoic in the face of a mob and simulated female passivity to contend with it. This strategy focuses attention on the Chinese as unchivalrous ruffians, and she asks herself, "Were they made in the image of God?" (YVB 119). Moreover, with her tendency to self-exoticism, she makes herself appear heroic, as if singled out for attack and prevailing against impossible odds.[26] Little, on the other hand, takes such incidents less dramatically, admitting that at first mud- and epithet-slinging mobs offer a sort of initiation rite: "There is a certain amount of excitement attached to it at first" (IC 256). Her description takes the heat out of the attack.

In situations that represent curiosity more that hostility, Little uses gendered strategies that tame the crowd and tempers their threatening image. In one episode, she takes an assertive approach: "The only one I have ever found effectual with a Chinese crowd . . . getting out of the [sedan] chair, standing quite still, [I] looked solemnly and sadly at first one, then another, till he wished the ground would cover him and retired. I fancy glasses heighten the effect" (IC 100). Her interactive approach has positive results. Treating the Chinese as misbehaving children enables her to establish personal authority. Although patronizing, her maternal gambit results in a far more benign picture of the Chinese than does Bird's. Another crowd-handling technique Little employs gives a vivid illustration of the nature of the curiosity seekers. Once followed by several hundred men as she walked in Chungking, she entered a courtyard and proceeded to photograph them as if that had been her purpose all along. The photograph, which illustrates her text, shows the men and boys agape and huddled non-threateningly in two groups in a sort of unenlightened stupor. For Little, the cool-headed tactic buys her freedom: "Many a walk since then have I taken through these same streets; and the people have got so accustomed to the sight of me, that they now do not turn around to look" (IC 82). The success of this ploy feminizes the conquest theme in colonial travel writing.

Commenting on the motive for Chinese attacks, Bird and Little reach different conclusions on the relative importance of race and gender. Apparently agreeing with Knollys that the Chinese instinctively cower before European men, Bird opines: "I doubt very much whether this and many similar ebullitions would have occurred if I had had a European man with me" (YVB 213). However, when traveling in the interior of Szechuan, the Littles are frequent targets of hostilities. Innkeepers refuse them hospitality if there are no women's quarters, and once Mrs. Little has to be passed off as a man in order for them to get a room for the night. In her analysis, the foreign woman is not so much an affront to Chinese sensibilities as she is simply an oddity: "All across the mountains there had been a great wondering as to what I was, and I had often heard the country people beseeching the coolies to tell them" (IC 66). At one village, a man explains, "'We are nothing but mountain people, . . . and anything like you we have never seen before! So we just want to look'" (IC 60). The effect of this explanation is to de-demonize the Chinese mob. Instead of creating an image of a ferocious Oriental, Little depicts him as a curious onlooker, a country bumpkin and familiar character type.

Little's rhetorical techniques have the effect of making these episodes about both hostile and curious throngs nonthreatening, of describing Chinese culture in a way that crosses national borders. She employs some of these same techniques to describe a unique cultural practice—namely, *feng-shui*—which she seems to have adapted from her husband's way of treating it. She gives an example of a belief in Ichang that a pyramidal mountain overlooking the town "prevents their young men from passing examinations, and makes all their wealth pass into the pockets of strangers" (IC 211). Rather than dismissing the belief as superstition, she compares it with her own experience of applying for south-facing rooms in London and witnessing the manager's incredulity when she described the position of the summer sun in the heavens. Although Little does not associate any intellectual or economic consequences with the position of the sun in a London summer, she suggests that the Chinese consideration of environment "is wiser than our own disregard of all such potent influences of nature" (IC 213). By relating the arcane *feng-shui* to common urban ignorance about the natural world, Little metamorphosizes orientalism into everyday experience and thus diminishes its power as symbol of subalternate difference.

Little's observations about both the domestic and public spheres lead her to return to the subject of women often in her travel and description books. Her novel had treated the Chinese woman more as an artifact than as a person. Other travel writers are largely silent about Chinese women, for language, education, and custom made it difficult for foreigners to get to know them. Silence also stems from the hypocrisy lurking behind the sexual exploitation of Chinese women, the silence that Little breaks in *A Marriage in China*. Few male writers of Victorian travel accounts venture the enthusiasm for Chinese women found in Downing's *Fan-Qui in China*, based on his experience in Canton in the 1830s: "They are unaffected children of nature, and therefore often possess those higher qualities of the sex."[27] Robert Fortune's longest passage about Chinese women is a set piece about the termagant wife who works herself into such a passion that she falls into a swoon; Bird includes a similar anecdote. As the decades of Western presence in China wore on, the image of Chinese women, like many things Chinese, took on a negative quality, as with Knollys, who, it will be remembered, disparages the women at a Chinese dinner party.

Little responds to that sort of negativism when introducing a defense of the virtue of Chinese women: "It is the custom of most men to write of the mock modesty of the women of China" (IC 168). Praising women's manners, she defends even those who lead "a vicious life" as being the victim of others who sold them into slavery (IC 170). Her nonfiction demonstrates a personal involvement with Chinese life and offers a more complete picture of Chinese women than any of the other travelers discussed above.

Little's defense of Chinese women derives from a privileged position that lends authority to force of conscience. Her associations were with what may be called middle-class Chinese women, the wives of the merchants and bureaucrats with whom her husband dealt in Chungking, though from 1895 on she also had formal contacts with educated and affluent Chinese women on her own account, due to the women's movement she influenced. She made an effort to enter into Chinese life in a way that the "twenty-years-in-the-country-and-not-know-a-word-of-the-language" Europeans did not. She learned to speak and read some Chinese, and, when in Szechuan, she modified her clothing to accommodate Chinese sensibilities (often noting that European men's clothing was considered far more indecent than European women's).[28] On more than one occasion, she takes the Chinese point of view against fellow Europeans, as in this outburst after hearing about antiforeign activities: "Why should we insist upon the Chinese swallowing our ugly clothes and ugly houses before they receive our beautiful gospel of glad tidings, I never can understand, except by reminding myself that that gospel never came from Shanghai or New York, but from that very Asia where still truth and beauty seem to Asiatics synonymous and interchangeable" (IC 244). Such subjectivity arises from the effort she and her husband made to understand China. Not only did they live in Chungking, fourteen hundred miles from the amenities of the "Model Settlement" in Shanghai, but they were engaged in local life. Little's empathy with Chinese women even has an aura of the privileged insider to it.

Little's chapter "The Position of Women" in *Intimate China* combines this sense of privilege and empathy. The chapter begins with three stories of women given official recognition posthumously: a mother with numerous male offspring, a dutiful daughter who sacrifices a bit of her flesh to make a soup for her dying mother, and a group of women war heroes in the

Taiping era. Little took the stories too literally, for these are the women of legend, of whom more recent versions may be found in *Half the Sky,* of the Maoist era. The flesh-soup sacrifice is ubiquitous in Chinese folklore, and it appears in Western fiction about China, from Oliver Ready's *Ch'un-kwang: A Tale of Chinese Love and Tragedy* (1905) to Amy Tan's *The Joy Luck Club* (1989). An adaptation of the women war heroes, not unlike Maxine Hong Kingston's *Woman Warrior* (1977), may be found in Lewis Wingfield's *The Lovely Wang* (1886). Little can be faulted for failing to understand the propaganda technique aimed at controlling women, though Hitler's gold-star mothers and Chairman Mao's similar rewarding of women's reproductivity suggest that she would have had to be quite farseeing to do so.

Little overlooks the propaganda level of these heroism stories partly because she wants to suggest that they demonstrate a reverence for women's contribution to family and society that probably would not be recognized in the West. Though they are memorialized only years after their deeds, "in most other countries they would have remained unnoticed to all time" (IC 168). In her zeal to bolster the status of women in China, Little later stretches credulity to the extreme. She notes that a woman who kills her husband is condemned to death by "a thousand cuts," "but though this shows the horror entertained of so dastardly a deed, yet in reality, even for such a crime as this, she is put to death first and cut in pieces afterwards" (IC 180). Little may have looked too hard for evidence of an elevated status of women in China, but the spirit of her inquiry is noble. Her positive approach has the disadvantage of ignoring problems, yet it has the salutary effect of supporting an underprivileged half of society.

If Little does not describe the life of Chinese women as lamentable, it may be because she unconsciously parallels the situation of European and Chinese women. In both her novels and manners-and-customs books, she criticizes idle colonial wives. The heroine in *A Marriage in China,* just arrived in China, is appalled by the European women's attention to wardrobe: "'I thought that was what ladies in harems amused themselves with'" (MiC 46). In this novel, the wives of merchants devote themselves to tennis and teas, flirting with single men, shopping in Shanghai, and frequent escapes to spas in Japan.[29] Another of Little's China novels, *A Millionaire's Courtship,* puts an even more biting attack in the mouth of the do-gooder heroine: English wives don't read, speak Chinese, show an interest in English politics, do housekeeping, or care for their children. Though Little does not draw a specific connection, she describes Chinese women of the middle classes in much the same way. They "do little beyond suckling children and making shoes. . . . They smoke and gossip, give and go to dinner parties, and one of their great delights is to go on pilgrimages to distant shrines" (IC 178). Little deliberately sets out to defend Chinese women, but she stops short of identifying them with European women. Race is too big a hurdle for her to overcome; she can only be an advocate from a position of superiority.

The other half of the satiric picture of women's occupation, or lack of it, is the demand for meaningful work. On this subject, Little again draws unconscious comparisons between Chinese and European women. She puts New Woman sentiments into the speeches of her fictional characters like Mrs. Stuckey, who asks Lilian: "'Do you have a mission?' . . . 'Or is being beautiful enough?'" (MiC 221). Little approves of Chinese women laboring in Shanghai factories and those working as trackers towing boats upstream at least in part because she is sometimes stymied in her own search for meaningful occupation. At her Szechuan farm, for example, she tries to participate in women's activities such as making plant-fiber cloth, but the women keep their distance: "They all talked about me in their local Chinese, saying to one another, 'She does not understand!' which alas! was true" (DCF 11). She fills the vacuum in her life by writing, as she explains in the introduction to *My Diary in a Chinese Farm:* "I was shut up in the one Farm house sitting room, so I started a Diary for much the same reason, probably, that I have often observed people do on a Sea Voyage." A search for meaningful occupation links her own life, her fictional characters, and Chinese women.

Finally, Little's estimation of the position of women in China arises from her sense that in some situations the Chinese wife enjoys greater power and distinction than an English wife. In the tradition of farm wives in other countries, the Chinese farm wife is the manager, and a similar role is at times accorded the wife of a Chinese merchant. Once when Mr. Little has to go downriver from Chungking for a time, his Chinese clerks, "greatly to my surprise," believe that Mrs. Little should keep the seals and the money and manage the business: "They seem to think this quite natural, and what a Chinese lady would do" (DCF 73). In a reverse situation—that is, European men commenting on the role of Chinese women in business transactions—European men are likely to condemn Chinese women as harridans: "Foreign men often get the idea that women rule the roost in China" because "some old woman of the family" is likely to delay a real estate deal (IC 179). These encounters with the seemingly more liberal attitude of Chinese men and the prejudice of European men toward the position of women arouses Mrs. Little's sense of solidarity with all women: "But it must be remembered what a dull, mulish, obstinacy is that of the Chinese man, and that somehow or other the Chinese woman has to get on with him" (IC 180). The homeliness of this husband joke suddenly puts East and West on the same footing. Little's own sense of powerlessness prompts her to reach across the racial divide. Cultural difference fades for the moment, while gender forges bonds.

How far does this ability to understand the point of view of the Chinese woman go? Despite Little's effort to understand the Chinese woman, on the whole it is on a general or theoretical level. She rarely names the Chinese, suggesting an inability to individualize people, though there are some superb snapshots, as of the Buddhist nuns who invite her to observe their ordination rites. Despite the affectionate gestures of Chinese women, Little's lack of fluency in the language limits her ability to socialize with them. It is too much to look for an intimate portrait of a Chinese woman in the vein of Shostak's *Nisa,* and yet, as far as Anglo-Chinese life goes, Little achieves a great deal in understanding and relating to Chinese women on their own terms.

Little crowns her effort to understand the position of Chinese women by becoming actively engaged on their behalf. She does this in an audacious assault on footbinding, one of the "greatest curses in China" (IC 143). As a symbol of difference, nothing can match the image this practice gave China as perverse and stagnant, and yet footbinding held a horrible fascination for Victorians. Every travel book dwells on the "universal" practice, partly because the erotic appeal of the bound foot and its tiny shoe is compatible with the "more familiar sexual fixation on boots and shoes," as Arthur Waley notes in the foreword to Howard Levy's book on footbinding.[30] As a result, modesty and voyeurism conspire with humanitarianism to give footbinding a prominent place in books about China: an English-woman's "limb" is nowhere pictured, but many works are illustrated with drawings and photographs of a Chinese leg adorned in its silk trousers and the bound foot in its ornate slipper.[31] This fetishistic interest can also be seen in the Western taste for porcelain snuffboxes and pincushions in the form and ideal size, three inches, of the bound foot.[32] In addition, Victorian writers often minimize the suffering imposed by footbinding by comparing it with other ways of distorting nature in the name of beauty, such as tattooing or, more frequently, the corset, which some maintained was worse because it caused internal injuries and weak offspring.

At the same time, Victorians condemned footbinding as a barbaric custom. The practice is "utterly opposed to the natural instincts of mankind," Arthur Smith writes in *Village Life in China*.[33] The Church Mission in Hankow, Little reports, refused to accept girls with bound feet, though Roman Catholic orphanages and the American Episcopal Church countenanced it so as to make the girls marriageable (IC 145–48). Lay writers are typically condemnatory but detached. Knollys, for example, says the physiological effects of footbinding "may interest Darwinites" (ELC 73). Cumming and Bird emphasize their distance from Chinese women by referring to the bound foot as a hoof, but Bird takes issue with Dr. Wells Williams, an authority on China, who says in *The Middle Kingdom* that footbinding "is more an inconvenient than a dangerous custom" (YVB 236). She adds that the "set-off against the miseries of footbinding is the extreme comfort of a Chinese woman's dress" (YVB 238). In contrast, the merchant Archibald Little writes far more sensitively than these missionaries and globetrotters about the suffering of little girls robbed of their childhood and "the enfeeblement of mothers" the custom produces (TYG 302). Mrs. Little says her effort to do something about footbinding "owed its inception" to him (GFY xiii).

In April 1895, Mrs. Little founded T'ien Tsu Hui, the Natural Feet Society, which she describes in *Intimate China* and *The Land of the Blue Gown*. Heretofore, Little notes, nonmissionary foreign women were uninvolved in the abolition movement, but she persuaded a group of Shanghai matrons (at a meeting that Isabella Bird also attended) to join this worthy cause.

Little provided the leadership and organizational skills not only to make the antifootbinding effort succeed but also to mobilize women in the foreign community to unite with Chinese women in the broader cause of elevating their status. Her society composed a pamphlet that, to satisfy decorum, they had translated into "the dignified Wenli of the Chinese classics," rather than any of the vernacular languages (IC 150). With donations from both wealthy foreigners and Chinese, they distributed ten thousand copies to all parts of China. Little also catalogued numerous examples of those who like the Manchu had never practiced footbinding and of individual women and villages that had now abandoned it.

Armed with information and the fire of conviction, she took her message on tour. She started in the river cities in central China with which she was most familiar, next going to Canton, Macao, and the treaty ports. The meetings she convened borrowed devices from temperance rallies: Placards with antifootbinding slogans written by famous Chinese dignitaries decorated the walls. After her speech, she solicited testimonies from those unbound and got individuals to sign on formally as members of the antifootbinding society. At Hankow, the brashness of her activities almost overwhelmed her, "realising to the fullest extent exactly how strange, how unheard of, these Chinese officials must consider a woman addressing them at all," especially on the "exceptionally indelicate subject—women's feet" (LBG 201). The audience of dignitaries, some with large retinues, so intimidated her interpreter that he was unable to speak, but luckily a missionary came to her rescue. With an all-female audience, however, she was more relaxed and could make jokes "at which the whole room tittered" (LBG 203).

She demonstrated the kind of political savvy needed to insure success by enlisting the support of well-placed Chinese. Her biggest coup was securing the endorsement of Li Hung-chang, arguably the most influential man in China in the second half of the nineteenth century.[34] At the imposing height of six feet four inches, dressed in an ermine-lined gown and sable cape, he "so entertained and charmed" her that she had some difficulty getting him to listen to the subject of her mission (LBG 208). At Swatow, she found her picture in a Chinese magazine. By the time she reached

Foochow and Soochow, the antifootbinding movement had taken on an aura of inevitability.

It took considerable self-assurance and not a little temerity for Little to crusade against such a deeply rooted custom. She cites stories on the origin of the practice, which is believed to have originated in the twelfth century with a court dancer who bound her feet in silk to dance on a golden lotus. Although Little's crusade was motivated by both feminism and humanitarianism, she surprisingly rejects as a "popular error" the idea that "the custom was introduced in order to prevent women from gadding about" (IC 134).[35] Ironically, her own words echo a Southern Sung poem that links the cause and effect she disputes: "'Why must the foot be bound? / To prevent barbarous running around!'"[36] Her own examples of the way bound feet limited women's movement should have made her understand the connection between physical disability and emotional suppression. But if Little was more concerned about the literal maiming of women than the implications of preventing a woman from "running around," her achievement is no less meritorious.

The maiming started early, on girls aged three to seven, and consisted of a torturous process of bending the four smaller toes under the sole of the foot, then forcing the heel toward the big toe, making the foot into an inverted *v*. Little shows that the custom was practiced with a different degree of severity in some parts of China, depending on family occupation, so that laboring girls were sometimes spared the more extreme forms of footbinding. The process had severe physiological effects that not infrequently caused death. Little's haunting story of a little girl who looks at her with an "expression of hopeless rage and agony and hate" crystallizes the image of a brutal custom (LBG 229). The objects of all this pain were the "golden lilies" that required ritualized attention, produced a tottering gait, and inspired a considerable erotic literature.

"Mrs. Little apparently remained blissfully unaware" that footbinding had "a directly sexual significance," writes a modern critic, implying that she should not or would not have engaged in her humanitarian campaign had she known the bound foot was an object of eroticism.[37] The charge of naïveté is exaggerated, though, as shown in Little's concerns when writing antifootbinding propaganda: "Were we appealing to the men or the women? ... We knew of course—we all sat sadly weighted by the thought —that feet are the most *risque* subject of conversation in China, and no subject more improper can be found there" (IC 150). Beyond eliminating suffering, unbinding feet also implied the freeing of Chinese women to control their own sexuality. This, and the radicalness of attacking a taboo subject, place Little's Natural Feet Society in the vanguard of women's liberation movements.

Within a few years, Chinese women assumed leadership of the movement, then added the establishment of girls' high schools to their liberation cause. In the autumn of 1897, the foreign women in Little's Natural Feet Society were invited by a group of high-ranking Chinese women to support the founding of the first high school for women in Shanghai. This event marked "the beginning of an interchange of civilities between foreign and Chinese ladies such as had never occurred before" (IC 553). Little's leadership was recognized by her being made vice president of the Women's Conference in Shanghai in 1900. She later used the success of the antifootbinding movement to argue for women's suffrage in England.[38]

Little's applying the principles of conventional gentlewoman's charity work to a social cause aimed at enhancing the lives of colonized people offers an alternative to the negative stereotype of Women of the Empire. Some of her contemporaries were mocking and resentful of that alternative, as a comment in the *Rattle* suggests: "One does not see at first glance how it is going to work. On the same lines, might we suggest that any European lady known to paint her face or to wear bloomers should be put on a milk-diet?"[39] The feminized orientalism that Little represents also rankles Nigel Cameron, who, though giving her grudging credit for her antifootbinding work, complains that without "anything better to do" than to write "lengthy, portentous books," she "belongs to a school of popular writers on China whose influence in Europe and America was probably much greater than sinologues would like to acknowledge."[40] The idea that writing books that had an effect on public opinion should be disparaged as the work of those without "anything better to do" is itself an artifact of a past era. It underlines the strength of custom that Alicia Little, and more importantly Chinese women, had to overcome to attack footbinding.

In 1902, Tz'u Hsi, the empress dowager, signed a proclamation banning footbinding (on her part, a formal act only; she was never known to harbor humanitarian sentiments). Mrs. Little's Natural Feet Society did not singlehandedly end footbinding, but it popularized a cause whose time had come. All abolition attempts, including those in the early years of the Ch'ing dynasty, had failed, but it was now understood in China that modernization required an improvement in the status of women. An initial objection Li Hung-chang made to Little predicts and regrets this modernization: "'If you unbind the women's feet you'll make them so strong, and the men so strong too, that they will overturn the dynasty'" (LBG 210). The 1911 revolution that finally ended the Ch'ing dynasty also essentially brought an end to footbinding.[41] China had been accused by the West for the greater part of the nineteenth century of being a stagnant society in thrall to unyielding custom. Little and the antifootbinding movement encouraged a sea change in that society—a change that coalesced with the socialist movement that would sweep twentieth-century China. If a cause of "losing the empire" was the undermining of the status quo, then Little and the European women involved in the antifootbinding movement may be seen as subversives who assisted that loss.

Poppies and Terraced Rice Fields. Photo by Alicia Little, *Intimate China*.

Conclusion

An Opened China

VICTORIAN TRAVELERS both rejoiced in and held reservations about an opened China. They supported the imperialist mission, premised on free trade and sustained by military force, yet treaty provisions dealing with the opium trade and missionaries gave them pause. The travelers believed that Western influence, ideas, and development were good for China, but to varying degrees they also express admiration for certain elements in Chinese culture. Representative of such inconsistent views is Archibald Little, who goes so far as to suggest that Britain ought to have "had the courage to usurp the dragon throne" in the so-called Second Opium War (TYG 302). However, in the first chapter of his first book he says the belief "that order, justice, and a high state of civilization is the monopoly of Christian nations ceases to be held upon a close study of this people" (TYG 40). The travelers have difficulty in reconciling their admiration for China's durable civilization with their support of westernizing it. They have divided opinions about both the long opening of China and their personal experience there.

Once envisioned as a magical place of luxury and refinement for its rulers and of utopian peace and prosperity for its people, "Cathay" became for the Victorians an ironic term designating a decaying civilization. They increasingly imbued the Orient with baleful images, even as they earmarked it for humanitarian efforts. Travelers "orientalized" the Chinese by attributing to them characteristics they deemed opposite of those displayed by Westerners, which served not only to define difference but to justify the political reality of Britain and the West encroaching on China's sovereignty.

Negative images of China in travelers' accounts became more persistent and serious as Western influence increased. Fortune, who went to China in 1843, had no doubt that he and the British were superior to the Chinese, and yet he idealized China's social organization and found the country a rich repository of natural and manmade objects. Thirty years later, Cumming's enthusiasm for China was challenged by the dirt and difference of Peking, and her departure has a sense of urgency to it. Bird, on the other hand, in part experiences China as an oriental version of the patriarchal forms she sought to escape by traveling abroad. Knollys, unable to recognize social structures or familiar associations in the oriental subject, finds China bereft of human feeling, dehumanized. Even the Littles, who associated with the Chinese more than most Westerners, believe that specific cultural practices present an unbridgeable gap between East and West.

In the accounts of these travelers, one of the most frequent denominators of racial difference is cleanliness. As the cult of cleanliness swept over England, installation of sanitation systems in cities and homes and attention to personal hygiene became hallmarks of a civilized society. Conversely, the lack of attention to public and personal cleanliness increasingly was associated with lower-class inferiority. Transposed to the East, this concept became associated with racial difference. The development of this

association can be observed by comparing Fortune's writings from the
1840s and 1850s with those of the travelers who saw China in the 1870s
and 1890s.

Fortune makes few comments on dirtiness, but all the other travelers
frequently mention the subject. Archibald Little uses it for the conclusion
of his *Mount Omi and Beyond,* a book that chronicles the journey he and his
wife took to visit the religious shrines and aboriginal people in far-western
Szechuan. In a passage echoing Bird at a similar juncture in her China
travel, Little concludes: "Returning once more to populous and prosperous Szechuan proper, after a delightful fortnight spent in the clean, dry
country beyond the pass, I am once again oppressed by the filthy condition
of the towns and people" (MOB 267). He continues at length on this theme,
adding opium smoking, "cripple-footed women," and "the stagnation of
Chungking" to punctuate his journey's end with images of cultural difference in China. He was ill during part of the journey to Mt. Omi. This,
combined with the frustration he was experiencing with his steamboat enterprise and the hostilities of the 1890s, had an embittering effect on him.
As a result, the final image he chooses to leave of this journey at the end of
the nineteenth century is of dirt and racial inferiority as the defining difference of China.

The cumulative effect of negativity toward an opened China may be
judged by the conclusion of a 1910 *Cook's Handbook for Tourists to Peking.*
After describing the four parts of Peking, it mentions that the Chinese city
is "little worthy of special attention," except that it represents "the subject
races" set off from the ruling races.[1] The *Handbook* ends with several lists
of tourist information, such as the Chinese words for Western food, place-
names for the foreign legations, and the Chinese phrases for these "Useful
Expressions":

> Do not trouble me.
> I do not require you.
> Do not hurt me.
> Be patient.
> He did it on purpose.
> What is that to you?

The "Useful Expressions" assume an aggressiveness on the part of both the Chinese and the tourist, and obnoxiousness is answered with obnoxiousness. The expressions are shrill reminders of the transvaluation of "Cathay" to the land of the "Chinaman." Victorian travel accounts that denigrate China's moral and cultural life while supporting those of Britain and the West must take some responsibility for dismantling the former image of China.

Ironically, though, as negativism increased, as the image of China in the West deteriorated, there was a simultaneous assertion of its power and prediction of its rebirth. The political fear expressed by the phrase "yellow peril" and the "invasion scare" novels, born partly out of guilt for shattering old China and partly out of the surge in Japan's strength and colonizing actions in China and Korea, contribute to the rebirth scenario. In her conclusion, Bird attempts to forecast a positive renewal for China, but the structure of her book undermines the idea. She ends the description of her quite spectacular sojourn through Szechuan to Lesser Tibet on an ambivalent note: "My journey on the whole had been one of extreme variety and interest" and thankfulness "for the deep and probably abiding interest in China and the Chinese" (YVB 495). "Extreme variety" is a modest way to sum up an arduous journey that included surviving physical attack, and it makes the "abiding interest" raw-edged.

Sensing that this ending does not reconcile her personal experience with the Chinese and the effects of imperialism on China, the inveterate traveler adds chapter after chapter: one on opium, one on missionaries, and finally "Concluding Remarks" that argue China is not in decay and "is certainly at the dawn of a new era" (YVB 534). However, she cannot resist a caveat: "Whether the twentieth century shall place her where she ought to be, in the van of oriental nations, or whether it shall witness her disintegration and decay, depends very largely on the statesmanship and influence of Great Britain." The image of a populous nation with its ancient civilization being dependent on Britain for its renewal reinforces the negative image of China that Bird ostensibly sets out to disable.

All the travelers, whatever the length of their stay, share an essential purpose of traveling: sightseeing, seeking out the unusual, the picturesque, and the "exotic," looking at the Chinese as a sort of museum specimen. On one level, late-nineteenth-century travel was a counterpart of the ethnographic museum displays of the same period, supposedly for the scientific and comparative study of culture. These displays, according to Coombes in "The Recalcitrant Object," combined "aesthetic pleasure, exotic delectation and spectacle," and "visible 'evidence' of racial inferiority."[2] Sightseeing in China is similarly fraught with ideological implications on both sides. First, the parameters of sightseeing—what might be seen by whom and when—are inscribed in Chinese culture. A country governed by rulers hidden away in the Forbidden City, with magnificent retreats and temples barred to the eyes of its populace, a population to which home means a walled compound housing several generations of family, all suggest a culture constructed around the ideas of secrecy and privilege. It suggests a prizing of secrecy so powerful that, as Archibald Little noted in his Yangtze River tour, it is difficult to ascertain the simplest facts about the country and people.

Opening China to the Victorians meant both a literal and metaphoric throwing open of the gates and going behind the walls of forbidden places. That highly charged entering of forbidden space in 1860, the French and British sacking of the imperial retreat, Yüan Ming Yüan, was as important symbolically as it was materially a sign of China's capitulation to the West. The walls of Peking next became the venue for a foreigner's stroll, and then Europeans trudged through the Temple of Heaven where once only the emperor was allowed to walk. Sightseeing in the imperial precincts became the conqueror's right, an assertion of foreign power over a weakened China.

Sightseeing in China suggested a violation of space, and this was almost immediately supercharged with pictures that could open its cultural life to the view of almost anyone. The artist William Alexander, who had accompanied Lord Macartney on his mission in 1792–94 to capture images of China for the folks back home, depicted the Chinese as robust and colorful, the country as placid and picturesque. Toward the end of the nineteenth century, travelers came armed with cameras, and subjectivity had a new medium. Now both images of scenic interest and tourist mementos, such as group shots commemorating an event, could be mass-produced. The "paparazzi" phenomenon also quickly developed, as photographers looked for an unusual image or the demeaning evidence of a subject nation. A man with a horribly deforming case of elephantiasis, squinting at the camera in shame, poses helplessly, and the photo is reproduced again and again in travel books. Bird's photographs include a miserable beggar woman peering out of a straw-mat hut and of soldiers looking foolishly unmilitary, while Little illustrates her account of footbinding with photographs of deformed, unshod feet. Documenting cultural difference, such photographs suggest that an "open China" meant a China with no secrets at all.

However exploitative the travelers' viewing of China may be at times, it is given piquancy by the Chinese ability to return it by "occidentalizing" the foreigner. The Chinese were expert at a kind of reciprocal gaze and travelers often found themselves surrounded by curiosity-seeking crowds. At best it meant village boys following travelers, examining their clothes and belongings or simply gaping at the sight of the alien in their midst. Fortune took being turned into a tourist attraction with a good humor that ingratiated him to the sociable Chinese. However, Cumming felt it contaminating, Bird was unnerved by it, and the Littles' were exasperated when a group of young men peered at them through the loosely joined slats of the ceiling as they ate and slept. There is a certain irony in the outsiders who are making use of a country and its people as spectacle, recreation, and object of exploration or cultural research being themselves objectified in this way. In a sense the travelers equate Chinese curiosity about them as an informal version of the ethnographic exhibitions mentioned above, and it does not please them. Bird and Alicia Little respond with explanations of how they handled being "occidentalized."

Chinese culture had, in a sense, institutionalized racialism in its age-old appellations for the foreigner as "barbarian" and "foreign devil." Even if Victorian travelers learned no other Chinese words, they soon recognized these terms. Assured of their own superiority, travelers typically accepted the epithets as a sign of ignorance, a joke. However, as the century wore on and more missionaries, traders, and travelers roamed the Middle Kingdom, as state revenues declined and opium addiction increased, the Chinese resorted to means beyond traditional epithets to avenge their wounded pride. As a result, travelers often depict themselves as victims of racialist behavior.

Besides directing their curiosity toward the traveler, the Chinese took action in a more menacing form toward the end of the century. The mobs harassing Bird and the Littles reflect a change in the climate of public opinion in China. Inflamed by the anti-foreign, anti-missionary propaganda churned out by Chou Han and frustrated with the corruption of their own government, Chinese mobs were rehearsing, as it were, a momentous overturning of dynastic rule. Travelers served symbolically as enemies of the people as much as hated objects of intrinsic difference.

My conclusions on the way travelers treat race and the image of China have not so far specifically taken gender and occupation into account. I wish now to consider those factors in travelers' views. Helen Callaway has written in "Ethnography and Experience" that anthropology is not genderless subjectivity, "that women and men may take up different topics" and that a narrative "necessarily unfolds in terms of gendered experience and its inequalities of power and privilege."[3] This observation on the work of modern professionals also applies to the writing of Victorian travelers/ amateur ethnologists in China. Gender shapes the point of view and experience of these travelers.

Perhaps most conspicuously, gender shapes experience in making women more likely than men to be targeted for hostilities and insults by the Chinese. Bird gets struck, chased, and harassed several times. Mrs. Little experiences hostilities even when traveling with her husband and attempting to avoid notice by sitting enclosed in a sedan chair covered head to foot with Chinese fur robes. The novelty of Western women in remoter parts of China made them a curiosity. In addition, Western women suffered from the effect of the low status of women in China. Archibald Little includes a telling anecdote of Chinese men pushing and shoving ahead of women tottering on their bound feet, laden with heavy burdens, when disembarking a river steamer. He was disgusted that the Chinese had no "angel in the house" idealization of woman's role.

Though the subordination of women in Chinese culture had a bearing on the treatment of Victorian women travelers, Englishwomen did not necessarily feel an affinity for their Chinese sisters. The travelers' education, their freedom to escape the forms impinging on them at home in their wanderings abroad, and of course their sense of racial and cultural superiority, made it difficult for the globetrotters Cumming and Bird to empathize with Chinese women. Their comments about Chinese women are general and distant. It falls to Alicia Little, whose marriage to a merchant and many years in China permitted her to observe domestic life there, to draw on her feminist and humanitarian instincts in the behalf of Chinese women. She transcends the boundaries of culture to show parallels between the position of Chinese and European women, showing how both are used in the furtherance of Western imperialism, united ironically as Women of the Empire.

Englishmen say little about Chinese women in their travel accounts. This silence is curious in view of Mrs. Little's development of the issues of concubinage and Eurasian children in her novel *A Marriage in China*. The legendary self-effacement of Chinese women is perpetuated in the blanked-out space they inhabited in semi-colonial China. The differing views of English men toward Chinese women, like that of English women, corresponds with the nature of their investment in China. The globetrotting Knollys can be flip and sarcastic. With a livelihood at stake and personal circumstances that prompted discretion, Fortune—who left his wife at home during his long years abroad—and Archibald Little—whose wife was at his side in China (though with a somewhat mysterious silence about his life before her arrival there)—are brief and kind in their comments on Chinese women.

Mrs. Little's position as wife of a merchant also authorizes her to comment on European women in China. Her novels draw on her travel experience to depict the roles of the recent arrivee, long-term residents, and missionaries, partly as victim, partly as companion in the establishment of hegemony over China. Through her own experience and her fictional characters she explores the complexity and variety of colonial culture in a way that the globetrotters cannot.

Globetrotting women are often said to treat European wives in the colonies as colonized subjects themselves, as idle socialites chained to outmoded British forms. In China Cumming has no such criticism, and Bird takes English men to task more severely than the women. Her judgmental remarks on both male and female missionaries also make gender less significant than her curmudgeonliness. The accounts of these three women travelers in China display gender as a causative factor in their experiences there rather than evidence of a monolithic point of view.

The same may be said of the men, though the politics of empire rather than social life is the impetus for their differences. To close his account of his tour in China, Knollys berates "the 'twenty-years-in-the-country-and-speak-the-language' men who resent the most evident propositions enunciated by unprejudiced newcomers." The Anglo-Chinese have not only forgotten the Western world but are unaware of their own ignorance, he says; therefore, their views cannot be trusted. Knollys's attack reflects the mutual distrust between globetrotters and colonists, between the holiday-makers and those whose work is abroad. The globetrotters think of themselves as an informal oversight committee of those carrying out the imperial mission. Knollys's final words on China highlight the uneasiness between the two groups of Englishmen there, which in turn mirrors the dubious-ness of this mission.

Englishmen, with the power of military victory on their side, fared better among the Chinese than Englishwomen. Fortune's unaffected friend-liness and Little's command of the language enable these men to move freely in China, to converse with the Chinese, to accept Chinese hospital-ity and experience something of Chinese domestic life. Knollys's contact with the Chinese is fleeting and formal, yet he has occasion to exercise his arrogant claim of the "natural command" of the Englishman over the East-ern races.

The command of the English is, however, challenged by that institu-tion in China, the interpreter-guide, who operates as a sort of chief of staff and essential facilitator of all travel arrangements, and whom travelers must employ even if they speak the language. Bird found herself virtually ruled by her interpreter, and Knollys reduced to almost adolescent dependency on his. Both Fortune and Archibald Little were distrustful of this person-age who transcends the master-servant relation. The interpreter is a sym-bol of the tentativeness of Western authority in China. In turn, travelers compensate for this tentativeness by representing Chinese men as effete. Their queue, their flowing clothes, but more than anything, their position as a subject race contrasts with the Englishman's self-image as aggressive and virile.

Though European men enjoyed greater authority and freedom in their sojourn in China than European women, the women were more moved to humanitarian concerns than their male counterparts. Cumming raised funds for Rev. Murray's work for the blind in China, Bird set up hospitals and infirmaries with her own money, and Alicia Little crusaded against footbinding. In their concern for the sick and unfortunate in Chinese society, these women exhibit traditional women's work, an interest in nursing, religion, and social problems. Of the male travelers, only Knollys mentions medical missions, though his purpose is to gather grist for his missionary criticism rather than support humanitarian work. Rather than humanitarianism per se, Archibald Little wants to help China by developing it. He spends a good deal of his own money towards that end, but he still would like a financial return on his investment. Fortune, in contrast, never mentions foreign humanitarian efforts in China, instead believing that China could export some of its cultural practices to the West.

In addition to determining their treatment of gendered issues and their relation to Chinese people, gender also plays an important role in the selection of topics travelers cover in their accounts. At first glance it seems that travelers tend to discuss similar material, but there are significant distinctions in emphasis and point of view. Though all the travelers have a good deal to say about trade, opium, and missionaries, their perspective is gendered. Fortune and Little deal with their occupational interest in trade. Partly in deference to Archibald Little, from whom she learned much about the condition of trade in China, Bird goes out of her way to discuss the topic. However, her admonishing young clerks, like Cumming scolding the mercantile community for its failure to support missionaries, shows her concentrating on the feminine, human resource side of trade.

On the central topic of the opium trade, beyond the fact that it spurs violent debate and far from unanimous conclusions, gender determines perspective. The men strongly support it and the women oppose it, though Mrs. Little's reticence on the subject suggests a family dispute that she does not want to get into print. As a trade item, opium was wildly successful with an estimated seventy to eighty per cent addiction in Szechuan by the end of the century. Travelers all weigh the economic and moral dimensions of opium use and the opium trade.

The linkage between the opium trade and missionaries in the various treaties made with China added to the controversy and level of polemics which mark Victorian travel books about China. Even Robert Fortune connects these in a chapter advocating a tough response to the Chinese tak-ing of the *Arrow*. Force should be used, he argues, to "bring the Chinese within the pale of nations, to extend our commerce, and to open up the country to missionary labor and scientific research" (RaC 433). The gen-dered response to missionaries shows men associating them with politics and remarking on their relative failure, while women travelers discuss more affective concerns. The women all discuss the human dimension of mis-sionary work, missionaries' living conditions and the isolation and lone-liness of people far from home. The disparate views of travelers about missionary work—only Fortune and Cumming support missionary work without reservation—stems from their misgivings about westernizing Chi-nese culture.

Time and purpose in China rather than gender determines the way trav-elers treat some topics. Globetrotters emphasize difference and distance between themselves and the Chinese by commenting on topics aimed at exoticizing the Orient. Knollys and Bird inspect prisons and describe rough Chinese justice; Cumming relates tales of cruelty and horror. English residents are more likely to admire the Chinese philosophy of life, seen in Fortune's idealizing of rural life and Archibald Little's admiration for Con-fucian ethics. The globetrotters ridicule ancestor worship, while Fortune thinks it a sign of filial feeling and the Littles, generally accepting of Chinese ethics, barely mention it. Autobiography in the sense of length of time and purpose in China is a strong determinant of subjective positions on Chinese culture.

The more open or accessible China became to the West, the more in-sistently travelers described it as stagnant. Fortune thought dilapidated temples were a sign that China had ceased to develop, but this is not an important theme in his books. Toward the end of the Victorian period, however, travelers find evidence of an unchanging China both in cultural continuity and anti-machine, anti-change expressions, from the ubiqui-tous blue clothes of the populace, to the omnipresence of the ancient clas-sics, to Luddite action against railroads. Archibald Little ends his *Through the Yang-tse Gorges* by quoting Pliny to characterize an unchanging China. Though not unkindly meant, the description implies that China is stuck in a remote past, a dead world.

It is left to Cumming, however, to provide the most striking image of China as a dead world. Her departure trope is as resonant as that of her arrival in Shanghai in a cold, muddy December. Visiting Peking at the end of her six-month tour, she feels enervated by the uncomfortable journey, wearied by pre-dawn sightseeing excursions, and choked by the dust, dirt, and crowds of the city. She celebrates her leave-taking with a fifteen-page description of the boat journey to Japan marked by cleansing rain, balmy weather, and homespun European shipmates. During a week's calm an eerie incident reminiscent of the "Rime of the Ancient Mariner" provides an allegorical image of China as Cumming's final comment on that country:

> Not one sail have we sighted in these seven days; but when the mist was most dense, and a brooding silence which we could almost feel seemed to rest upon the waters, a large skeleton junk floated noiselessly close past us, its great black ribs looking weird and spirit-like, like one of Gustave Doré's strange fantasies. There could be little doubt that all her crew had perished,—at all events, no living thing remained on her. Had we struck her in the night we should inevitably have foundered, so we inferred that our good angels had been faithful watchers. (WIC 512)

The "skeleton junk" emerging out of a "brooding silence" is a ghost ship, a decaying "ship of state" representing China. In Coleridge's poem, the be-calmed sea and ghost ship are part of the phantasmagoria caused by the Mariner's violation of nature, his killing the bird that "brings the wind and rain." Cumming's imagery, in contrast, has no hint that those threatened— the junk could destroy "us" if "we struck her in the night"—are at fault. In Cumming's closing trope, the Europeans' "good angels" protect them from the haunting vengeance of the "spirit-like" junk, i.e. China. In the end, she reflects a fear of reprisal from China much as Knollys does in his fear of being outnumbered, of pushing his military bearing too far.

In general, travelers supported the forced opening of China. They were proud of the evidence of merchants' success, their modern factories and warehouses and palatial homes, and their rapid transformation of Hong Kong and Shanghai into modern European metropolises. They saw war,

commerce, modern development, and humanitarianism as necessary Western expansionism and ultimately of benefit to China even as they quarrel
with one another on how that expansionism might best be fostered, and
whether missionaries or merchants might best be blamed for its failures.

Struggling with the failure of their own government to protect them
from outside force as well as from its own depredations on its people, the
Chinese enacted a series of civil wars during which foreigners, particularly
missionaries, often found themselves the scapegoat. However these attacks
looked to others, and whatever history has shown were the actual causes,
travelers like Archibald Little blamed the missionaries for bringing them on
by trying to change a social ethic that did not need to be changed. Missionaries, on the other hand, blamed the merchants and the opium trade for
poisoning the minds of the Chinese which in turn fomented the attacks on
themselves. This division of opinion within the foreign community reflects
the uncertain moral ground on which Britain and the West had proceeded
in their dealings with China. These different subjectivities and the competing "truths" about China continue into the twentieth century.

Yet for all the division of opinion among travelers and for all the complaints about China and criticism of its infrastructure, the Victorians were
united in finding much to admire in China and the Chinese. Some element
of the myth of China remained. The two travelers in whom the myth is
felt most strongly, the belief in China as an El Dorado, are Robert Fortune
and Archibald Little. They stayed on or returned again and again because
they found something of value in China beyond the call of business. Evidence lies in their appreciation of Chinese aesthetics, a subject for which
the globetrotters show disdain. Fortune's appreciation lies primarily in the
methods with which the Chinese learned to manipulate nature, Little's
in the harmonizing of art and nature, and both men are attracted to the
philosophical underpinning of Chinese culture. For Fortune, this is sensed
in a practical way in his view of family and social organization. Little has
a deeper, more intellectual grasp of the Confucian ethic which he believes
is in no way inferior to Western ethical systems.

All of the travelers admire the natural beauty of China, whether a hillside of blooming azaleas, picturesque mountains, or the splendor of the
Yangtze gorges. They admire the conquering of nature in China seen in its

canals, terraced fields, and lush agriculture and are in awe of the laborer, his strength, indefatigability, and cheerfulness. They applaud "democratic China" with its classless mingling of all types of people, its uniform customs and modest clothing. Of its ancient gifts to the West—gunpowder, paper, silk, porcelain, and tea, all improved by Western technology—travelers after Robert Fortune, in the way that students forget the role of the teacher in their education, have little to say.

Notes

Introduction: Opening China

1. Dec. 3, 1842, 469.

2. For the historical background on China, I am indebted to John K. Fairbank, *China: A New History* (Cambridge, Mass.: Belknap Press, 1994); John K. Fairbank, Edwin O. Reischauer, and Albert M. Craig, *East Asia: Tradition and Transformation,* rev. ed. (Boston: Houghton Mifflin, 1989); Immanuel C. Y. Hsü, *The Rise of Modern China,* 4th ed. (New York: Oxford University Press, 1990); Alain Peyrefitte, *The Immobile Empire,* trans. Jon Rothschild (New York: Knopf, 1992); Jonathan D. Spence, *The Search for Modern China* (New York: Norton, 1990); and Bodo Wiethoff, *Introduction to Chinese History* (London: Thames & Hudson, 1975).

3. Peyrefitte, *Immobile Empire,* 402.

4. China's examination system based on the teachings of Confucius was abolished in 1905.

5. The Vikings may have acquired Chinese coins through their trade in Constantinople; no one has ever suggested that the Vikings sailed the China Sea.

6. As a continuation of such resistance, Henry Pu Yi, China's last emperor, explains his naïveté about basic geographical knowledge in his propagandistic autobiography *The Last Manchu,* ed. Paul Kramer, trans. Kuo Ying Paul Tsai (New York: Pocket Books, 1987). Whether this self-criticism reflects the sensibilities he acquired in years of Communist "re-education" is unclear.

7. Sander Gilman argues that the idea of Chinese imperviousness to Westernization, and consequently an authentically *Chinese* civilization, is a mirage, since they accepted or modified many Western scientific, medical, and aesthetic practices; "Lam Qua and the Development of a Westernized Medical Iconography," *Medical History* 30 (1986): 57–69.

8. These signs of decline in the Manchu dynasty are explored in Hsü, *Rise of Modern China,* 122–27.

9. The image of China in the West has been the subject of a number of studies,

including those of Mary Gertrude Mason, *Western Concepts of China and the Chinese, 1840–1876* (New York: Seeman Printery, 1939); Harold R. Isaacs, *Scratches on Our Minds: American Images of China and India* (New York: John Day, 1958); Raymond Dawson, *The Chinese Chameleon: An Analysis of European Conceptions of Chinese Civilizations* (London: Oxford University Press, 1967); Jerome Ch'en, *China and the West: Society and Culture 1815–1937* (Bloomington: Indiana University Press, 1979); and Colin Mackerras, *Western Images of China* (Hong Kong: Oxford University Press, 1989). Ranging over all of Europe in a multitude of disciplines, Mason's work is breathtaking in scope.

10. The remark appears in Gulliver's description of English life in his sojourn among the Houyhnhnms in *Gulliver's Travels,* pt. 4, ch. 6.

11. Charles Lamb's essay dates from 1823. A declining image of China in English literature starting with Defoe and Dr. Johnson is traced by Zhang Longxi in "The Myth of the Other: China in the Eyes of the West," *Critical Inquiry* 15 (autumn 1988): 121–23.

12. See my article "China in Dickens," *Dickens Quarterly* 8 (Sept. 1991): 99–111.

13. John Stuart Mill, *On Liberty,* ed. David Spitz (New York: Norton, 1975), 67.

14. The changing image of China in British literary expressions over the course of a century and a half can also be traced in its chinoiserie as graceful Chinese Chippendale eventually gave way to vulgar curios; for the changing taste in chinoiserie, from the decor of the music room at the Brighton Pavilion to a Chinese dairy for the fifth duke of Bedford at Woburn, see Hugh Honour, *Chinoiserie: The Vision of Cathay* (London: John Murray, 1961), 198–204, and Patrick Conner, *The China Trade 1600–1800* (Brighton: Royal Pavilion, Art Gallery & Museums, 1986), 62–64.

15. Bai Shouyi, ed., *An Outline History of China* (Beijing: Foreign Languages Press, 1982), 424. A concise summary of the extent and cost of the China trade to the British is found in Hsü, *Rise of Modern China,* 148–50. The fuller story is in Michael Greenberg, *British Trade and the Opening of China 1800–1842* (Cambridge: Cambridge University Press, 1951).

16. Spence summarizes these global economic effects in *Search for Modern China,* 20.

17. The following summary of the Canton System of Trade owes to Hsü, *Rise of Modern China,* 139–55; and Spence, *Search for Modern China,* 120–22. The mechanism of the China trade is described by Carl L. Crossman, *The Decorative Arts of the China Trade* (Woodbridge, Suffolk: Antique Collectors Club, 1991), 16–18.

18. Contemporary views of the Macartney embassy include that of John Barrow, the comptroller on the mission; and the journal of Macartney's twelve-year-old page, Thomas Staunton, who learned Chinese during the voyage and became invaluable as an unofficial interpreter. Macartney's expedition has been exhaustively recounted with the benefit of Chinese sources by Peyrefitte, *Immobile Empire;* s.a.

Hsü, *Rise of Modern China,* 155–63. It may be added that attempts by European nations to establish diplomatic relations with China also failed.

19. Greenberg, *British Trade and the Opening of China,* 105; emphasis in original.

20. Fairbank, Reischauer, and Craig cite this data in *East Asia,* at 450 and 582. After 1879, opium imports from India declined due to domestic production. Hsü provides further details on the economics of opium use on both the individual and national levels (*Rise of Modern China,* 168–73).

21. The causes of opium addiction in China are discussed in Fairbank, Reischauer, and Craig, *East Asia,* 450; Hsü, *Rise of Modern China,* 168–69; and Spence, *Search for Modern China,* 129.

22. C. Toogood Downing, *"Fan-Qui" in China, 1836–37,* 3 vols. (1838; reprint, Shannon: Irish University Press, n.d.), 3:171.

23. Sunqua was one of the most important painters involved in the Western trade, according to Crossman, *Decorative Arts,* 406 ff. Sunqua's specialties were ships, port views, and landscapes. A number of his paintings are held by the Peabody Museum.

24. New York: New York University Press, 1977, bk. 4, ch. 3. Michael Cotsell, "Carlyle, Travel, and the Enlargements of History," in *Creditable Warriors,* ed. Michael Cotsell (London: Ashfield Press, 1990) reminds us of an earlier passage in *Past and Present* (bk. 3, ch. 15) that gives a "relaxed account of the lucid reasonableness" of the Chinese (95). As Emerson says, "consistency is the hobgoblin of little minds."

25. Alexander's pictures were the one success of Macartney's mission and gave the English some of their first realistic images of Chinese people, places, crafts, and cultural practices. A modern reprint of these pictures can be found in William Alexander and George Henry Mason, *Views of 18th Century China Costumes* (1800; reprint, London: Studio Editions, 1988).

26. 9 July 1842, 131.

27. *Illustrated London News,* 6 Aug. 1842, 196.

28. *Illustrated London News,* 12 Nov. 1842, 420.

29. *Times* (London), 21 Nov. 1842, 5a.

30. For contemporary treatment of this treaty, see the *Times* (London, 1842), 21 Nov. 5a; 23 Nov., 4d; 26 Nov., 5e; 1 Dec., 5e; and 17 Dec., 5c.

31. Britain and the United States relinquished their "extra-territorial rights" in China in 1942.

32. In recognition of its effective status, in the following chapters I occasionally refer to the whole of China as a colonial nation, though of course only Hong Kong was formally a colony.

33. This account of the provisions of the treaties of 1858–60 follows that of Hsü, *Rise of Modern China,* 108–215, and Spence, *Search for Modern China,* 180–81.

34. Downing, *"Fan-Qui" in China, 1836–37,* 3:194.

35. *Illustrated London News,* 4 June 1842, 56.

36. Gutzlaff's indirect inspiration for the Taipings is noted by Jonathan D. Spence, *God's Chinese Son: The Taiping Heavenly Kingdom of Hong Xiuquan,* (New York: Norton, 1996), 177.

37. The work and writings of missionaries has been treated in numerous studies. Among these studies are the census-like work of Kenneth Scott Latourette, *History of Chinese Missions* (1929; reprint, New York: Russell & Russell, 1967), which is extremely useful for understanding the scope and depth of mission work in China. Pat Barr, *To China with Love: The Lives and Times of Protestant Missionaries in China 1860–1900* (London: Secker & Warburg, 1972) is an appealing narrative of British missions; Nigel Cameron, *Barbarians and Mandarins: Thirteen Centuries of Travellers in China* (New York: Walker/Weatherhill, 1970) provides somewhat acerbic sketches of several missionaries; Kathleen L. Lodwick, *Crusaders against Opium: Protestant Missionaries in China, 1874–1917* (Lexington: University Press of Kentucky, 1996) focuses on a specific cause missionaries pursued. The impact of Christianity on China is the subject of Paul A. Cohen's *China and Christianity* (Cambridge: Harvard University Press, 1963) and Jacques Gernet's *China and the Christian Impact: A Conflict of Cultures,* trans. Janet Lloyd (Cambridge: Cambridge University Press, 1985).

38. Mrs. Pruen's description of the Miao is found in *The Provinces of Western China* and is retold by Mrs. Little in *In the Land of the Blue Gown* (1902; reprint, London: Everett, 1912), 189–94. The Miao rebelled against Han rule several times over the centuries, and after each loss were driven further south and west.

39. The total foreign population of Shanghai in 1912 was 144,754, including 75,210 Japanese and 45,908 Russians, according to *China, An Official Guide to Eastern Asia* (Tokyo: Imperial Japanese Government Railway, 1915), 4:xxxiii.

40. I refer to Isabella Bird throughout by her maiden name, by which she is most well known. She was unmarried when she made her first brief visit to China in 1878. When she returned in 1895, she was a widow, publishing her China book as Mrs. Bishop.

41. My approach is influenced by Patrick Brantlinger's work on colonial literature in *Rule of Darkness: British Literature and Imperialism, 1830–1914* (Ithaca: Cornell University Press, 1988).

42. Although the subject of Edward Said's *Orientalism* (New York: Vintage, 1979) is the European interpretation of the Middle East, as James Clifford notes, the book "operates in a number of registers," *Predicament of Culture* (Cambridge: Harvard University Press, 1988), 256.

43. Said, *Orientalism,* 20.

44. Victorian travelers felt no compunction in explaining China, but a century later Roland Barthes was nonplused by it; *Alors la Chine?* (Paris: C. Bourgois, 1975). It may be added that Lisa Lowe's deconstruction of Barthes's text as the

refutation of the European hermeneutic is a tour de force; *Critical Terrains: French and British Orientalisms* (Ithaca: Cornell University Press, 1991).

45. The anticolonialist approach has pitfalls, as exemplified by the lurid illustrations in Sander Gilman's "Black Bodies, White Bodies . . ." that have the unfortunate effect of revictimizing the subjects of the original exploiting colonialists; Henry Louis Gates Jr. ed., *"Race," Writing and Difference* (Chicago: University of Chicago Press, 1986), 223–61.

46. "The Myth of the Other: China in the Eyes of the West," 124.

47. Homi Bhabha, "The Other Question . . . ," *Screen* 24 (1983): 21.

48. Satya P. Mohanty, "Colonial Legacies, Multicultural Futures: Relativism, Objectivity, and the Challenge of Otherness," *PMLA* 110 (Jan. 1995): 111.

49. Mary Louise Pratt, "Scratches on the Face of the Country; or What Mr. Barrow Saw in the Land of the Bushmen," *Critical Inquiry* 12 (1985), 159. Pratt expands this discussion of the gaze in *Imperial Eyes* (London: Routledge, 1992), chs. 3–4. Barrow, it should be added, was also part of Lord Macartney's entourage on the 1792 expedition to China.

50. Dennis Porter, *Haunted Journeys: Desire and Transgression in European Travel Writing* (Princeton: Princeton University Press, 1991), 247.

51. Claude Lévi-Strauss, *Tristes Tropiques,* trans. John and Doreen Weightman (1955; reprint, Harmondsworth: Penguin Books, 1992). For some, such as historian Barbara Tuchman, representational authority and genre-crossing in travel writing are problematic, as she explains in the introduction to her travel account, *Notes from China* (New York: Collier Books, 1972): "This is what I vowed I would never do—put ephemeral journalism between the covers of a book." Her account is about a tour of China undertaken after publishing *Stillwell and the American Experience in China, 1911–45* (New York: Macmillan, 1971).

52. Although the travel writer/ethnographer may aim for objectivity, reflexivity remains. Like impossible-to-disguise handwriting, Kirsten Hastrup says in "Writing Ethnography: State of the Art" that "Self and other, subject and object are categories of thought, not discrete entities"; *Anthropology and Autobiography,* ed. Judith Okley and Helen Callaway (London: Routledge, 1992), 117. This theme is also pursued in Clifford, *Predicament of Culture,* 26–31; and Geertz, *Works and Lives* (Stanford, Calif.: Stanford University Press, 1988).

53. See Pratt, "Fieldwork in Common Places," in *Writing Culture: The Poetics and Politics of Ethnography,* ed. James Clifford and George E. Marcus (Berkeley: University of California Press, 1986), 37–38; Renato Rosaldo "From the Door of His Tent: The Fieldworker and the Inquisitor," in *Writing Culture,* ed. James Clifford and George E. Marcus (Berkeley: University of California Press, 1986), 92; Hastrup, "Writing Ethnography" 119; Porter, *Haunted Journeys,* 246–67; Geertz, *Works and Lives,* 73–83.

54. See the entries on Travel and Tourism in Sally Mitchell's *Victorian Britain:*

An Encyclopedia (New York: Garland, 1988) on the emergence of mass tourism in the age of the railroad and steamship.

55. Cumming explains her dilemma in a letter to her publisher Chatto & Windus 29 Oct. 1884; I am indebted to Michael Bott, keeper of archives and manuscripts at the University of Reading, for transcriptions of Cumming's letters.

56. "Mrs. Bishop's Will" appears in the *Times* (London), 15 Dec. 1904, 7c.

57. Lexington: University Press of Kentucky, 1983. In *The Ethnographic Imagination* (London: Routledge, 1990), Paul Atkinson builds on Adams's argument by showing how sociologists use literary and rhetorical forms (i.e., character, irony, etc.) to present their findings.

58. Ali Behdad, *Belated Travelers: Orientalism in the Age of Colonial Dissolution* (Durham, N.C.: Duke University Press, 1994), 75. This is akin to Clifford's idea of allegory, the "stories built into the representational process," in ethnographic writing ("On Ethnographic Allegory," 100).

59. [Elizabeth Eastlake], "Lady Travellers," *Quarterly Review* 76 (June 1845): 99.

60. [W. G. Blaikie], "Lady Travellers," *Blackwood's Magazine* 160 (July 1896): 49–66; Dorothy Middleton, *Victorian Lady Travellers* (1965; reprint, Chicago: Academy, 1982).

61. Dea Birkett, *Spinsters Abroad: Victorian Lady Explorers* (London: Blackwell, 1989); Sara Mills, *Discourses of Difference: An Analysis of Women's Travel Writing and Colonialism* (London: Routledge, 1993); Susan Morgan, *Place Matters: Gendered Geography in Victorian Women's Travel Books about Southeast Asia* (Brunswick, N.J.: Rutgers University Press, 1996); Pratt, *Imperial Eyes.*

62. Paul Fussell, *Abroad: British Traveling between the Wars* (New York: Oxford University Press, 1980); Porter, *Haunted Journeys, 17.*

63. Eric J. Leed, *The Mind of the Traveler* (New York: Basic Books, 1992), 121–29; James Buzard, *The Beaten Track: European Tourism, Literature, and the Ways to 'Culture' 1800–1918* (Oxford: Clarendon Press, 1993), 138–52.

Chapter One
Gathering in China: Robert Fortune

1. The description of the exhibition appears in Wm. B. Langdon, *A Descriptive Catalogue of the Chinese Collection Now Exhibiting at St. George's Place, Hyde Park Corner . . .* 10th ed. (London, 1842), and the *Illustrated London News,* 6 Aug. 1842, 204–5. The popularity of the exhibition is suggested by the note that fifty thousand copies of the catalogue had already been sold. According to Richard D. Altick in *The Shows of London* (Cambridge: Harvard University Press, 1978), the exhibition had been organized by an American entrepreneur, Nathan Dunn, a wealthy tea merchant who had refused to deal in opium. The exhibition had first been shown

in Philadelphia and remained in Hyde Park for several years, but eventually the objects were dispersed and the pagoda itself dismantled (Altick, 292–94).

2. *Illustrated London News,* 3 Dec. 1842, 469.

3. Yedo, or Yeddo, is the former name of Tokyo.

4. The value of rare plants is mentioned in a review of *Three Years' Wanderings* by Gilbert F. Lewis, "Fortune's *China: Gardening,*" in the *Edinburgh Review* 88 (Oct. 1848), 409. Fortune traveled to Manilla, struggled through nearly impenetrable mountain thickets, and endured schools of leeches and leg injuries to match the find of the "Queen of Orchids." He was rewarded with an incredible one-hundred-bloom plant, for which he paid one dollar (TYW 337).

5. See the Lindley Correspondence, 27 May 1846: "I hear the Kew people are giving away great quantities of my Chinese plants. Do you know if they *give them away as their own . . . ?*"

6. Letter from the RHS to RF, 23 Feb 1843; at the end of TYW, he notes that this is probably an embellishment of a variety of peach grown near Shanghai that has an eleven-inch circumference and weighs twelve ounces (404).

7. Pratt, *Imperial Eyes,* 38–39.

8. Fortune finally found a yellow camellia years later in a garden about ten miles from Shanghai: "It is certainly a most curious plant, although not very handsome" (JTC 339).

9. Fortune's horticultural work is well documented. Bretschneider gives the most inclusive list of Fortune's collection of living plants in *History of European Botanical Discoveries* (London: Sampson Low, Marston, 1898), 403–518; and his collecting work is also treated by Alice M. Coats, *The Quest for Plants* (New York: McGraw Hill, 1969); E. H. M. Cox, *Plant Hunting in China* (London: Oldbourne, 1945); Miles Hadfield, *Pioneers in Gardening* (London: Routledge & Kegan Paul, 1955); Charles Lyte, *The Plant Hunters* (London: Orbis, 1983); Dawn Macleod, "A Mystery Solved: New Light on Robert Fortune," *The Garden,* May 1992, 214–17; and Ernest H. Wilson, *China: Mother of Gardens* (1929; reprint, New York: Benjamin Blom, 1971).

10. Letters from RHS to RF, 6 Mar, 1845.

11. The Swedish botanist Linnaeus was the first to identify tea as *camellia sinensis,* later named *Thea sinensis;* William H. Ukers, *All about Tea,* 2 vols. (New York: Tea and Coffee Trade Journal Company, 1935), 1:205–6 and 1:223. It is generally agreed that there is but one genus of the tea plant and that it originated in India and southern China (Ukers, 1:5–6 and 1:497–98).

12. Ukers, *All about Tea* recapitulates the history of the tea monopoly (1:67–85). This is an astonishingly thorough resource on all aspects of tea. It includes "A Chronology of Tea" starting in 2737 B.C. and a bibliography with more than thirteen hundred titles. Samuel Ball, *An Account of the Cultivation and Manufacture of*

Tea in China (London: Longman, Brown, Green, & Longmans, 1848) is authoritative if less inclusive than Ukers; Alexander Michie, *The Englishman in China during the Victorian Era,* 2 vols. (Edinburgh: Blackwood, 1900) is helpful as a contemporary resource on the economics of tea importation and tea plantations in India: the "supplanting of Chinese by Indian tea [is] . . . an interesting example of the encroachment of Western enterprise on the ancient province of Eastern habits" (1:184).

13. John Keay, *The Honourable Company: A History of the English East India Company* (New York: Macmillan, 1991), 551.

14. Fortune says in a footnote that he learned of Medhurst's journey "since this was written" (JTC 20).

15. The Bohea mountains help form the border of Fokien, Chekiang, and Kiangsi Provinces. The famous mountain Woo-e-shan (Wuyi Shan), which Fortune visited, is near this area.

16. Michie, *Englishman in China,* 1:131.

17. [Dominick Murphy], review of *Three Years' Wanderings in China*, *Dublin Review* 23 (Sept. 1847): 71. In his second book, Fortune corrects his mistake about indigo being used to dye tea; the substance used was Prussian blue (JTC 95).

18. The Japanese developed a tea export trade that, like the Chinese, peaked in the 1870s and 1880s, then declined due to the competition with tea from India and Ceylon. The main market for Japanese green tea was the United States; William G. Beasley, *The Rise of Modern Japan* (New York: St. Martin's, 1990), 113; Ukers, *All about Tea,* 2:211–29.

19. Michie, *Englishman in China,* 1:185; Wilson, *China: Mother of Gardens,* 376.

20. William Gardener, "Robert Fortune and the Cultivation of Tea in the United States," *Arnoldia* 31 (1971): 1–18, explains the role of the U.S. Patent Office and Fortune's hopes for establishing an American tea plantation.

21. Letters to Joseph Holt, 19 Feb. 1859; *Letters, Reports, Essays;* Agric. Dept., U.S. Patent Office, vols. 20–21 (1858–60); U.S. National Archives.

22. Letters to Joseph Holt, 24 May 1859; vols. 20–21 (1858–60); U.S. National Archives.

23. 1 Aug. 1858; vols. 20–21 (1858–60); U.S. National Archives.

24. Gardener, "Robert Fortune and Cultivation," 13; Letter to W. D. Bishop, 5 Aug. 1859; U.S. National Archives.

25. Although the U.S. made no attempt to develop tea plantations, it attempted to mollify Fortune by telling him tea trees were being cultivated in home gardens. Tea bushes were raised in half a dozen southern states, but interest in tea plantations in the United States was never rekindled after the Civil War (Ukers, *All about Tea,* 1:213).

26. Before the Suez Canal opened, there were two routes to the Orient from England. One was around the Cape of Good Hope, which Fortune seems to have taken for each of his journeys. The other route was to sail to Egypt, travel over-

land to Suez, and then sail through the Red Sea. After calling in at Aden, the journey continued to points east. Cumming took this route twice, once to Fiji. During that journey, she saw no land for six weeks. Because of the monsoons, sailing during the summer and early autumn was avoided.

27. The unwritten story of his wife Jane Penney and their six children may explain Fortune's reticence about his personal life in his books. Recently, Dawn Macleod found a great-granddaughter of the Fortunes from whom she obtained long-buried family information and an 1866 family photograph with the two youngest children, Thomas and Alice. Macleod also clears up the confusion about Fortune's date of birth, 1812, as owing to his own desire to veil the fact that his parents were married less than three months before his birth; "A Mystery Solved," 214–17.

28. As Fortune's discourse slides from scientific cataloguing and Latin nomenclature into novelistic techniques of the picturesque, he is naturalized into the Chinese setting, illustrating David Spurr's point about the "mobility" of the definition of naturalization; *The Rhetoric of Empire* (Durham, N.C.: Duke University Press, 1994), 168.

29. [Lewis], "Fortune's *China,*" 418.

30. [William Orr], "Fortune's Wanderings in China," review of *Three Years' Wanderings, Chamber's Edinburgh Journal* 7 (1847): 299.

31. Coats, *Quest for Plants,* 110; Hadfield, *Pioneers in Gardening,* 135; Lyte, *Plant Hunters,* 69; Cox, *Plant Hunting in China,* 92.

32. *Pictures from Italy,* The New Oxford Illustrated Dickens (London: Oxford University Press, 1957), 301, 322.

33. Charles Dickens, *Bleak House,* eds. George Ford and Sylvere Monod (New York: Norton, 1977), 137; the overcrowded cemetery Dickens had in mind was attached to St. Martin's-in-the-Fields (*Bleak House* 901).

34. Such a transformation in the traveler-collector is explained by Stephen Bann in "Travelling to Collect" as a result of the "oscillation of the subjective states that he imposes on the world, and the world imposes on him"; *Travellers' Tales,* ed. George Robertson, et al. (London: Routledge, 1994), 160.

35. Crossman, *Decorative Arts of the China Trade,* 19; by 1860, English and Continental factories were producing high-quality porcelain designed for Western taste, and by 1876 the China trade was virtually over; see also introduction, n. 14, on chinoiserie.

36. The display of genuine Chinese porcelains and bronzes next to Victorian-era counterfeits in the Victoria and Albert Museum puts Fortune's artifact collecting into perspective, although most counterfeits were produced after Fortune's years in China. The first counterfeit T'ang ceramics were produced in China in 1912, according to Honour, *Chinoiserie,* 223.

37. See "Robert Fortune: The Collector," *Gardener's Chronicle* 155 (11 Jan 1964)

for details on Fortune's earnings (34–35). Gardener writes that Fortune's commission was a pound per hundred for plant stock propagated from his collections; other plants were auctioned at Covent Garden. Fortune frequently makes an issue of money with his employers. His correspondence held at the RHS shows that his salary from 1843 to 1846 was £100 a year, plus expenses of £500 a year. The East India Company paid £500 a year beyond expenses and the United States paid £300 salary with £800 credit for expenses.

38. The Spanish dollar, a large silver coin, was the foreign-exchange currency in China during Fortune's time. His expense account for 1845 suggests a parity between the Spanish dollar and the pound; however, in 1857 he says $60 is approximately the equivalent of £20 (RaC 297).

39. Yi-fu Tuan, *Topophilia* (Englewood-Cliffs: Prentice Hall, 1974), 4.

40. I use the translation of the *Tao Te Ching* by D. C. Lau (London: Penguin Books, 1976).

41. This is not to say that Fortune is alone in espousing such views. One of his friends in China was a fellow Scotsman, John Scarth, whose *Twelve Years in China* (1860; reprint, Wilmington: Scholarly Resources, 1972) expounds sympathetically on Chinese education and philosophy. Scarth ridicules gunboat diplomacy. He resided in China from 1847 to 1859 and wrote three books about China. He also provided a number of illustrations for Fortune's third book.

42. Zhang Longxi, "The Myth of the Other: China in the Eyes of the West," *Critical Inquiry* 15 (autumn 1988): 131.

43. The most comprehensive account of the Taiping Rebellion is that of Franz Michael and Chung-li Chang, *The Taiping Rebellion: History and Documents,* 3 vols. (Seattle: University of Washington Press, 1966, 1971). More recently, Jonathan D. Spence, *God's Chinese Son,* gives a compelling account of this episode in Chinese history. A Maoist interpretation of the Taiping Rebellion is developed in *An Outline History of China,* Shouyi, ed., 436–42; Bai extends the period of conflict, saying it began in 1844 and was not ended until 1868.

44. Coats, *Quest for Plants,* expresses confusion about Fortune's final journey: "we do not even know whether he went straight from China to Japan in 1860 or went home in the interval" (110). Fortune's correspondence with the U.S. Department of Patents indicates he made a separate trip to China in 1858–59 and returned to London by September 1859. Also, an obituary cites an anecdote after his return from his American-sponsored journey that indicates he made two separate journeys to the East between 1858 and 1860: "'Well Fortune, surely home for good now!' 'No,' said the traveller, 'I have just learned the Japanese ports are open to Europeans, and I go there on Thursday,'" *Trans. Botanical Society Edinburgh* 45 (Nov. 1880): 162.

45. Gordon's account of the looting and the "Looty" detail are cited from

Cameron, *Barbarians and Mandarins*, 352–53. Nothing but broken stones and pillars remain, and the original drawings of the palaces and gardens are housed in France.

46. *At Home in Fiji* (Edinburgh: Blackwood, 1881); Rudyard Kipling, *Kim* (Garden City, N.Y.: Doubleday, Doran, 1931), 80.

47. The instruments remain in place today on the East corner of the old city wall in Beijing. Constance Cumming found the Chinese instruments the more interesting in her 1878 visit. Father Ricci had earlier admired the superior craftsmanship of the Song dynasty instruments, but the Chinese had lost the knowledge of how to use them. Verbiest's instruments combined European and Chinese design. Western knowledge of early Chinese scientific achievements is indebted to the work of Joseph Needham, *Science and Civilization in China,* 4 vols. (Cambridge: Cambridge University Press, 1954–62); for Verbiest's work on the observatory, see Needham, IV. 436–39.

48. Fortune died in 1880, aged seventy-eight.

Chapter Two
Westward the Course of Empire: Archibald John Little

1. "Westward the course of empire takes its way" is from Bishop George Berkeley, "On the Prospect of Planting Arts and Learning in America."

2. Matthew Arnold, *Culture and Anarchy* in *The Portable Matthew Arnold,* edited by Lionel Trilling (New York: Viking Press, 1949), 538; such negative images have led Martin Weiner, in *English Culture and the Decline of the Industrial Spirit 1850–1980* (Cambridge: Cambridge University Press, 1988), to argue that at midcentury British culture started turning against the industrial spirit and toward the gentrification of the industrialist. Positive portraits of men engaged in business are typically confined to minor characters such as Dickens's characters Pancks in *Little Dorrit* and Silas Wegg in *Our Mutual Friend.*

3. Dilke believes the merchants' response to the murder of the missionaries "injudicious" and exaggerated, but to prove he is not a "thick and thin apologist for the Chinese," he assails them on what today are termed human-rights abuses; Sir Charles Wentworth Dilke, *Greater Britain* (London: Macmillan, 1894), 592, 600. A rather strong picture of worst-case traders in colonial Zaire that makes Anglo-Chinese merchants models of restraint by comparison appears in Adam Hochshild, "Mr Kurtz, I Presume," *New Yorker* 14 (Apr. 1997): 40–47.

4. Mrs. Archibald Little, *Intimate China* (London: Hutchinson, 1899), 10; Mrs. Little says that during the tea-tasting season, "we talked tea at breakfast and tiffin and dinner, and we took it at five and considered its quality. But that would not make the people at home give up Indian tea, with all its tannin and nerve-poisoning

qualities" (10); the peak year of China's tea trade was 1888, when three hundred million pounds of tea were exported (Ukers, *All about Tea,* 2:99). A nostalgic account of the old tea trade that supports Mrs. Little is Jason Goodwin's *A Time for Tea* (New York: Knopf, 1991), a modern travel book using the tea trade as its premise. Tea tasting, Goodwin notes, is "a minor legacy of the British Empire" (206).

5. Mrs. Little published this collection of her husband's writings, as well as edited his *Across Yunnan,* after his death.

6. Biographical details about Little (1838–1908) are in the foreword by R. S. Gundry and the editorial note by Mrs. Little, both in *Gleanings from Fifty Years in China* (v–x and xi–xiv); see also Archibald Little's obituary in the *Times,* 6 Nov. 1908, 15c.

7. *Through the Yang-Tse Gorges or Trade and Travel in Western China* (London: Sampson Low, Marston, Searle, & Rivington, 1888); Little's *Mount Omi and Beyond* (London: Heinemann, 1901) chronicles journeys Little and his wife undertook in western Szechuan in 1892 and 1897. This book includes descriptions of scenery and cultural artifacts and travel details, but lacks the enthusiasm and textual layers of his first book. His book *The Far East* (Oxford: Clarendon Press, 1905), part of a "Regions of the World" series, is a reference book.

8. Blakiston was the first Englishman to go up the Yangtze beyond Hankow. Baber, whose expertise in the Chinese language made him quite indispensable, was a consular official at the British legation in Peking. He charted 840 miles of the river, ending at Pingshan, in March and June 1861. Hosie, another British consul, wrote *Three Years in Western China* (London: G. Philip, 1890) as well as official reports on the status of the opium trade.

9. The German Baron Ferdinand von Ricthofen, who traveled in China in 1872, contributed the most thorough of European surveys of western China during that era. Rev. Virgil Hart's *Western China* (Boston: Ticknor, 1888) covers much the same material as his English compatriots but highlights Buddhism and the religious monuments on Mount Omi rather than geography.

10. This is not to minimize the steamy summer heat of places such as the "three furnaces," the cities forming modern Wuhan. Mrs. Little ironizes the inconsistent and sometimes irrational reaction to the summer sun in her comments on Englishwomen's beachwear (it included corsets and gloves) at a seaside resort in China in *Land of the Blue Gown* (1902; reprint, London: Everett, 1912).

11. Tim Wright attributes the late development of China's coal industry to the lack of technology, political debilitation of the Chinese state, and Western imperialism; *Coal Mining in China's Economy and Society 1895–1937* (London: Cambridge University Press, 1984), 3–5.

12. He also translated a legend, "The Rat's Plaint," and a farce, "Borrowing Boots," which may be found in *Gleanings from Fifty Years in China.*

13. Among the hundreds of contemporary articles and books on both sides of the opium-trade debate, one of the wilder ones is Arthur Y. Davenport, *China from Within: A Study of the Opium Fallacies and Missionary Mistakes* (London: T. F. Unwin, 1904). Also, as Britain was gradually reducing its opium sale to China in 1909, the British consul Alexander Hosie optimistically predicted that opium production and use would soon end; *Despatch . . . Respecting the Opium Question* (London: Harrison, 1909); for later assessments of opium-reform policies, see Meribeth E. Cameron, *The Reform Movement in China 1898–1912* (Stanford, Calif.: Stanford University Press, 1931), 136–59; Lodwick, *Crusaders against Opium,* 148–80; and Spence, *Search for Modern China*, 257.

14. Little's optimistic view of civil strife wore thin as attacks against foreigners in the 1890s escalated; the Littles lost all their "worldly goods in China" in a riot (IC 533).

15. On Frederick Ward, see Caleb Carr, *The Devil Soldier* (New York: Random House, 1991); on Gordon and the Ever-Victorious Army, see Spence, *God's Chinese Son*, 328–31; the sentimental hero of the Victorian age for his valor at Khartoum, Gordon's rather strange military career and personal life are recounted by the Bloomsbury historian Lytton Strachey in *Eminent Victorians* (New York: Modern Library); Kathryn Tidrick, *Empire and the English Character* (London: Tauris, 1992), mentions Gordon's unusual habit of never carrying a weapon into battle (39–41).

16. The missionaries' case against merchants is discussed in chapters 3 and 4.

17. Little's enthusiasm for the beauties of Chungking might have puzzled those who went there with Chiang Kai-shek when he moved his wartime capital to what Sterling Seagrave says was then a "shabby Yangtze river town"; *The Soong Dynasty* (New York: Harper & Row, 1985), 363. Today it is an industrial center, and thanks to an ambitious local administration that annexed the entire county, the world's largest city.

18. Due to opposition from other countries over some of the treaty provisions, the British Parliament did not ratify the convention until 1885. In *Opium and the People,* Berridge and Edwards throw light on the complicated negotiations over import duties on opium contained in the treaty (182–83).

19. After the Suez Canal opened in 1869, sailing time to China was cut to twenty-one days (seventeen to India). Hannah Davies, a missionary, kept a detailed account of a journey that began in London, 13 Oct. 1893, stopped in India, arrived at Hong Kong 19 November, and ended in Szechuan 8 December. Her unaffected diary, part of *Among Hills and Valleys in Western China* (London: S. W. Partridge, 1901), captures the wonder, homesickness, and religious zeal that prompted so many to make the same journey.

20. A similar account of boat hauling appears in the eighth-century diary kept by the Japanese monk Ennin, translated by Edwin O. Reischauer (New York:

Ronald Press, 1955). I am indebted to Dennis Marshall for calling this to my attention.

21. Not all Victorians agreed with the view of British merchants; as mentioned earlier, in *Greater Britain* Dilke writes scathingly of those who think the Chinese should "revolutionize in our favour" (594).

22. E. V. G. Kiernan, *British Diplomacy in China 1880 to 1885* (1939; reprint, New York: Octagon Books, 1970), 267.

23. Henry Knollys (chapter 4) also writes about the Woosung railroad. He was acquainted with the British engineer who built it, which may explain his hystrionics about the "bigoted conservatism" of the Chinese who destroyed it; *English Life in China* (London: Smith, Elder, 1885), 129, 198.

24. Kiernan, *British Diplomacy in China 1880 to 1885,* 24.

25. On the Tsungli Yamen, see Spence, *Search for Modern China,* 199–204, and Hsü, *Rise of Modern China,* 268–69; on the chastisement of Prince Kung, see Hsü, 306–10.

26. Pioneering seems to have been frequently recognized in China: Rudyard Kipling, in *From Sea To Sea,* 2 vols. (New York: Doubleday, Page & Co. 1925), 2:265, says he toured the Hong Kong harbor during his brief visit there in 1897 in the *Pioneer*.

27. Mrs. Little sat out the time in London writing a biography of Li Hung-chang. Mr. Little, who appears in a photograph with the "Fortification Staff at the British Legation, Peking, 1900," calls the Boxer uprising "lamentable" and casts many a stone at missionaries for bringing on the violence (GFY 289–307); for a thorough, documented account using both English and Chinese sources, see Joseph W. Esherick, *The Origins of the Boxer Uprising* (Berkeley: University of California Press, 1987).

28. According to Fairbank in *The Great Chinese Revolution* (New York: Harper & Row, 1987), there is some evidence that refutes the stagnation image of China, such as port activity in Shanghai in the early nineteenth century, that lends evidence to a view of a dynamic China (48–49); see also the treatment of this subject in the introduction.

29. R. K. Webb, *Modern England* (New York, Toronto: Dodd, Mead, 1972), 444.

30. By "gentry" Little means "landlords," men of wealth and property; by "literati" he means "intellectuals," the educated men of leisure. "Mandarins" belonged to the highest rank of civil officials and government and military officers, all of whom attained their posts through the rigid examination system; see the helpful entry on mandarins in Dyer J. Ball, *Things Chinese Or, Notes Connected with China,* 5th edition, revised by E. Chalmers Werner (London: John Murray, 1926). Although mandarins are often villainized by Westerners, Little sympathizes

with those who are blamed for a drought and the subsequent failure of winter crops (TYG 154).

31. Little is also frustrated with the pace of change in Britain; he insists that it urgently needs to adopt the metric system in order to compete in world markets (GFY 45–49). It hardly need mentioning that the United States still resists such a change. For her part, Mrs. Little urges manufacturers to date tinned goods, an idea that took nearly a century for the United States to embrace.

32. Mrs. Little's account of the transition to Chinese dress appears in *My Diary in a Chinese Farm* (Shanghai, Tokyo: Kelly & Walsh, 1898). The Littles' life and travel in China is discussed more fully in chapter 6.

33. Pratt, *Imperial Eyes,* 204–5.

34. Some might argue that Little's claims are in the spirit of what Spurr has called colonialism's need to "reaffirm its value in the face of nothingness"; *Rhetoric of Empire,* 109; however, Little would probably be heartened by Pascal Bruckner's case against "Third Worldism," which argues that both the "anti-European Inquisition and aggressive Eurocentrism" must be examined with skepticism; *The Tears of the White Man: Compassion as Contempt,* translated by William R. Beer (New York: Free Press; London: Collier Macmillan, 1986), 149.

35. In the twentieth century, a railway system was constructed rapidly in China. One result was that an overland journey from Europe became relatively fast and economical. By 1915, the railway journey from London via Paris and Berlin to Shanghai took about fourteen days and cost £60 first class, £40 second class; *China: An Official Guide to Eastern Asia* (Tokyo: Imperial Japanese Government Railway, 1915), 4:xxiii.

Chapter Three
An Unbiased Stranger: Constance Gordon Cumming

1. After her six months in China, she would tour the Hawaiian Islands and visit the eastern United States before returning to Britain in 1880.

2. Constance Gordon Cumming, *Wanderings in China,* cheaper ed. (Edinburgh: Blackwood, 1900), 243.

3. [W. G. Blaikie], "Lady Travellers," *Blackwood's Magazine* 160 (July 1896): 63. Cumming's contemporary popularity is also attested to by her inclusion in W. H. D. Adams, *Celebrated Women Travelers of the Nineteenth Century* (London: W. Swan Sonnenschein, 1883); F. Hays, *Women of the Day* (London: Chatto & Windus, 1885); A. T. C. Pratt, *People of the Period,* 2 vols. (London: N. Beeman, 1897); and Victor G. Plarr, *Men and Women of the Time,* 15th ed. (London: G. Routledge, 1899).

4. Birkett, *Spinsters Abroad*; Maria H. Frawley, *A Wider Range: Travel Writing by Women in Victorian England* (London: Associated University Presses, 1994); Billie

Melman, *Women's Orients: English Women and the Middle East, 1818–1918* (Ann Arbor: University of Michigan Press, 1995). Cumming is conspicuous by her absence from Mignon Rittenhouse, *Seven Women Explorers,* (Philadelphia: J. B. Lippincott, 1964); Luree Miller, *On Top of the World: Five Women Explorers in Tibet* (New York: Paddington Press, 1976); Marion Tinling, *Women into the Unknown* (New York: Greenwood Press, 1989); Shirley Foster, *Across New Worlds* (New York: Harvester Wheatsheaf, 1990); Mills, *Discourses of Difference*; Middleton, *Victorian Lady Travellers,* dismisses Cumming with the complaint that her books are "almost unreadable, so informative are they" (5).

5. Cumming is related to the type of woman traveler described by Lady Eastlake in 1845: "well-read, solid thinking,—early rising—sketch-loving"; "Lady Travellers," *Quarterly Review* 76 (June 1845): 102.

6. Kirsten Hastrup, "Writing Ethnography: State of the Art," in *Anthropology and Autobiography,* ed. Judith Okley and Helen Callaway (London: Routledge, 1992), 119; Clifford writes in "On Ethnographic Allegory" that in spite of "ethnography's narrative of specific differences," self-revelation is inherent in the text; *Writing Culture: The Poetics and Politics of Ethnography,* ed. James Clifford and George E. Marcus (Berkeley: University of California Press, 1986), 101.

7. The short stories in *Yellow and White* (Boston: Roberts; London: John Lane, 1895) set in Hong Kong and Macao are preoccupied with decadence and violence; a survey of several images of Hong Kong depicted in late Victorian and early-twentieth-century fiction has been done by C. Mary Turnbull, "Hong Kong: Fragrant Harbour, City of Sin and Death," *Asia in Western Fiction,* ed. Robin W. Winks and James R. Rush (Honolulu: University of Hawaii Press, 1990), 117–36.

8. Catherine Barnes Stevenson, *Victorian Travel Writers in Africa* (Boston: Twayne, 1982), 5.

9. Birkett, *Spinsters Abroad,* discusses women travelers' tendency to contrast themselves with European residents in distant lands (85–97).

10. Constance Gordon Cumming, *In the Himalayas and on the Indian Plains,* new ed. (London: Chatto & Windus, 1886), 238.

11. Cumming's lazy streak is in evidence frequently in her travel. While touring in the Himalayas years earlier, she insisted on being carried though the other woman in the party, like the men, walked. Cumming's bearers finally absconded and she was forced to return on foot.

12. Cumming had toured the Hebrides with her younger brother in 1868, then visited a sister in India in 1870–71 and friends in Ceylon in 1872–74. Bird copied Cumming's tour of the Hebrides in 1871 and in 1879 went to Ceylon inspired, she said, by Cumming's paintings of it.

13. Quoted from Anna Stoddart, *The Life of Isabella Bird* (London: John Murray, 1906), 105.

14. Fussell, *Abroad*, 47–50; Buzard, *Beaten Track,* 4–7; the analysis of the touristic impulse by Dean MacCannell, *The Tourist: A New Theory of the Leisure Class* (New York: Schocken Books, 1976) provides an important underpinning to these works and my own study of travelers.

15. Excepting her volumes on the Hebrides and India, Cumming published her travel accounts only after completing her years of travel in 1880.

16. Cumming died in 1924. After her years of travel she settled in Crieff, Scotland.

17. Blaikie, 62; [Robert K. Douglas], review of *Wanderings in China, The Academy* 721 (27 Feb. 1886): 141.

18. Jonathan Culler, *Framing the Sign: Criticism and Its Institutions* (Norman: University of Oklahoma Press, 1988), 155.

19. If Cumming's opinion differs from Fortune on aesthetics, she appears to owe him a debt in other ways, for she seems to have cribbed material on tea, azaleas, and silkworms from his *Three Years' Wanderings.*

20. Nancy C. Lutkehaus, "Margaret Mead and the 'Rustling-of-the-Wind-in-the-Palm-Trees School' of Ethnographic Writing," in *Women Writing Culture,* ed. Ruth Behar and Deborah A. Gordon (Berkeley: University of California Press, 1995), 190. Comparing Cumming to Mead is not whimsical, for some of Cumming's observations about Samoa anticipate Mead, as does Cumming's tendency to use her observation for didactic application to home culture, as Mead does in her recommendations about education. Cumming may be seen in the tradition of other women ethnographers as well: Cole shows how Ruth Landes was dismissed as writing "unscientific travelogue and a personal memoir," in "Ruth Landes and the Early Ethnography of Race and Gender" in Behar and Gordon, *Women Writing Culture,* 168; Florinda Donner's *Shabono* and Marjorie Shostak's *Nise: The Life and Words of a !Kung Woman* have faced similar criticism.

21. Lévi-Strauss mocks such an impulse as misguided nostalgia: "So I can understand the mad passion for travel books and their deceptiveness. They create the illusion of something which no longer exists but still should exist"; *Tristes Tropiques,* 38.

22. Edinburgh: Blackwood, 1882.

23. *The Private Life of Victorian Women: Autobiography in Nineteenth-Century England* (New York: Harvester Wheatsheaf, 1989), 15.

24. Spence mentions these pioneering Chinese women doctors in *Search for Modern China*, 209–10.

25. *Discourses of Difference,* 96.

26. Cumming's reaction to Shanghai confirmed that of Cook's Round-the-World tour in 1872. The tour may be said to have "officially" opened China as a tourist destination, though as a result of miscalculations, the tour missed Canton

and allowed only a glance at Hong Kong. Further details on the China portion of Cook's tour are in Piers Brandon, *Thomas Cook* (London: Secker & Warburg, 1991), 144–46, and Edmund Swinglehurst, *Cook's Tours* (Poole, Dorset: Blandford Press, 1982), 68.

27. Ithaca: Cornell University Press, 1986; the chapter on "The City: The Sewer, the Gaze, and the Contaminating Touch" centers on bourgeois "scopophilia" and fear of the lumpen proletariat.

28. Anne McClintock's analysis of how soap became entwined with race and the imperial trade mission also explores this paradigm; *Imperial Leather* (New York: Routledge, 1994), 207–31.

29. Edgar Snow, *Red Star over China* (1938; revised and enlarged, New York: Grove, 1973); Stephen Spender and David Hockney, *China Diary* (New York: Harry N. Abrams, 1982) alter the pattern when they compare Xi'an to a 1930s provincial French town.

30. Cumming says nine out of ten are smokers; the missionary Virgil Hart in *Western China* estimated a million addicts in 1879; in *Despatch from His Majesty's Minister in China . . . Respecting the Opium Question in China* (London: Harrison & Sons, 1909), the British consul Alexander Hosie put the level at 6.64 percent of adults in 1906; more dispassionate observers typically estimated 40 percent of all Chinese and 80 percent of Szechuanese were habitual opium smokers at the end of the century; see Lodwick, *Crusaders against Opium*, 139, 18.

31. The famous illustrator of Dante's *Inferno,* Doré, with Blanchard Jerrold, also produced *London, A Pilgrimage* in 1872.

32. Virginia Berridge and Griffith Edwards, *Opium and the People: Opiate Use in Nineteenth-century England* (London: Allen Lane/St. Martin's Press, 1981) detail the extent of opium use in nineteenth-century England among both the high and low, including a long list of famous Victorian users (55–60); Barry Milligan, *Pleasures and Pain: Opium and the Orient in Nineteenth-century British Culture* (Charlottesville: University Press of Virginia, 1995) shows that opium consumption as depicted in literature from Coleridge to Conan Doyle reflects attitudes toward the Orient; Andrew Blake, "Foreign Devils and Moral Panics," *The Expansion of England,* ed. Bill Schwarz (London: Routledge, 1996), 240–49, gives an impassioned summary of the effects of Britain's opium policy.

33. Twenty years later Bird would frankly note the ineffectiveness of this cure, citing as her source Dr. Main, who ran the Hangchow hospital (YVB 26).

34. Lodwick, *Crusaders against Opium,* 144.

35. C. R. Haines, *A Vindication of England's Policy with Regards to the Opium Trade* (London: W. H. Allen, 1884), 100; James Bromley Eames, *The English in China* (1909; reprint, London: Curzon; New York: Barnes & Noble, 1974), 581.

36. Donald Matheson, *What Is the Opium Trade?* (Edinburgh: Thomas Constable, 1857), 14.

37. Latourette, *History of Christian Missions*, 406.

38. Both Cumming and Bird use reports by Protestant and Catholic missionaries on numbers of converts as a way of lending support to missionary work (WiC 148–50, 437; YVB, 508). As evidence of missionaries' difficulties, Cumming mentions the Baldwins, who labored for thirty years before gaining more than a handful of converts (WiC 127).

39. Constance Gordon Cumming, *The Inventor of the Numeral-Type for China* (London: Simpkin, Marshall, Hamilton, & Kent, 1898) and *Work for the Blind in China* (London: James Nisbet, 1888). Murray combined his missionary's zeal with a remarkable aptitude for language and the patient ingenuity of the workingman to invent a reading system for the blind in China. Cumming saw the hand of Providence in her meeting the Rev. Murray, who served as her guide in Peking. Once back in England, she began publicizing his work as a method of fundraising for him, an effort redoubled after his presses were destroyed in an anti-Christian riot. She reproduces essentially the same biographical information in five books and pamphlets of different title, and in *The Inventor of the Numeral-Type* boasts of having raised £2,000 for him by 1887.

40. Cumming's views contrast with what Birkett says is "a general feeling against missionary influence and aims" among women travelers in Africa and Asia (*Spinsters Abroad* 152).

41. Cumming mentions her breakfast drink in *A Lady's Cruise in a French Man-of-War*.

42. Constance Gordon Cumming, *Fire Fountains: The Kingdom of Hawaii*, 2 vols. (Edinburgh: Blackwood, 1883); Cumming spent three months in northern California in 1878. She stayed in San Francisco in October 1879 only long enough to find a boat bound for Honolulu.

43. An alternative explanation for "the obsessive debasement of the Other in colonial discourse," the Other as id, is offered by Spurr: The debasement "arises not simply from the fear and the recognition of difference but also, on another level, from a desire for and identification with the Other which must be resisted"; *Rhetoric of Empire*, 80.

Chapter Four
The Pen and the Sword: Major Henry Knollys

1. Knollys held the rank of major at the time he traveled in China. He became a lieutenant colonel in 1888 and brevet colonel in 1893. He is styled Colonel Sir Henry Knollys, K.C.V.O. in the notice of his death at age eighty-nine (*Times*, 4 Mar. 1930: 11c).

2. In support of this characterization, French verses that Knollys himself had written several years earlier are cited (*Times* 8 Mar. 1930, 17). A description of his

funeral and account of his estate are also published in the *Times,* 8 Mar. 1930, 19d and 2 June 1930, 9d.

3. Knollys's writings on military subjects include *Incidents in the Sepoy War* (1873), *Life of General Sir Hope Grant* (1894), a training manual on *The Elements of Field Artillery* (1877), and journal articles on the English officer and soldier "as he was" in *Blackwood's Edinburgh Magazine* 158 (Oct. 1895): 527–39 and 158 (Dec. 1895): 850–65.

4. A contemporary reviewer rebukes Knollys for producing "a thoroughly bad book—inaccurate, inconsistent, full of exaggerations" and later welcomed Cumming's *Wanderings in China* "as a counter-blast"; *Athenaeum* no. 3033 (12 Dec. 1885): 768, and *Athenaeum* no. 3043 (20 Feb. 1886): 258; Cumming, as mentioned previously, traveled in China in 1878–79 but did not publish her account immediately. Knollys's other travel writing includes *From Sedan to Saarbruck* (1872), *Sketches of Life in Japan* (1887), and several journal articles.

5. The "feminine" laundry detail and one or two uses of "we" in his chapter on Hong Kong are the only evidence that his wife may have accompanied him, though the rest of the account makes this seems unlikely. Knollys was twice married, to Louisa Eyre in 1876 (d. 1888) and to Flora Goodeve in 1909. He had no children.

6. J. M. Coetzee, *White Writing: On the Culture of Letters in South Africa* (New Haven: Yale University Press, 1988), 5.

7. Pratt, *Imperial Eyes,* 205.

8. Victorians were not unaware of the consequences of such open-season hunting. Cumming was proud of her famous big-game hunting brothers in Africa and India who bragged of killing twenty-five tigers in a day, but she worried about the impact of hunting on such a scale; *Memories* (Edinburgh: Blackwood, 1904).

9. The phrase has been used as an essay title by Joseph Wood Krutch.

10. Edinburgh: Blackwood, 1875.

11. Lord Elgin was the nephew of the man who brought the Parthenon friezes, the "Elgin marbles," to England.

12. *Incidents in the China War of 1860,* 214. Modern accounts of the final onslaught on Peking appear in Fairbank, Reischauer, and Craig, *East Asia,* 477–78, and Hsü, *Rise of Modern China,* 215.

13. *Incidents in the China War of 1860,* 225.

14. Hsü, *Rise of Modern China,* 215.

15. Mary Gertrude Mason, *Western Concepts of China and the Chinese,* 70.

16. Sir Charles Wentworth Dilke, *Greater Britain* (London: Macmillan, 1894), 398; Captain William Gill, *The River of Golden Sand,* condensed by Edward Colborne Baber, ed. Col. Henry Yule (London: John Murray, 1883), 14.

17. Arthur H. Smith, *Chinese Characteristics,* 5th ed., revised (New York,

Chicago, Toronto: Fleming H. Revell, 1894); Oliver G. Ready, *Life and Sport in China* (London: Chapman & Hall, 1904).

18. Knollys's allusions to Darwin reflects his involvement with contemporary culture: Gertrude Himmelfarb notes that "By 1876 . . . the Darwinian revolution was virtually accomplished"; *Darwin and the Darwinian Revolution* (New York: Norton, 1968), 253.

19. Darwinian thought resonated somewhat differently within China. During the 1890s, educated Chinese were fixated on social Darwinism that included a racial (i.e., anti-Manchu) element; see Spence, *Search for Modern China,* 300–301.

20. An example from Swift's "The Lady's Dressing Room" may suffice: Strephon is punished for peeping on Celia using her chamber pot: "His foul Imagination links/Each Dame he sees with all her Stinks."

21. *The History of Sexuality Volume 1: An Introduction,* translated by Robert Hurley (New York: Vintage Books, 1978), 151.

22. Pratt, "Scratches on the Face of the Country": 139.

23. Houston A. Baker, "Caliban's Triple Play," in *"Race," Writing, and Difference,* Henry Louis Gates Jr., ed., 394.

24. This is not to ignore the fact that the Hong Kong Botanical Garden *was* established by Englishmen.

25. Gill, *River of Golden Sand,* 39.

26. This partial list includes expressions by Knollys that are similar to those found in numerous other accounts; for example, Isabella Bird, *The Yangtze Valley and Beyond* (1899; reprint, Boston: Beacon Press, 1987), 10; R. H. Graves, *Forty Years in China* (1895; reprint, Wilmington, Del.: Scholarly Resources, 1972), 57; John Scarth, *Twelve Years in China* (1860; reprint, Wilmington: Scholarly Resources, 1972), 96. Mason's descriptive list shows that a kind of character study by consensus occurs in midcentury travel and description books; *Western Concepts of China and the Chinese,* 137–45.

27. Smith, *Chinese Characteristics,* 196. An important difference between Smith and Knollys is the former's balancing of Chinese traits viewed negatively by Westerners with those admired, such as politeness, cheerfulness, and patience.

28. *Chinese Characteristics,* 188, 193.

29. Even Spurr, *Rhetoric of Empire,* falls victim to the old habit in referring to "the (inscrutable) essence of the Chinese" (167).

30. Knollys repeats this unfeeling rationalization in his essay "A Chinese Ascot," in *Cornhill,* New Series 5 (July 1885): "habit begets indifference" (74).

31. *The Cuckoo Clock* (1877; reprint, London: Macmillan, 1980); Mrs. Molesworth was apparently inspired by figurines of nodding Chinese, "nodders," of which a large number were imported from Canton in the early nineteenth century; Crossman, *Decorative Arts,* 315–20.

32. Henry Mayhew, who produced *London Labour and the London Poor,* 4 vols. (London: Griffin & Bohn, 1861–62) is arguably the most influential of the Victorians who investigated and documented the life of the lower classes. Social exploration represented one class analyzing and reporting on a lower class, as Keating defines it in his editor's introduction to *Into Unknown England 1866–1913: Selections from the Social Explorers* (Manchester, England: Manchester University Press, 1976).

33. Keating, 14.

34. The chauvinism of travelers like Knollys perhaps inevitably led to counteraction, as shown by the "political witness" travelers in the twentieth century. In *Haunted Journeys,* Dennis Porter discusses travelers like T. E. Lawrence who merge reflections on government or political institutions with landscape and ethnographic description and would like to construct "an abroad at home" or lend support to countries "who are engaged in an heroic or utopian effort of reconstruction"; *Haunted Journeys*, 224.

35. Knollys's interpretation of the opium den may have been assisted by the contemporary belief that opium was not harmful to the Chinese because "the cruder nervous system of inferior races" eased deleterious effects of the drug on the Oriental; Nigel Leask, *British Romantic Writers and the East* (Cambridge: Cambridge University Press, 1992), 215.

36. *British Romantic Writers and the East,* 171.

37. W. Somerset Maugham, *On a Chinese Screen* (1922; reprint, New York: Paragon House, 1990), 61. Arguments on both sides of the opium debate are cited in other chapters. It may be added here that Fortune's friend John Scarth draws attention to the association of drugs and crime that permeates the modern debate on drugs, that the real evil of opium comes from the criminality engendered by the introduction of the drug, especially the extortionate practices of foreign traders; *Twelve Years in China* (1860; reprint, Wilmington: Scholarly Resources, 1972), 297.

38. *To China with Love,* 144.

39. Latourette, *History of Christian Missions,* 406, 479.

40. At another mission, Knollys finds Dr. Begg's discovery of Chinese "prophylactics for diminishing the number of births" (ELC 165) to be titillating rather than misguided.

41. Geertz, *Works and Lives,* 97.

42. Knollys exhibits the attitude that Francis Galton, *The Art of Travel; or, Shifts and Contrivances Available in Wild Countries* (London: John Murray, 1855) recommended a few decades earlier: "A frank, joking, but determined manner, joined with an air of showing more confidence to the savages than you really feel, is the best" (60).

43. Kaiser Wilhelm II coined the term "yellow peril" in reaction to the emer-

gence of Japan as a world power in the 1890s, and the term soon was applied to the potential power of China as well; cf. Jerome Ch'en's discussion of China as "'sleeping giant'" in *China and the West: Society and Culture 1815–1937* (Bloomington: Indiana University Press, 1979), 57–58.

Chapter Five
In Search of Elysium: Isabella Bird Bishop

1. Isabella Bird (Mrs. Bishop), *The Yangtze Valley and Beyond* (1899; reprint, Boston: Beacon Press, 1987).

2. Three full-length biographies document these facts repeatedly: Anna Stoddart, *The Life of Isabella Bird* (London: John Murray, 1906); Pat Barr, *A Curious Life for a Lady* (London: Macmillan and John Murray, 1970); and Evelyn Kaye, *Amazing Traveler* (Boulder: Blue Penguin, 1994). Bird's striking character has also been the subject of numerous shorter biographical essays, including W. H. D. Adams, *Celebrated Women Travellers* (London: W. S. Sonnenschein, 1883): "Miss Bird . . . carried in her bosom a man's heart, and was never wanting in courage or resolution" (433); Margaret Tabor, *Pioneer Women* (third series, London: Sheldon Press, 1930): her fame owed to her being small, delicate, and fearless while her pioneer work was in being able to impart to the reader "something of a thrill" (35); Middleton, *Victorian Lady Travellers*: "Her emotions were violent, her health precarious, and her energy phenomenal" (20); Marion Tinling, *Women into the Unknown* (New York: Greenwood Press, 1989), 47–55.

3. After her *Six Months in the Sandwich Islands* (1875) and *A Lady's Life in the Rocky Mountains* (1879), Bird won acclaim for her *Unbeaten Tracks in Japan* (1880), which describes her sojourn among the Ainu, the aboriginal people in the northern island of Hokkaido. Her incredible journey through Kashmir, Persia, Armenia, and Turkey (returning to London on the Orient Express) recorded in *Journeys in Persia and Kurdistan* (1891) took her through regions so little known that they had heretofore been marked "empty" on British maps. Her last journey was a thousand-mile trek on horseback across North Africa.

4. Ellen Moers, *Literary Women* (Garden City, New York: Anchor Books, 1977), 309; on the importance of Madame de Stael's *Corinne, or Italy* (1807) in nineteenth-century girlhood, see "Performing Heroinism: The Myth of Corinne," 261–319.

5. Bird complained in a letter to her publisher John Murray that the RHS committed "a dastardly deed" in again closing its membership to women (27 May 1893).

6. Archibald Little is also beholden to Baber; see chapter 2, n. 8.

7. For Bird's research concerns, see notes and letters to Murray, June–November 1899. In an age of often casual documentation of sources, she is almost obsessively careful to cite hers, and her reviewers credited her for it. The work took its toll,

however, and Bird told her publisher that she would write no more travels after YVB.

8. Jerome Ch'en, *China and the West: Society and Culture 1815–1937* (Bloomington: Indiana University Press, 1979), 207.

9. Aug. 1896, 56–57.

10. See Alison Blunt's discussion of Kingsley's attitudes on the subject in *Travel, Gender, and Imperialism: Mary Kingsley and West Africa* (New York: Guilford Press, 1994), 50 ff.

11. Morgan, *Place Matters,* 155.

12. Bird's comments seem attuned to contemporary debate, as indicated by similar ones in Ready's *Life and Sport in China* (1904). Both Bird and Ready seem to provide support for the thesis of Martin Weiner's *English Culture and the Decline of the English Spirit 1850–1980* (Cambridge: Cambridge University Press, 1988), that at the end of the nineteenth century there was a monied-middle-class flight from the work ethic to the old aristocratic ideal of the leisured gentleman.

13. Gill traveled in 1876. A similar route had previously been taken by T. T. Cooper. A number of Jesuits and other missionaries who were pouring into western China after the 1870s had earlier explored eastern Tibet.

14. Certainly Bird preferred her solo status. She hated domestic concerns and was at least partly motivated to start her 1889 tour to the subcontinent in order to escape them. Only once—her travel in Armenia as a "cover" for the reconnaissance work of Major Sawyer—did she agree to travel in tandem.

15. *Chinese Characteristics* (5th ed., rev. New York: Fleming H. Revell, 1894), 101.

16. Bird's avid interest in photography was repaid by a book offer. Her *Chinese Pictures* (London: Cassell, 1900) is a collection of dozens of her photos and explanatory notes on items of cultural interest, modes of transport, and people.

17. Perhaps Bird was growing crotchety, but in any case she sounds very different from the European women travelers in the Middle East whom Billie Melman discusses in *Women's Orients* (Ann Arbor: University of Michigan Press, 1995). Their visits to harems and their associations with Arab women are the main subject of Melman's analysis.

18. Melman points out that in Turkey, Bird "became quite addicted to the *chibouque,*" the long pipe used by Turkish women (129). Perhaps Bird used such a pipe in China as well.

19. A drawing of this costume appeared in *A Lady's Life in the Rocky Mountains.* There are many comments on this episode in Bird's life, including that of Birgitta Maria Ingemanson, "Under Cover: The Paradox of Victorian Women's Travel Costume," *Women and the Journey,* ed. Bonnie Frederick and Susan H. MacLeod (Pullman: Washington State University Press, 1993), 5–23.

20. At the end of *The Yangtze Valley and Beyond,* Bird camouflages her insensitivity to Chinese custom by self-importantly advising missionaries to defer to it, though in reality the missionaries she describes seem scrupulous in their effort to do so.

21. Lévi-Strauss, *Tristes Tropiques,* 122.

22. The Paoning dispensary was destroyed in a riot a few years later. Bird also established hospitals and dispensaries as memorials to Henrietta Bird and John Bishop in India and Africa. In her will, she bequeathed nearly £6,500 to various missions ("Mrs. Bishop's Will," *Times* [London], 15 Dec. 1904, 7c).

23. In *The Golden Chersonese,* Bird paints a horrifying picture of "antiquated quackery" in Chinese medical practices (91), but her publisher persuaded her to omit such material in *The Yangtze Valley and Beyond;* undated note among Bird's papers held by publisher John Murray.

24. Bird's sister Henrietta was the recipient of her passion, while guilt dominated her feelings toward her husband. Biographies by Stoddart and Stewart give details. More wide-ranging analysis of these two relationships appears in Barr's *A Curious Life for a Lady.* For details on the Baptist immersion, see Stoddart, *The Life of Isabella Bird,* 195.

25. For a narrative of this period of missionary history, see Peter Fleming, *The Siege at Peking* (New York: Dorset Press, 1959) and Barr, *To China with Love;* Joseph W. Esherick, *The Origins of the Boxer Uprising* (Berkeley: University of California Press, 1987) gives a scholarly account.

26. A more complete explanation of the stresses on Chinese society leading up to the Boxer Rebellion is in Hsü, *Rise of Modern China,* 387–89.

27. One might look no further than her clergyman father's strict sabbatarianism to find a reason for her disenchantment with missionaries.

28. In addition to the material on mission work in her China book, Bird gave a number of lectures on the subject; see A. T. Pierson, "Mrs. Bishop on Protestant Missions in China," *Missionary Review of the World* 23 (Sept. 1900): 675–79, and Mrs. Joseph Cook, "Mrs. Isabella Bird Bishop, Traveler and Friend of Missions," *Missionary Review of the World* 28 (July 1905): 501–3. Bird also wrote an introduction for *Among Hills and Valleys in Western China* (London: S. W. Partridge, 1901) by Hannah Davies, one of the missionaries she visited in Paoning-Fu.

29. Arthur Moule, *China as a Mission Field* (2nd ed, rev. London: Church Mission House, 1891), 47–44. According to Latourette, *History of Christian Missions,* there were 1296 Protestant missionaries in China in 1889; communicants numbered 55,093 in 1893 (406, 479). The official count of Roman Catholics in 1896–97 was 532,448, with 759 foreign missionaries and 409 native priests (329).

30. Bird expresses these views in a letter to Miss Cullen quoted by Stoddart, *The Life of Isabella Bird,* 319.

31. Bird preferred "in legendary British fashion, the company of horses" in Barr's estimation; *A Curious Life for a Lady,* 185.

32. On Bird's arrival in Japan, see Eva-Marie Kroller, "First Impressions: Travel Writing by Victorian Women," *Ariel* 21 (Oct. 1990): 87–99.

Chapter Six
Orientalizing Feminism: Mrs. Archibald Little

1. Helen Callaway, *Gender, Culture and Empire: European Women in Colonial Nigeria* (Urbana: University of Illinois Press, 1987). Lean's statement originally appeared in "Sayings in the Week," *Observer* (London), 24 Feb. 1985; Callaway notes that "the context is not revealed, unfortunately, nor Sir David's tone of voice."

2. Margaret Strobel, *European Women and the Second British Empire* (Bloomington: Indiana University Press, 1991), 2.

3. Alicia Helen Neva Bewicke, of a Leicestershire family, was born in Madeira in 1845. She died in 1926. Her novels include *Flirts and Flirts* (1868), *Lonely Carlotta* (1874), *Onwards! But Whither* (1875), and *Margery Travers* (1878).

4. The author is quoted in an obituary in the *Times,* 6 Aug. 1926, 17e. *Mother Darling* is the story of an obedient daughter coerced into marriage with a wealthy cad who moves his mistress into the home, then retains control of the children when the humiliated wife leaves.

5. Little's China books include three novels, four travel and description books, a biography of the Chinese statesman *Li Hung-Chang,* an English version of a Chinese tale, *The Fairy Foxes;* and a guide book of Peking. After her husband's death, she edited his *Across Yunnan* and *Gleanings from Fifty Years in China.*

6. *My Diary in a Chinese Farm* (Shanghai, Tokyo: Kelly & Walsh, 1898).

7. Mrs. Archibald Little, *Intimate China* (London: Hutchinson, 1899); *In the Land of the Blue Gown* (1902; reprint, London: Everett, 1912); *A Marriage in China* (London: George Bell, 1897).

8. The "no dogs or Chinese" prohibition in that Shanghai park is current in Chinese thinking as an indictment of British imperialism.

9. Perhaps British colonial novels were on the whole more reticent on the topic of interracial unions than the Dutch; see Jean Taylor's study of the interracial marriage in "The World of Women in the Colonial Dutch Novel" *Kabar Seberang* 2 (1977): 26–41. On interracialism in colonial novels set in Africa, see A. P. A. Busia, "Miscegenation as Metonymy: Sexuality and Power in the Colonial Novel," *Ethnic and Racial Studies* 9 (1986): 360–72.

10. Little's character Claude bears strong resemblances to Henry Cockburn, a vice-consul in Chungking in the 1880s. Cockburn's son Claud describes his father's China years in *A Discord of Trumpets: An Autobiography* (New York: Simon & Schuster, 1956), 18–25.

11. Strobel, *European Women,* 19–20. Callaway points out that the military had unwritten regulations to the same effect: cadets were not allowed to get married for three years; *Gender, Culture and Empire,* 20. According to Ann Laura Stoler, "Carnal Knowledge and Imperial Power: Gender, Race, and Morality in Colonial Asia," in *Gender at the Crossroads of Knowledge: Feminist Anthropology in the Post-modern Era,* ed. Micaela di Leonardo (Berkeley: University of California Press, 1991), the Dutch in the East Indies allowed only officers above the rank of sergeant major to marry (61).

12. *The China Punch,* 16 Oct. 1874, 15.

13. Stoler, "Carnal Knowledge and Imperial Power," 61. Banks and commercial establishments had similar prohibitions on their employees, though the restrictions varied somewhat from colony to colony as is demonstrated in the work of Callaway about Africa, Strobel about India, and Stoler about colonial Asia.

14. There were also strong class arguments in limiting marriage to higher ranking officers, thus avoiding the "proliferation of a lower-class European settler population"; Stoler, "Carnal Knowledge," 62.

15. Stoler, "Carnal Knowledge," 59. I use "concubine" and "concubinage" as terms for cohabitation and unmarried unions in China. Chinese polygamy, too, is typically referred to as concubinage.

16. Strobel, *European Women,* 3. The change in policy in India may be attributed to the fact that the former policy regarding racial and sexual separation was implicated in the mutiny of 1857; cf. Christopher Lane, *The Ruling Passion: British Colonial Allegory and the Paradox of Homosexual Desire* (Durham, N.C.: Duke University Press, 1995), 158.

17. Callaway, *Gender, Culture and Empire,* 49; Stoler, "Carnal Knowledge," 59; cf. Ronald Hyam, "Concubinage and the Colonial Service: The Crewe Circular (1909)," *Journal of Imperial and Commonwealth History"* 14 (1986): 170–86; and Lane, *Ruling Passion,* 158–59. The scandal over a pedophile, Hubert Silberrad, in Kenya in 1908 was the immediate cause of the Crewe circular of 1909 that attempted to legislate sexual conduct of those in the colonial service.

18. Lilian's secret wedding also represents one of the conventional dangers and rewards of the orphan-heroine in the Victorian novel; the convention has been linked to the changing image of women at the end of the nineteenth century by Kimberley Reynolds and Nicola Humble, *Victorian Heroines: Representations of Femininity in Nineteenth-century Literature and Art* (New York: New York University Press, 1991).

19. In the Indies, Stoler writes, "the majority of such children were not recognized by their fathers, nor were they reabsorbed into local communities" ("Carnal Knowledge," 78).

20. *China Punch,* 8 Nov. 1867, 96.

21. "Eurasian Schools and Asylums," *Cycle* 55 (6 May 1871): 628–29; the article

shows particular concern for Eurasian girls who, if pretty, will be sold into prostitution, and if not may be disposed of.

22. For a discussion of the "eugenics of empire," see Stoler, "Carnal Knowledge," 72–76.

23. *Englishwoman's Review,* new series 28 (15 Jan. 1897): 52. The reviewer notes that although Little finished her novel in 1893, it did not appear in England until 1896. The controversial subject matter may have deterred publication, but the novel's popularity caused it to be reprinted in 1897 and 1899. Cf. the review of *A Marriage in China* on its aesthetic merits, and its comparison to Rees's *Chun-Ti-kung* in "Chinese Stories," *Athenaeum* no. 3625 (17 Apr. 1897): 504–5.

24. Gayatri Chakravorty Spivak, "Can the Subaltern Speak?" *Marxism and the Interpretation of Culture,* ed. Lawrence Grossberg and Cary Nelson (Urbana: University of Illinois Press, 1988), 308.

25. Little's discourse illustrates Mills's observation that women travel writers "cannot be said to speak from outside colonial discourse," *Discourses of Difference*, 63.

26. Bird at times illustrates an idea suggested by Behda in *Belated Travelers* (75) that desire for "authentic" experience prompts some travelers to position themselves so as to strike a strong contrast to native culture, costume, and so on.

27. Downing, *"Fan-Qui" in China,* 3:191.

28. A photograph of Little in an early edition of *In the Land of the Blue Gown,* showing her youthful figure, tightly corseted and bustled, suggests her preferred self-image; however, in the same book she ridicules Englishwomen for adhering to corseted English dress even at the beach in the steamy heat of a Chinese summer. Apparently she was of two minds about Western and Eastern clothing.

29. Little does not put into her novel what she says in her travel book: "Nor was that flask of whisky forgotten that is such a support to the traveller, remaining always full under all emergencies because never wanted" (IC 351).

30. *Chinese Footbinding: The History of a Curious Erotic Custom* (New York: Bell, 1967).

31. Little uses photographs of both shod and unshod bound feet. In *Chinese Footbinding,* Levy uses stylized illustrations that are far less exploitative.

32. In *A Woman in China* (Philadelphia: Lippincott, 1914), Mary Gaunt mentions that her father (a military officer posted to China during the Boxer Rebellion) owned such a snuffbox; on the bound-foot pincushion, see Honour, *Chinoiserie,* 204.

33. Published 1899; reprint, New York: Greenwood Press, 1967, 261.

34. Inspired by this interview, Little wrote a biography, *Li Hung-Chang,* the first full-length English treatment of this consummate politician and leader in the drive to modernize China; (London: Cassell, 1903).

35. The connection between footbinding and a desire to punish and subdue women who had become too powerful was noted before the Victorian period by

Downing, *"Fan-Qui" in China,* 2:44–45. This is essentially Julia Kristeva's explanation in *About Chinese Women* (trans. Anita Barrows, New York: Urizen Books, 1977), in which she reasons back from Freud's interpretation of footbinding as female castration to exclude woman from the social order, to the matriarchal society that was situated in central China around 6000 B.C., to the association of earth with the feminine in Chinese cosmology and the yin/yang concept assigning the feminine a completely separate but completely harmonious role.

36. The lines are quoted from Levy, *Chinese Footbinding,* 41.

37. Cameron, *Barbarians and Mandarins,* 352.

38. Little makes an extended comparison between footbinding and woman's right to vote in "The Woman Suffragists": "There was nothing feminine or unfeminine about having the feet mutilated. . . . There is nothing feminine or unfeminine about voting"; *Times* (London), 24 Feb. 1908, 12d.

39. *Rattle,* Feb. 1897, 144. Attention in London to Little's work is shown by an enthusiastic account of the progress on antifootbinding by a lady (Little herself?) "just returned from England after a seven months' absence": "The Social Revolution in China," *Spectator* 80 (1898): 406, and reprinted as "Notes from Abroad," *Englishwoman's Review,* n.s. 29 (15 Apr. 1898): 128–30.

40. *Barbarians and Mandarins,* 351.

41. Levy, *Chinese Footbinding,* provides data on the demise of the custom that shows residual cases as late as 1937 (90–93). As a footnote to history, Little notes that the Taipings, nominal Christians, opposed footbinding, and wonders whether the success of their revolution might not have ended footbinding.

Conclusion: An Opened China

1. *Cook's Handbook for Tourists to Peking, Tientsin, Shan-Hai-Kwan, Mukden, Dalny, Port Arthur, and Seoul* (London: Simpkin, Marshall, Hamilton, Kent, 1910), 18.

2. Annie E. Coombes, "The Recalcitrant Object: Culture Contact and the Question of Hybridity," eds. Francis Barker, Peter Hulme, and Margaret Iversen, in *Colonial Discourse/Postcolonial Theory* (Manchester, England: Manchester University Press, 1994), 92. Timothy Mitchell cites a number of examples of oriental visitors "rendered up as objects to be viewed" in nineteenth-century Europe in "Orientalism and the Exhibitionary Other," ed. Nicholas B. Dirks, in *Colonialism and Culture* (Ann Arbor: University of Michigan Press, 1992), 290–93; and Richard D. Altick describes various nineteenth-century exhibitions that are ethnographic in orientation in *The Shows of London* (Cambridge: Harvard University Press, 1978).

3. "Ethnography and Experience: Gender Implications in Fieldwork and Text," in *Anthropology and Autobiography,* ed. Judith Okley and Helen Callaway (London: Routledge, 1992), 35–36.

Bibliography

Adams, Percy G. *Travel and the Evolution of the Novel.* Lexington: University Press of Kentucky, 1983.

Adams, W. H. D. *Celebrated Women Travellers of the Nineteenth Century.* London: W. S. Sonnensschein, 1883.

Alexander, William, and George Henry Mason. *Views of 18th Century China Costumes: History: Customs.* 1800. Reprint, London: Studio Editions, 1988.

Altick, Richard D. *The Shows of London.* Cambridge: Harvard University Press, 1978.

Arnold, Matthew. *Culture and Anarchy* in *The Portable Matthew Arnold.* Ed. Lionel Trilling. New York: Viking Press, 1949.

Atkinson, Paul. *The Ethnographic Imagination: Textual Constructions of Reality.* London: Routledge, 1990.

Bai, Shouyi, ed. *An Outline History of China.* Beijing: Foreign Languages Press, 1982.

Baker, Houston A. "Caliban's Triple Play." In *"Race," Writing, and Difference,* ed. Henry Louis Gates Jr., 381–95. Chicago: University of Chicago Press, 1986.

Ball, J. Dyer. *Things Chinese Or, Notes Connected with China.* 5th ed. Rev. by E. Chalmers Werner. London: John Murray, 1926.

Ball, Samuel. *An Account of the Cultivation and Manufacture of Tea.* London: Longman, Brown, Green, & Longmans, 1848.

Bann, Stephen. "Travelling to Collect: The Booty of John Bargrave and Charles Waterton." In *Travellers' Tales,* ed. George Robertson, et al., 155–63. London: Routledge, 1994.

Barker, Francis, Peter Hulme, and Margaret Iversen, eds. *Colonial Discourse/ Postcolonial Theory.* Manchester: Manchester University Press, 1994.

Barr, Pat. *A Curious Life for a Lady.* London: Macmillan and John Murray, 1970.

———. *To China with Love: The Lives and Times of Protestant Missionaries in China 1860–1900.* London: Secker & Warburg, 1972.

Barrow, John. *Travels in China.* London: Cadell & Davis, 1804.

Barthes, Roland. *Alors la Chine?* Paris: C. Bourgois, 1975.

Beasley, William G. *The Rise of Modern Japan.* New York: St. Martin's, 1990.

Behdad, Ali. *Belated Travelers: Orientalism in the Age of Colonial Dissolution.* Durham, N.C.: Duke University Press, 1994.

Behar, Ruth, and Deborah A. Gordon. *Women Writing Culture.* Berkeley: University of California Press, 1995.

Berridge, Virginia, and Griffith Edwards. *Opium and the People: Opiate Use in Nineteenth-century England.* London: Allen Lane/St. Martin's, 1981.

Bhabha, Homi. "The Other Question . . ." *Screen* 24 (1983): 18–36.

Bird, Isabella (Mrs. Bishop). *The Golden Chersonese.* 1883. Reprint, Singapore: Oxford University Press, 1990.

———. *The Englishwoman in America.* London: John Murray, 1856.

———. *The Hawaiian Archipelago: Six Months among the Palm Groves, Coral Reefs, and Volcanoes of the Sandwich Islands.* London: John Murray, 1875.

———. *A Lady's Life in The Rocky Mountains.* London: John Murray, 1879.

———. Letters and Papers. London: John Murray.

———. "Mrs. Bishop's Will." *Times* (London), 15 December 1904, 7c.

———. *The Yangtze Valley and Beyond.* London, John Murray, 1899. Reprint, Boston: Beacon Press, 1987.

Birkett, Dea. *Spinsters Abroad: Victorian Lady Explorers.* London: Basil Blackwell, 1989.

[Blaikie, W. G.] "Lady Travellers." *Blackwood's Magazine* 160 (July 1896): 49–66.

Blake, Andrew. "Foreign Devils and Moral Panics." In *The Expansion of England,* ed. Bill Schwarz. London: Routledge, 1996.

Blunt, Alison. *Travel, Gender, and Imperialism: Mary Kingsley and West Africa.* New York: Guilford Press, 1994.

Bramah, Ernest. *The Wallet of Kai Lung.* London: Grant Richards, 1900.

Brantlinger, Patrick. *Rule of Darkness: British Literature and Imperialism, 1830–1914.* Ithaca: Cornell University Press, 1988.

Bretschneider, E. *History of European Botanical Discoveries.* London: Sampson Low, Marston, 1898.

Bruckner, Pascal. *The Tears of the White Man: Compassion as Contempt.* Trans. William R. Beer. New York: Free Press; London: Collier Macmillan, 1986.

Busia, A. P. A. "Miscegenation as Metonymy: Sexuality and Power in the Colonial Novel." *Ethnic and Racial Studies* 9 (1986): 360–72.

Buzard, James. *The Beaten Track: European Tourism, Literature, and the Ways to 'Culture' 1800–1918.* Oxford: Clarendon Press, 1993.

Callaway, Helen. "Ethnography and Experience: Gender Implications in Field-work and Text." In *Anthropology and Autobiography,* ed. Judith Okley and Helen Callaway, 29–49. London: Routledge, 1992.

———. *Gender, Culture and Empire: European Women in Colonial Nigeria.* Urbana: University of Illinois Press, 1987.

Cameron, Nigel. *Barbarians and Mandarins: Thirteen Centuries of Travellers in China.* New York: Walker/Weatherhill, 1970.

Cameron, Meribeth E. *The Reform Movement in China, 1898–1912.* California: Stanford University Press, 1931.

Carlyle, Thomas. *Past and Present.* New York: New York University Press, 1977.

Carr, Caleb. *The Devil Soldier.* New York: Random House, 1991.

Ch'en, Jerome. *China and the West: Society and Culture, 1815–1937.* Bloomington: Indiana University Press, 1979.

China. An Official Guide to Eastern Asia. Vol. 4. Tokyo: Imperial Japanese Government Railway, 1915.

"Chinese Stories." Review of *Chun Ti-kung, His Life and Adventures* and *A Marriage in China. Athenaeum* no. 3625 (17 Apr. 1897): 504–5.

Clifford, James. "On Ethnographic Allegory." In *Writing Culture: The Poetics and Politics of Ethnography,* ed. James Clifford and George E. Marcus, 98–121. Berkeley: University of California Press, 1986.

———. *The Predicament of Culture: Twentieth-Century Ethnography, Literature, and Art.* Cambridge: Harvard University Press, 1988.

Coats, Alice M. *The Quest for Plants.* New York: McGraw Hill, 1969.

Cockburn, Claud. *A Discord of Trumpets: An Autobiography.* New York: Simon & Schuster, 1956.

Coetzee, J. M. *White Writing: On the Culture of Letters in South Africa.* New Haven: Yale University Press, 1988.

Cohen, Paul A. *China and Christianity.* Cambridge: Harvard University Press, 1963.

Cole, Sally. "Ruth Landes and the Early Ethnography of Race and Gender." In *Women Writing Culture,* ed. Ruth Behar and Deborah A. Gordon, 166–84. Berkeley: University of California Press, 1995.

Conner, Patrick. *The China Trade, 1600–1800.* Brighton: Royal Pavilion, Art Gallery and Museums, 1986.

———. *Oriental Architecture in the West.* London: Thames & Hudson, 1979.

Cook, Mrs. Joseph. "Mrs. Isabella Bird Bishop, Traveler and Friend of Missions." *Missionary Review of the World* 28 (July 1905): 501–3.

Cook's Handbook for Tourists to Peking, Tientsin, Shan-Hai-Kwan, Mukden, Dalny, Port Arthur, and Seoul. London: Simpkin, Marshall, Hamilton, Kent, 1910.

Coombes, Annie E. "The Recalcitrant Object: Culture Contact and the Question of Hybridity." In *Colonial Discourse/Postcolonial Theory*, ed. Francis Barker, Peter Hulme, and Margaret Iversen, 89–114. Manchester, England: Manchester University Press, 1994.

Cotsell, Michael. "Carlyle, Travel, and the Enlargements of History." In *Creditable Warriors,* ed. Michael Cotsell, 93–96. London: Ashfield Press, 1990.

Cox, E. H. M. *Plant Hunting in China.* London: Oldbourne, 1945.

Crossman, Carl L. *The Decorative Arts of the China Trade.* Woodbridge, Suffolk, England: Antique Collectors Club, 1991.

Culler, Jonathan. *Framing the Sign: Criticism and Its Institutions.* Norman: University of Oklahoma Press, 1988.

Cumming, Constance Gordon. *Fire Fountains: The Kingdom of Hawaii.* 2 vols. Edinburgh: Blackwood, 1883.

———. *In the Himalayas and on the Indian Plains.* New ed. London: Chatto & Windus, 1886.

———. *At Home in Fiji.* Edinburgh: Blackwood, 1881.

———. *A Lady's Cruise in a French Man-of-War.* Edinburgh: Blackwood, 1882.

———. Letters to Chatto & Windus 1884–1887. The Library, Archives and Manuscripts, University of Reading, England.

———. *Memories.* Edinburgh: Blackwood, 1904.

———. *Wanderings in China.* Cheaper edition. Edinburgh: Blackwood, 1900.

Cumming, Roualeyn. *Five years of a Hunter's Life in the Far Interior of South Africa.* New York: Harper, 1850.

Darwin, Charles. *Voyage of the Beagle.* 1845. Reprint, New York: P. F. Collier, 1937.

Davenport, Arthur Y. *China from Within: A Study of the Opium Fallacies and Missionary Mistakes.* London: T. F. Unwin, 1904.

Davies, Hannah. *Among Hills and Valleys in Western China.* London: S. W. Partridge, 1901.

Dawe, William Carlton. *Yellow and White.* Boston: Roberts Bros., London: John Lane, 1895.

Dawson, Raymond. *The Chinese Chameleon: An Analysis of European Conceptions of Chinese Civilizations.* London: Oxford University Press, 1967.

Dickens, Charles. *Bleak House.* Ed. George Ford and Sylvere Monod. New York: Norton, 1977.

———. *Pictures from Italy.* The New Oxford Illustrated Dickens. London: Oxford University Press, 1957.

Dilke, Sir Charles Wentworth. *Greater Britain.* London: Macmillan, 1894.

Dirks, Nicholas B., ed. *Colonialism and Culture*. Ann Arbor: University of Michigan Press, 1992.

[Douglas, Robert K.] "Wanderings in China." Review of *Three Years' Wanderings*. *The Academy* 721 (27 Feb. 1886): 141–42.

Downing, C. Toogood. *"Fan-Qui" in China, 1836–37*. 3 vols. 1838. Reprint, Shannon: Irish University Press, n.d.

Eames, James Bromley. *The English in China*. 1909. Reprint, London: Barnes & Noble, 1974.

[Eastlake, Elizabeth]. "Lady Travellers." *Quarterly Review* 76 (June 1845): 98–137.

Ennin's Diary: The Record of a Pilgrimage to China in Search of the Law. Translated by Edwin O. Reischauer. New York: Ronald Press, 1955.

Esherick, Joseph W. *The Origins of the Boxer Uprising*. Berkeley: University of California Press, 1987.

"Eurasian Schools and Asylums." *Cycle* 55 (6 May 1871): 628–29.

Fairbank, John K. *China: A New History*. Cambridge, Mass.: Belknap Press, 1994.

———. *The Great Chinese Revolution, 1800–1895*. New York: Harper & Row, 1987.

Fairbank, John K., Edwin O. Reischauer, and Albert M. Craig. *East Asia: Tradition and Transformation*. Rev. ed., Boston: Houghton Mifflin, 1989.

Fay, Peter Ward. *The Opium War, 1840–42: Barbarian in the Celestial Empire. . . .* New York: Norton, 1976.

Fleming, Peter. *The Siege at Peking*. New York: Dorset Press, 1959.

Forrest, Denys. *The World Tea Trade: A Survey of the Production, Distribution, and Consumption of Tea*. Cambridge: Woodhead-Faulkner, 1985.

Fortune, Robert. *A Journey to the Tea Countries*. 1852. Reprint, London: Mildmay Books, 1987.

———. Letters from the Royal Horticultural Society to Robert Fortune. 23 Feb. 1843; 6 Mar. 1845. Library of the Royal Horticultural Society, London.

———. Letters from Robert Fortune to the Royal Horticultural Society. 1 July 1842, 6 Mar. 1845, 16 Aug. 1845. Library of the Royal Horticultural Society, London.

———. Letters from Robert Fortune, 1846–1880. Lindley correspondence. Library Archives. Royal Botanic Gardens, Kew, England.

———. Letters to Joseph Holt, 1 Aug. 1858, 19 Feb. 1859, and 24 May 1859; to W. D. Bishop, 5 Aug. 1859 and 6 Sept. 1859. *Letters, Reports, Essays*. Agric. Dept., U.S. Pat. Off. vols. 20–21 (1858–60). U.S. National Archives.

———. *A Residence among the Chinese*. London: John Murray, 1857.

———. *The Tea District of China*. London: John Murray, 1953.

———. *Three Years' Wanderings in the Northern Provinces of China.* London: John Murray, 1847.

———. *Yedo and Peking.* London: John Murray, 1863.

Foster, Shirley. *Across New Worlds: Nineteenth-Century Women Travellers and Their Writings.* New York: Harvester Wheatsheaf, 1990.

Foucault, Michel. *The History of Sexuality, Volume I: An Introduction.* Trans. Robert Hurley. New York: Vintage Books, 1990.

Frawley, Maria H. *A Wider Range: Travel Writing by Women in Victorian England.* London: Associated University Presses, 1994.

Fussell, Paul. *Abroad: British Traveling between the Wars.* New York: Oxford University Press, 1980.

Galton, Francis. *The Art of Travel; or, Shifts and Contrivances Available in Wild Countries.* London: John Murray, 1855.

Gardener, William. "Robert Fortune and the Cultivation of Tea in the United States." *Arnoldia* 31 (1971): 1–18.

———. "Robert Fortune: The Collector." *Gardener's Chronicle* 155 (11 Jan. 1964): 34–35.

Gaunt, Mary. *A Woman in China.* Philadelphia: Lippincott, 1914.

Geertz, Clifford. *Works and Lives: The Anthropologist as Author.* Stanford, Calif.: Stanford University Press, 1988.

Gernet, Jacques. *China and the Christian Impact: A Conflict of Cultures.* Trans. Janet Lloyd. Cambridge: Cambridge University Press, 1985.

Gill, Captain William. *The River of Golden Sand.* Condensed by Edward Colborne Baber. Ed. Col. Henry Yule. London: John Murray, 1883.

Gilman, Sander. "Black Bodies, White Bodies . . ." In *"Race," Writing, and Difference,* ed. Henry Louis Gates, Jr., 223–61. Chicago: University of Chicago Press, 1986.

———. "Lam Qua and the Development of a Westernized Medical Iconography." *Medical History* 30 (1986): 57–69.

Goodwin, Jason. *A Time for Tea: Travels through China and India in Search of Tea.* New York: Knopf, 1991.

Graham, Gerald S. *The China Station: War and Diplomacy, 1830–1860.* Oxford: Clarendon Press, 1978.

Graves, R. H. *Forty Years in China.* 1895. Reprint, Wilmington, Del.: Scholarly Resources, 1972.

Greenberg, Michael D. *British Trade and the Opening of China, 1800–1842.* Cambridge: Cambridge University Press, 1951.

Hadfield, Miles. *Pioneers in Gardening.* Routledge & Kegan Paul, 1955.

Haines, C. R. *A Vindication of England's Policy with Regards to the Opium Trade.* London: W. H. Allen, 1884.

Half the Sky. Beijing: Women of China, 1985.

Hart, Rev. Virgil. *Western China.* Boston: Ticknor, 1888.

Hastrup, Kirsten. "Writing Ethnography: State of the Art." In *Anthropology and Autobiography,* ed. Judith Okley and Helen Callaway, 116–33. London: Routledge, 1992.

Himmelfarb, Gertrude. *Darwin and the Darwinian Revolution.* New York: W. W. Norton, 1968.

Hochshild, Adam. "Mr. Kurtz, I Presume." *New Yorker,* 14 Apr. 1997, 40–47.

Honour, Hugh. *Chinoiserie: The Vision of Cathay.* London: John Murray, 1961.

Hosie, Alexander. *Despatch from His Majesty's Minister in China . . . Respecting the Opium Question in China.* London: Harrison & Sons, 1909.

———. *Three Years in Western China.* London: G. Philip & Son, 1890.

Hsü, Immanuel C. Y. *The Rise of Modern China.* 4th ed. New York: Oxford University Press, 1990.

Hyam, Ronald. "Concubinage and the Colonial Service: The Crewe Circular (1909)." *The Journal of Imperial and Commonwealth History"* 14 (1986): 170–86.

———. *Empire and Sexuality: The British Experience.* Manchester, England: Manchester University Press, 1990.

Ingemanson, Birgitta Maria. "Under Cover: The Paradox of Victorian Women's Travel Costume." In *Women and the Journey,* ed. Bonnie Frederick and Susan H. MacLeod, 5–23. Pullman: Washington State University Press, 1993.

Isaacs, Harold R. *Scratches on Our Minds: American Images of China and India.* New York: John Day, 1958.

Kaye, Evelyn. *Amazing Traveler.* Boulder: Blue Penguin, 1994.

Keating, P. J., ed. *Into Unknown England, 1866–1913: Selections from the Social Explorers.* Manchester: Manchester University Press, 1976.

Keay, John. *The Honourable Company: A History of the English East India Company.* New York: Macmillan, 1991.

Kiernan, E. V. G. *British Diplomacy in China 1880 to 1885.* 1939. Reprint, New York: Octagon Books, 1970.

Kingston, Maxine Hong. *The Woman Warrior.* New York: Vintage Books, 1977.

Kipling, Rudyard. *From Sea to Sea.* 2 vols. New York: Doubleday, Page, 1925.

———. *Kim.* Garden City, N.Y.: Doubleday, Doran, 1931.

Knollys, Henry. "China's Reputation Bubble." *Blackwoods* 156 (Nov. 1894): 714–26.

———. "A Chinese Ascot." *Cornhill* 5 (new series), (July 1885): 73–83.

———. *English Life in China.* London: Smith, Elder, 1885.

———. *Incidents in the China War of 1860.* Edinburgh: Blackwood, 1875.

———. "The Rival 'Foreign Devils.'" *Blackwoods* 168 (Nov. 1900): 719–28.

Kristeva, Julia. *About Chinese Women.* Trans. Anita Barrows. New York: Urizen Books, 1977.

Kroller, Eva-Marie. "First Impressions: Travel Writing by Victorian Women. *Ariel* 21 (Oct. 1990): 87–99.

Lamb, Charles. "Old China." In *English Romantic Poetry and Prose.* Selected and edited by Russell Noyes, 618–21. New York: Oxford University Press, 1956.

Lane, Christopher. *The Ruling Passion: British Colonial Allegory and the Paradox of Homosexual Desire.* Durham: Duke University Press, 1995.

Lao-Tzu. *Tao Te Ching.* Trans. D. C. Lau. London: Penguin Books, 1976.

Latourette, Kenneth Scott. *A History of Christian Missions in China.* 1929. Reprint, New York: Russell & Russell, 1967.

Leask, Nigel. *British Romantic Writers and the East.* Cambridge: Cambridge University Press, 1992.

Leed, Eric J. *The Mind of the Traveler: From Gilgamesh to Global Tourism.* New York: Basic Books, 1992.

Lévi-Strauss, Claude. *Tristes Tropiques.* Trans. John and Doreen Weightman. 1955, 1973. New York: Atheneum, 1974; Reprint, Harmondsworth, England: Penguin Books, 1992.

Levy, Howard S. *Chinese Footbinding: The History of a Curious Erotic Custom.* New York: Bell, 1967.

[Lewis, Gilbert F.] "Fortune's *China:* Gardening." Review of *Three Years' Wanderings. Edinburgh Review* 88 (Oct. 1848): 403–29.

Little, Archibald John. *The Far East.* Oxford, England: Clarendon Press, 1905.

———. *Gleanings from Fifty Years in China.* Philadelphia: J. B. Lippincott, 1910.

———. *Mount Omi and Beyond: A Record of Travel on the Thibetan Border.* London: Heinemann, 1901.

———. *Through the Yang-Tse Gorges, or Trade and Travel in Western China.* London: Sampson Low, Marston, Searle, & Rivington, 1888.

Little, Mrs. Archibald [Alicia]. *The Fairy Foxes: A Chinese Legend.* Yokohama, Shanghai: Kelly & Walsh, n.d.

———. *Guide to Peking.* Tientsin: Tientsin Press, 1904.

———. *Intimate China.* London: Hutchinson, 1899.

———. *In the Land of the Blue Gown.* 1902. Reprint, London: Everett, 1912.

———. *Li Hung-Chang.* London: Cassell, 1903.

———. *A Marriage in China.* London: George Bell & Sons, 1897.

———. *A Millionaire's Courtship.* London: T. Fisher, Unwin, 1906.

————. *My Diary in a Chinese Farm.* Shanghai, Tokyo: Kelly & Walsh, 1898.

————. *Out in China!* London: Treherne, 1902.

————. *Round My Peking Garden.* London: T. Fisher, Unwin, 1905.

————. "The Woman Suffragists." *Times* (London), 24 Feb. 1908, 12d.

Lodwick, Kathleen L. *Crusaders against Opium: Protestant Missionaries in China, 1874–1917.* Lexington: University Press of Kentucky, 1996.

Lowe, Lisa. *Critical Terrains: French and British Orientalisms.* Ithaca: Cornell University Press, 1991.

Lutkehaus, Nancy C. "Margaret Mead and the 'Rustling-of-the-Wind-in-the-Palm-Trees School' of Ethnographic Writing." In *Women Writing Culture,* ed. Ruth Behar and Deborah A. Gordon, 186–206. Berkeley: University of California Press, 1995.

Lyte, Charles. *The Plant Hunters.* London: Orbis, 1983.

MacCannell, Dean. *The Tourist: A New Theory of the Leisure Class.* New York: Schocken Books, 1976.

Mackerras, Colin. *Western Images of China.* Hong Kong: Oxford University Press, 1989.

Macleod, Dawn. "A Mystery Solved: New Light on Robert Fortune." *Garden* (May 1992): 214–17.

McClintock, Anne. *Imperial Leather.* New York: Routledge, 1994.

Mason, Mary Gertrude. *Western Concepts of China and the Chinese, 1840–1876.* New York: Seeman Printers, 1939.

Matheson, Donald. *What Is the Opium Trade?* Edinburgh: Thomas Constable, 1857.

Maugham, W. Somerset. *On a Chinese Screen.* 1922. Reprint, New York: Paragon House, 1990.

Mayhew, Henry. *London Labour and the London Poor.* 4 vols. London: Griffin & Bohn, 1861–62.

Melman, Billie. *Women's Orients: English Women and the Middle East, 1818–1918.* Ann Arbor: University of Michigan Press, 1995.

Merrill, Lynn L. *The Romance of Victorian Natural History.* New York: Oxford University Press, 1989.

Michael, Franz, and Chung-li Chang. *The Taiping Rebellion: History and Documents.* 3 vols. Seattle: University of Washington Press, 1966, 1971.

Michie, Alexander. *The Englishman in China during the Victorian Era.* 2 vols. Edinburgh: Blackwood, 1900.

Middleton, Dorothy. *Victorian Lady Travellers.* 1965. Reprint, Chicago: Academy, 1982.

Mill, John Stuart. *On Liberty.* Ed. David Spitz. New York: Norton, 1975.

Miller, Luree. *On Top of the World: Five Women Explorers in Tibet.* U.S.: Paddington Press, 1976.

Milligan, Barry. *Pleasures and Pain: Opium and the Orient in Nineteenth-century British Culture.* Charlottesville: University Press of Virginia, 1995.

Mills, Sara. *Discourses of Difference: An Analysis of Women's Travel Writing and Colonialism.* London: Routledge, 1993.

Mitchell, Sally. *Victorian Britain: An Encyclopedia.* New York: Garland, 1988.

Mitchell, Timothy. "Orientalism and the Exhibitionary Other." In *Colonialism and Culture,* ed. Nicholas B. Dirks, 290–315. Ann Arbor: University of Michigan Press, 1992.

Moers, Ellen. *Literary Women.* Garden City, N. Y.: Anchor Books, 1977.

Mohanty, Satya P. "Colonial Legacies, Multicultural Futures: Relativism, Objectivity, and the Challenge of Otherness." *PMLA* 110 (Jan. 1995): 108–18.

Molesworth, Mrs. *The Cuckoo Clock.* 1877. Reprint, London: Macmillan, 1980.

Morgan, Susan. *Place Matters: Gendered Geography in Victorian Women's Travel Books about Southeast Asia.* Brunswick, N.J.: Rutgers University Press, 1996.

Moule, Arthur. *China as a Mission Field.* 2nd ed, rev., London: Church Mission House, 1891.

[Murphy, Dominick.] Review of *Three Years Wanderings in China. Dublin Review* 23 (Sept. 1847): 59–77.

Needham, Joseph. *Science and Civilization in China.* 4 vols. Cambridge: Cambridge University Press, 1954–62.

[Orr, William.] "Fortune's Wanderings in China." Review of *Three Years Wanderings. Chamber's Edinburgh Journal* 7 (1847): 299–301.

Payn, James. *By Proxy.* 2 vols. London: Chatto & Windus, 1878.

Peterson, M. Jeanne. *Family, Love, and Work in the Lives of Victorian Gentlewomen.* Bloomington: Indiana University Press, 1989.

Peyrefitte, Alain. *The Immobile Empire.* Trans. Jon Rothschild. New York: Knopf, 1992.

Pierson, A. T. "Mrs. Bishop on Protestant Missions in China." *Missionary Review of the World* 23 (Sept. 1900): 675–79.

Plarr, Victor G. *Men and Women of the Time.* 15th ed. London: Routledge, 1899.

Porter, Dennis. *Haunted Journeys: Desire and Transgression in European Travel Writing.* Princeton: Princeton University Press, 1991.

Pratt, A. T. C. *People of the Period.* 2 vols. London: N. Beeman, 1897.

Pratt, Mary Louise. *Imperial Eyes.* London: Routledge, 1992.

———. "Scratches on the Face of the Country; or What Mr. Barrow Saw in the Land of the Bushmen." *Critical Inquiry* 12 (1985): 119–43.

———. "Fieldwork in Common Places." In *Writing Culture: The Poetics and Politics of Ethnography,* ed. James Clifford and George E. Marcus, 27–50. Berkeley: University of California Press, 1986.

Pu Yi, Henry. *The Last Manchu.* Ed. Paul Kramer. Trans. Kuo Ying Paul Tsai. New York: Pocket Books, 1987.

Ready, Oliver G. *Life and Sport in China.* London: Chapman & Hall, 1904.

———. *Ch'un-kwang: A Tale of Chinese Love and Tragedy.* London: Chapman & Hall, 1905.

Rees, Claude A. *Chun Ti-kung, His Life and Adventures.* London: Heinemann, 1896.

Review of *A Marriage in China,* by Mrs. Archibald Little. *English Woman's Review,* n.s., 28 (15 Jan. 1897): 51–52.

Review of *Yedo and Peking,* by Robert Fortune. *Living Age* 77 (1863): 186–88.

Reynolds, Kimberley, and Nicola Humble. *Victorian Heroines: Representations of Femininity in Nineteenth-century Literature and Art.* New York: New York University Press, 1993.

Rittenhouse, Mignon. *Seven Women Explorers.* Philadelphia: J. B. Lippincott, 1964.

"Robert Fortune." *Gardener's Chronicle* 13 (17 Sept. 1880): 487–89.

Rosaldo, Renato. "From the Door of His Tent: The Fieldworker and the Inquisitor." In *Writing Culture,* ed. James Clifford and George E. Marcus, 77–97. Berkeley: University of California Press, 1986.

Said, Edward. *Orientalism.* New York: Vintage, 1979.

Sanders, Valerie. *The Private Life of Victorian Women: Autobiography in Nineteenth-Century England.* New York: Harvester Wheatsheaf, 1989.

Scarth, John. *Twelve Years in China.* 1860. Reprint, Wilmington: Scholarly Resources, 1972.

Scidmore, Elisa. *China: The Long-Lived Empire.* New York: Century, 1900.

Seagrave, Sterling. *The Soong Dynasty.* New York: Harper & Row, 1985.

Shiel, M. P. *The Yellow Danger.* New York: Fenno; London: Grant Richards, 1899.

Shostak, Marjorie. *Nisa: The Life and Words of a ¡Kung Woman.* Cambridge: Harvard University Press, 1981.

Smith, Arthur H. *Chinese Characteristics.* 5th ed. rev. New York: Fleming H. Revell, 1894.

———. *Village Life in China.* 1899. Reprint, New York: Greenwood Press, 1967.

Snow, Edgar. *Red Star over China.* 1938. Reprint, New York: Grove, 1973.

Spence, Jonathan D. *God's Chinese Son: The Taiping Heavenly Kingdom of Hong Xiuquan.* New York: W. W. Norton, 1996.

———. *The Search for Modern China.* New York: W. W. Norton, 1990.

Spender, Stephen, and Hockney, David. *China Diary.* New York: Harry N. Abrams, 1982.

Spivak, Gayatri Chakravorty. "Can the Subaltern Speak?" In *Marxism and the Interpretation of Culture,* ed. Lawrence Grossberg and Cary Nelson, 271–313. Urbana: University of Illinois Press, 1988.

Spurr, David. *The Rhetoric of Empire: Colonial Discourse in Journalism, Travel Writing, and Imperial Administration.* Durham, N.C.: Duke University Press, 1994.

Stallybrass, Peter, and Allon White. *The Politics and Poetics of Transgression.* Ithaca: Cornell University Press, 1986.

Stevenson, Catherine Barnes. *Victorian Travel Writers in Africa.* Boston: Twayne, 1982.

Stewart, Agnes Grainger. "Some Recollections of Isabella Bishop." *Blackwood's Edinburgh Magazine* 176 (Nov. 1904): 698–704.

Stoddart, Anna. *The Life of Isabella Bird.* London: John Murray, 1906.

Stoler, Ann Laura. "Carnal Knowledge and Imperial Power: Gender, Race, and Morality in Colonial Asia." In *Gender at the Crossroads of Knowledge: Feminist Anthropology in the Postmodern Era,* ed. Micaela di Leonardo, 51–101. Berkeley: University of California Press, 1991.

Strachey, Lytton. *Eminent Victorians.* New York: Modern Library, 1918.

Strobel, Margaret. *European Women and the Second British Empire.* Bloomington: Indiana University Press, 1991.

Swift, Jonathan. *Gulliver's Travels.* London: Oxford University Press, 1963.

Swinglehurst, Edmund. *Cook's Tours.* Poole, Dorset: Blandford Press, 1982.

Tabor, Margaret. *Pioneer Women.* Third Series. London: Sheldon Press, 1930.

Tan, Amy. *The Joy Luck Club.* New York: Putnams, 1989.

Taylor, Jean. "The World of Women in the Colonial Dutch Novel." *Kabar Seberang* 2 (1977): 26–41.

Tidrick, Kathryn. *Empire and the English Character.* London: Tauris, 1992.

Tinling, Marion. *Women into the Unknown: A Sourcebook on Women Explorers and Travelers.* New York: Greenwood Press, 1989.

Thurin, Susan Schoenbauer. "China in Dickens." *Dickens Quarterly* 8 (Sept. 1991): 99–111.

———. "Constance Gordon Cumming." *British Travel Writers, 1876–1909.* Dictionary of Literary Biography, vol. 174, ed. Barbara Brothers and Julia Gergits, 67–96. Detroit: Bruccoli Clark Layman, 1997.

Tuan, Yi-fu. *Topophilia.* Englewood Cliffs: Prentice Hall, 1974.

Tuchman, Barbara W. *Notes from China.* New York: Collier Books, 1972.

————. *Stillwell and the American Experience in China, 1911–45.* New York: Macmillan, 1971.

Turnbull, C. Mary. "Hong Kong: Fragrant Harbour, City of Sin and Death." In *Asia in Western Fiction,* ed. Robin W. Winks and James R. Rush, 117–36. Honolulu: University of Hawaii Press, 1990.

Ukers, William H. *All about Tea.* 2 vols. New York: Tea and Coffee Trade Journal Company, 1935.

Webb, R. K. *Modern England.* New York, Toronto: Dodd, Mead, 1972.

Weiner, Martin J. *English Culture and the Decline of the Industrial Spirit, 1850–1980.* Cambridge: Cambridge University Press, 1988.

Wiethoff, Bodo. *Introduction to Chinese History.* London: Thames & Hudson, 1975.

Wilson, Ernest H. *China: Mother of Gardens.* 1929. Reprint, New York: Benjamin Blom, 1971.

Williams, S. Wells. *The Middle Kingdom.* 1883. Reprint, New York: Paragon, 1966.

Wingfield, Hon. Lewis. *The Lovely Wang: A Bit of China.* New York: Henry Holt, 1886.

Wright, Tim. *Coal Mining in China's Economy and Society, 1895–1937.* London: Cambridge University Press, 1984.

Zhang, Longxi. "The Myth of the Other: China in the Eyes of the West." *Critical Inquiry* 15 (autumn 1988): 108–31.

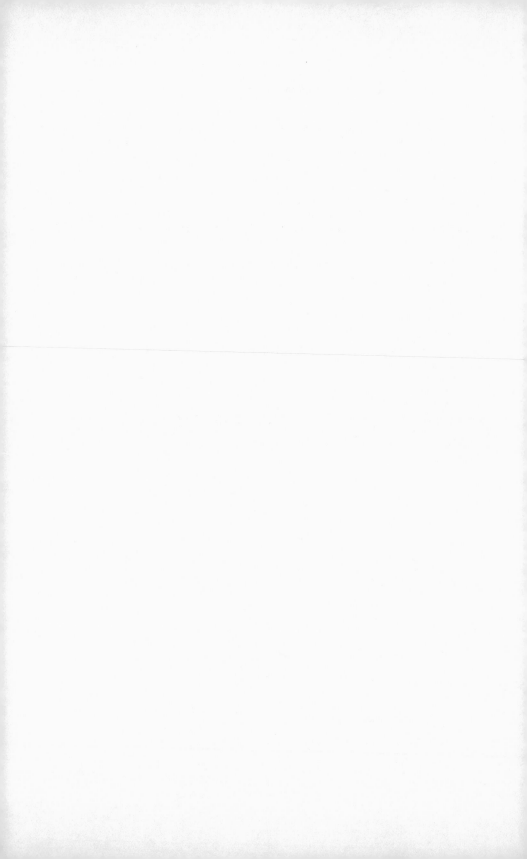

Index